T0291396

THE
PIONEER MERCHANTS
of SINGAPORE

Johnston, Boustead, Guthrie and Others

THE

PIONEER MERCHANTS
of SINGAPORE

Johnston, Boustead, Guthrie and Others

R. E. Hale

W💿 World Scientific

NEW JERSEY · LONDON · SINGAPORE · BEIJING · SHANGHAI · HONG KONG · TAIPEI · CHENNAI · TOKYO

Published by

World Scientific Publishing Co. Pte. Ltd.
5 Toh Tuck Link, Singapore 596224
USA office: 27 Warren Street, Suite 401-402, Hackensack, NJ 07601
UK office: 57 Shelton Street, Covent Garden, London WC2H 9HE

National Library Board, Singapore Cataloguing in Publication Data
Name(s): Hale, R. E. (Richard Edward)
Title: The pioneer merchants of Singapore : Johnston, Boustead, Guthrie and others / R. E. Hale.
Description: Singapore : World Scientific Publishing Co. Pte. Ltd., 2022.
Identifier(s): ISBN 978-981-12-4712-5 (hardcover) | 978-981-12-4713-2 (ebook for institutions) | 978-981-12-4714-9 (ebook for individuals)
Subject(s): LCSH: Merchants--Singapore--History. | Singapore--Commerce--History.
Classification: DDC 381.095957--dc23

British Library Cataloguing-in-Publication Data
A catalogue record for this book is available from the British Library.

Supported by

The views expressed here are solely those of the author in his private capacity and do not in any way represent the views of the National Heritage Board and/or any government agencies.

For any available supplementary material, please visit
https://www.worldscientific.com/worldscibooks/10.1142/12546#t=suppl

Desk Editor: Nicole Ong

Typeset by Stallion Press
Email: enquiries@stallionpress.com

For FCYK

About the Author

Richard Edward Hale was Chairman of the Singapore International Chamber of Commerce from 1993 to 1995, and a member of the National Parks Board for eight years. In 1993, he was made Officer of the Order of the British Empire by Queen Elizabeth II and two years later was awarded the Singapore Public Service Star (BBM).

His career after two years active national service in the Royal Navy (1956–1958) lasted 37 years with HSBC, including stints in Hong Kong, Japan, Malaysia, France & Germany. He was stationed in Singapore for 3 years in the seventies and then for 9 years from 1986. While still a banker he was the first recipient of the Singapore Green Leaf Award in 1991. Retiring from commercial banking in 1995 he was elected non-executive director of various public companies including Sembcorp Industries Ltd, CapitaLand Ltd and the private company Wildlife Reserves Singapore Pte Ltd.

He is now fully retired and in addition to other hobbies researches the history of Singapore people and places in the 1800s.

His first book, *The Balestiers: The first American Residents of Singapore* was published in 2016. His second, *Fraser's Hill and Lewis J. Fraser of Singapore* was published in Malaysia in 2018.

Preface

This book was originally intended to cover the life and times of Alexander Laurie Johnston but at the request of the publishers has been expanded to cover Edward Boustead, Alexander Guthrie and 11 other merchants operating in Singapore at some stage during the first 10 years of the East India Company administration. I have relied almost entirely on original records. You will find few references to other published sources and no list of volumes perused as there have been almost none. The views expressed here are solely my own in my private capacity and do not, in any way, represent the views of the National Heritage Board and/or any government agency.

My thanks are due to the National Heritage Board for their support, to Chua Hong Koon and my editor Nicole Ong at World Scientific and to the kind people who have helped in my research or read parts of the text and made many helpful suggestions. In no particular order these were Mark Smith and other staff at the Shetland Museum & Archives, Mrs Genevieve McCully, Mrs Vivienne Tan, Professor Tommy Koh, David Man of New York whose information on Boustead has been invaluable, Pierre Moccand, Tan Teng Teng, Francis Dorai, Colin Harris of the Bodleian Library, staff at the National Library of Scotland, David Boswell, Mrs Ann Pickett, and last but far from least Chiew Yuan Keng. If by ill chance and failing memory I have left somebody out I hope they will forgive me.

Contents

Introduction

With the backing of the Governor General in Calcutta, representing the 'Supreme Government' of the Honorable East India Company, but with the active opposition of authorities in Penang, Sir Stamford Raffles sailed precipitately from Penang on 19th January 1819 bound 'to the eastward'. Sailing via Malacca and the Carimon Islands he arrived off Singapore on the afternoon of 28th January. By 7th February he had signed a treaty leasing a small coastal stretch of land for the establishment of a 'factory' or business settlement and departed for Penang, leaving Major Farquhar in control as Resident. He was to report to Raffles whose official position was Lieutenant Governor of Bencoolen, a British possession on the southwest coast of Sumatra.

This time-consuming and inefficient reporting line lasted until June 1823, when Farquhar was replaced by Dr John Crawfurd who reported to the Governor General in Calcutta. He signed a new treaty in 1824 under which the Company obtained full sovereignty over the whole island of Singapore and some neighbouring islets.

In 1826 Singapore and Malacca were combined administratively with Penang, to which they now reported, becoming a new presidency on par with Calcutta, Bombay and Madras and termed 'The Straits Settlements'. This proved to be an expensive experiment. Not enough revenue could be generated to cover the running costs of a presidency with its officialdom and elaborate judicial system. It was therefore officially cancelled on

25th May 1830 and downgraded to a residency under the Bengal Presidency at Calcutta.

The offices and titles of Governor and Resident Councillor were thereupon removed. The official now in charge was the Resident who was assisted by a Deputy Resident and Assistant Residents in Singapore and Malacca. Nobody in authority had thought ahead and realised that the Charter of Justice under which the whole judicial system functioned specified the original titles. As these no longer existed the whole system closed down for over two years, despite the united efforts of the merchants, until the titles were reinstated in 1832.

Although much has been written about Sir Stamford Raffles and some about Lt. Col. Farquhar, almost nothing has been published about the early merchants of all races operating in Singapore between 1819 and 1829, the first 10 years after its initial acquisition by the East India Company, and their later careers. This book is designed to fill that gap with as much verifiable information as possible based entirely on original sources, many newly discovered.

Alex Johnston (Figure 1), almost the first European merchant here, arrived in Singapore in 1820 and retired to Scotland in 1841. As far as I know he has never featured prominently, if ever, elsewhere. I was fortunate to discover, hidden in the Shetland Islands Archives, United Kingdom, some letters from Andrew Hay to his own brother. Hay, who was Johnston's first employee and later business partner, wrote in detail and sheds light on much which, otherwise, would have been lost to us. In one he gives the text of a letter, not recorded elsewhere, which Raffles wrote to London recommending Johnston as a man with whom one could safely do business. In addition to Johnston's biography there is a large section of his recollections as imagined based on the author's research, recalling his days in Singapore while in retirement in Scotland two years prior to his death in 1850. These include new information on individuals such as S. G. Bonham, Tan Che Sang, Naraina Pillai, and Claude Queiros.

Edward Boustead, who arrived in 1828, had 'the house of twenty–seven pillars' built by Coleman, and later lived for a short while in a large house facing the Esplanade, was briefly US Consul before moving back to England in 1851. His son by a Malay mistress sued his executors after his death in 1888 and the previously ignored file in the United Kingdom

National Archives on that court case gives us much interesting information on the early days of Singapore.

Alexander Guthrie was a Scot who came to Singapore in 1821 from the Cape of Good Hope where he had worked for a Captain Harrington, who was formerly the master of the vessel in which Raffles first went to Penang. Although as compared with Boustead and Johnston not as much detailed information about him is available, much of it is new.

The last section of the book records in shorter form the known facts and careers of some other individuals of the period including certain Indo-European and Chinese merchants.

The currencies in use were many and varied, as explained in the text, but it should be noted that the $ sign refers throughout to the Spanish Dollar which was in circulation generally at this period.

The names of places given in the text are as they were known in the early 1800s. Rhio refers to the island of Bintang and its main village Tanjung Pinang, and should not be confused with the present province of Riau. Batavia is now Jakarta and Tappanooly is now Sibolga.

Dramatis Personae

Alexander Laurie Johnston

ABDULLAH Munshi	Malay language teacher
BALESTIER, J	Merchant. American Consul from 1836.
BERNARD, F. J.	Son–in–law of William Farquhar
BONHAM, Lieutenant George	Army officer. Half–brother of S. G. Bonham
BONHAM, S. G. (known as Sam)	The East India Company. Writer. Later Governor
BOUSTEAD, E.	English merchant from Cumberland
CHOA Chong Long	Chinese merchant from Malacca
CHURCH, Thomas	The East India Company
COLEMAN, G. D.	Irish architect. Later surveyor
CRAWFURD, Dr John	Succeeded William Farquhar as Resident
DAVIS, Captain C. E.	Son–in–law of William Farquhar. Cantonment Adjutant
DUNCAN, W. S.	Shetland Islander. Merchant
ELLIOT, Mrs Clara	Wife of Captain Elliot serving in China
FARQUHAR, A.	Son of William Farquhar. Later Merchant

FARQUHAR, Major William.   Resident
(later Lt. Colonel)

FLINT, Captain W.   Brother–in–law of Raffles. Master
        Attendant

FRASER, James   Merchant

FULLERTON, R.   The East India Co. Later Governor

GUTHRIE, Alexander   Scottish merchant

HAY, Andrew   Shetland Islander. Merchant. Partner
        with Johnston

HULL, L. Nilson   Secretary to Raffles and brother of
        his wife.

HUNTER, Robert   Merchant

HUSSEIN, Sultan   Sultan of Singapore

IBBETSON, R.   The East India Company

JACKSON, Lieutenant P.   Artillery Lieutenant

JARDINE. William   Merchant in China

JOHNSTON, Alexander Laurie   Scottish merchant

MACKENZIE, Graham   Merchant

MAXWELL, J. A.   Merchant

METHVEN, Captain C.   East India Company Army Officer

MONTGOMERIE, Dr William   Surgeon

MORGAN, John   Merchant

MURCHISON, K   The East India Company

NAPIER, D. S.   Merchant

NAPIER, William   Brother of D. S. Napier. Lawyer

PALMER, John   Merchant & Financier in Calcutta

PEARL, Captain James   Naval Officer

PRESGRAVE, E.   East India Company Formerly in
        Bencoolen

PRINCE, John   Resident Councillor, Singapore
        1827

PURVIS, J.	Scottish merchant
QUEIROS, Claude	Merchant. Agent for John Palmer
RAFFLES, Sir Stamford	The East India Company
RALFE, Lieutenant H	Artillery officer East India Company
READ, C. R.	Merchant — Partner with Johnston
REED, R. P.	The East India Company. Writer
SCOTT, C.	Merchant
SKELTON, P.	Merchant at Batavia
TAN Che Sang	Hokkien merchant
TEMENGGONG	Sultan's Chief Administrator
THOMAS, Charles	Merchant
TRAVERS, Captain O. T.	East India Company Bencoolen

Shetland Islands

Lerwick

Brechin

Perth

The Clyde

Edinburgh

Dumfries

Peebles

Isle of Man

Irthington

Camlork

Cumberland

Manchester

Tullamore

Birmingham

Essex

Liverpool

London

Alexandria

Basra

Madeira

Suez

St Helena

Cape Town

Cape Agulhas

Simonstown

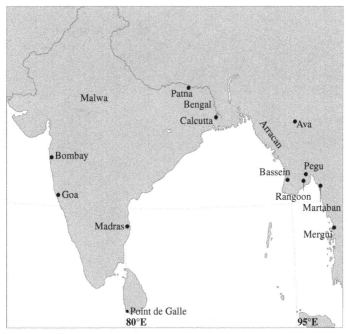

Malwa

Patna

Bengal

Calcutta

Ava

Arracan

Bombay

Bassein

Pegu

Goa

Rangoon

Martaban

Madras

Mergui

Point de Galle

80°E

95°E

xxi

1. Palembang
2. Minto
3. Gasper Island
4. Banten
5. Batavia
6. Malacca
7. Cucob
8. Endau
9. Sedili
10. Cape Ramunia
11. Rhio
12. Lingin
13. Gallang
14. Carimon Islands
15. Bulang Bay

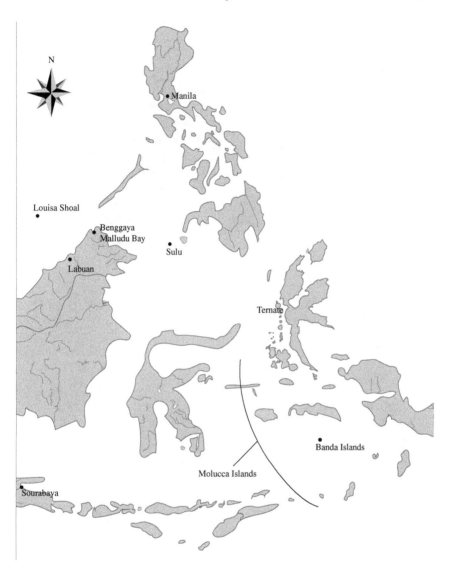

Abbreviations

JMBRAS   Journal of the Malayan Branch of the Royal Asiatic Society
SSR   Straits Settlements Records

List of Illustrations

1. A. L. Johnston. Print by D. J. Pound from a painting by George Chinnery painted during ALJ's visit to Macao. National Portrait Gallery, London.
2. Singapore town. Part of a map marked 'Rec'd 18 June 1825' in the British Library London.
3. Deptford, England, where *Earl Fitzwilliam* was built in 1786. Private Collection.
4. The circular announcing the formation of the firm A. L. Johnston & Co.
5. Map hand-drawn by Andrew Hay showing the properties held by A. L. Johnston & Co. in 1827, with lots highlighted as the original markings are too faint to show up.
6. Sloop *Clive* salvaging opium clipper *Sylph* off Batam Island, by W. J. Huggins. Source: National Maritime Museum, Greenwich, London.
7. Excerpt from *Singapore Free Press*, advertising the Jardine. Source: *Singapore Free Press*, 1836.
8. 1846 Kampong Rochor by J. T. Thomson. Courtesy of the Hocken Collections, University of Otago. Source: John Thomson 1846
9. Silver dollar of Charles IV of Spain 1806.
10. Print taken from a painting by Francois-Edmond Paris of the French frigate *La Favorite* which called in at Singapore from 18th to 25th August 1830. This shows not only the drawbridge over the river but also on the right Methven's godown which was still used by Government

at the time. Courtesy of the National Museum of Singapore, National Heritage Board.

11. August 1830 Singapore with Boat Quay godowns on the left. Courtesy of the National Museum of Singapore, National Heritage Board.

12. Dr John Crawfurd, much later in life. National Portrait Gallery, London.

13. Dutch Guilder 1786.

14. Ruins of the Canton Factories after the Fire. China trade painting – Public domain, via Wikimedia Commons.

15. HEIC ship Repulse in East India Dock 25 September 1839. © National Maritime Museum, Greenwich, London.

16. The Peter Wilkins print of Cruickshank's sketch with Morgan's identification of the participants. Courtesy of the National Museum of Singapore, National Heritage Board.

17. Orchid Tree or Pride of Burma (Amherstia nobilis Wallich.) flowering branch with separate fruit and sectioned ovary. Chromolithograph by P. Depannemaeker, c. 1885, after B. Hoola van Nooten. Source: Wellcome Collection. Attribution 4.0 International (CC BY 4.0).

18. Robert Fullerton (1773–1831). St Marylebone Parish Church, London.

19. An example of one of C. R. Read's tokens, his name being inscribed below the cockerel figure.

20. Wood engraving by Heinrich Leutemann of Coleman's surveying party under attack by a tiger. Courtesy of the National Museum of Singapore, National Heritage Board.

21. The former Keng Teck Whay building, 150 Teluk Ayer Street. © Frank Chiew.

22. Alexander L. Johnston and friends at Tanjong Tangkap, Singapore. © Frank Chiew.

23. Edward Boustead (1800–1888). Public domain, via Wikimedia Commons.

24. Robert Wise & Co. Notice. Excerpt from the Singapore Chronicle. Source: Singapore Chronicle, 10 December 1831.

25. George Bennett & Siamang Illustration. Source: Bennett, G. (1834) Wanderings in New South Wales, Batavia, Pedir Coast, Singapore, and China: Being the Journal of a Naturalist in Those Countries During 1832, 1833, and 1834, Vol 2. Richard Bentley, New Burlington Street, London, pp. 142–173.

Part 1

Alexander Laurie Johnston

Chapter 1

Alexander Laurie Johnston — Biography

One of the first Europeans to set up business in Singapore, Johnston is an enigmatic figure about whom we have but few reliable details. He was greatly respected by and popular in all communities as he was seen to be both fair–dealing and kind, behaviour which was no more common then than it is today. It was a free-wheeling community of many races dedicated to making money fast, not necessarily by the most ethical methods, and in the first few years at least after its founding in 1819 members of the quickly increasing population had no intention of making it their permanent home.

Sir Stamford Raffles had sailed from Penang aboard the ship *Indiana* which he had chartered there from Captain James Pearl, under an agreement made earlier with John Palmer, a powerful mogul in Calcutta. She set off for the Carimon Islands to rendezvous with the survey vessels *Investigator* and *Discovery* and three other vessels, *Nearchus*, *Mercury* and *Ganges*, finding them as planned on 27th January 1819. The squadron sailed eastward the next morning, anchoring off St John's Island some eight hours later. Landing first on 28th January, Raffles signed an agreement with the Temenggong on 30th January, raised the Union Jack and disembarked the troops from the *Nearchus*. This was followed, when Sultan Hussein had arrived from Rhio, by a treaty signed on 6th February allowing the establishment of a '*factory*' within a two-mile stretch of shoreline and '*inland to the extent of a point–blank range of a cannon shot*'. Further clarification was made in June specifying that the lands covered stretched from Tanjong Katong in the east to Tanjong Malang in the west. The long-term future of the port was far from assured, given the fury of the Dutch authorities in Batavia over its establishment, and the less than lukewarm attitude towards it taken by the East India Company officials in both Penang and Calcutta. This uncertainty was only removed by the signature in London in March 1824 of a treaty allocating the Malay Peninsula to the British and leaving Sumatra and all south of the equator to the Dutch.

At first the settlement was small and Europeans few. Raffles had clear ideas for its development. His first visit had been brief, leaving for Penang on 7th February 1819 just a day after signing the treaty with the Sultan, leaving Major (later Lieutenant Colonel) Farquhar in charge as Resident. He returned on 31st May, giving instructions on how he wished the town to develop, until 28th June when he left for Bencoolen on the southwest coast of Sumatra to resume his duties as Lieutenant Governor, having been absent from it for many months.

Tools and provisions were sent from Penang and some attap-roofed, mat-walled timber houses were quickly built. Captain Pearl, following a hint given, had loaded *Indiana* with bricks as ballast and sold them at high prices. Raffles reserved a plot of land for his brother-in-law Captain William Flint, his designated Master Attendant, who did not arrive in the Settlement until 24th April 1820. This plot at the mouth of the Singapore River was later registered in Flint's name. It was the narrow neck of land, fronting both the sea and the river, between the rocky point and a small jungle covered hill on the right (south) bank. Looking westwards, one could see what was going on up-river and, looking eastwards, see the arrival of shipping in the roads. To the west, beyond the house which Flint quickly had built at his own expense, rose the low hill where today Raffles Place is situated, which soon afterwards was flattened. The rocks and soil, together with rocks from the river near the point, were deposited to create what is now Boat Quay. According to Munshi Abdullah, Raffles stayed in this house with his sister and brother-in-law, at the start of his last visit, from October 1822 to January 1823 while his own bungalow was being built on Government Hill.

William Jardine who visited Singapore in May 1819, only three months after the signing of the treaty, felt that its prospects were good. As he wrote to M. Larruleta & Co. in Calcutta on 24th May, he was:

'of the opinion that a person settling here for a few months with a few thousand dollars as a circulatory medium (which they greatly want) might carry on business to great advantage. I dare say that opium might now be retailed at $1300 per chest but there is no one individual who could afford to buy so large a quantity as a chest; the sale of which must be the work of many days. Mr Bernard, son-in-law of the Major [Farquhar], who is Master Attendant [until Flint's arrival], is an inexperienced youth and knows not to take advantage of his opportunities. I offered to sell him opium for Government bills on Bengal but could not prevail on him to venture on a purchase.'[1]

Jardine who, as is well known, was based in Macao and Canton, went on to make his fortune shipping trade goods and quantities of opium to China and selling it from fast ships trading up and down that coast. He was born in Dumfriesshire in 1784, one of five children of a farmer who died when Jardine was nine. Thanks to help from his elder brother, although money had been short, he was able to graduate from the Edinburgh Medical School in 1802 and joined the East India Company as Surgeon's Mate. Employees of the company were allowed to trade for their own account to a certain extent and so, having made good use of the cargo space allowed for trade goods and built up his own capital, he left their service in 1817 when he was 33 and became an independent trader.

Whether or not Jardine and Johnston knew each other at this time is not recorded, nor is the exact date when Johnston first landed in Singapore. Captain O. T. Travers, who had arrived from Bencoolen expecting, as appointed by Raffles, to take over as Resident from Farquhar, mentions Johnston in his journal for June 1820 as arriving that month in *Marchioness of Wellesley* and that he was strongly recommended by Travers' friends including Philip Skelton of Batavia.

---

[1] Trocki, Carl, A. 1990. *Opium & Empire: Chinese Society in Colonial Singapore, 1800–1910*. Cornell University Press, pp. xiv, 260.

The vessel also brought several other new settlers including the Calcutta merchant John Palmer's supposed natural son and protégé Claude Queiros. Travers mentions Johnston departing for Bengal in the same ship at the beginning of July. She called at Penang from 18th to 23rd July and arrived in Calcutta on 30th August.[2] Johnston took with him several of Travers' letters and returned to Singapore to settle in November.[3] He is said to have established himself as merchant that month, but in the absence of laws &ca this would seem to have had no official foundation other than his possibly obtaining approval from the Resident to reside in Singapore.

Johnston was about 18 months younger than Raffles, and a year or so older than Jardine, having been born at Cumlorg (per East India Company records) in the Isle of Man on New Year's Day 1783. His father, James Johnston farmed at Camlork and died there in 1784 leaving his widow Elizabeth Laurie Johnston (born 1752) with three children, William, Jane and Alexander and pregnant with a fourth (Joan). His executor and the guardian of his children was his wife's father Alexander Laurie or Lowrie of Ernespie.[4] The family in Dumfriesshire was reputed to be highly respectable but Johnston was a widespread surname and details of his paternal relations have not been traced. It was to this part of Scotland that he returned in his retirement many years later. Where and how he was educated are also not known. He entered the service of the East India Company aged 12 as a midshipman aboard *Earl Fitzwilliam* (803 tons) (Figure 3) and sailed East on 9th July 1795, leaving behind a country which had been at war with the French for two years, where the harvest was failing, and shortages of grain led to bread riots. He arrived back 19 months later on 18th February 1797 to find the Bank of England suspending cash payment. Even in those days 12 was an early age to be sent away but he remained with the ship when she sailed once more from Torbay on 22nd September 1797.

---

[2] *The Asiatic Journal and Monthly Miscellany*, Volume 11, Wm. H. Allen & Company, 1821. p.277.

[3] SSR N1 315 British European inhabitants residing in Singapore who have no licenses.

[4] His mother's sister Margaret married John William Pew of Hillowton in Galloway. The Pew family bore arms 'Arg, a lion passant sat between three fleurs de lis gu' and a crest of 'A griffins head erased". See *Heraldic Illustrations* by J & J. B. Burke Vol.2 Pl. LXXXV. They had a son Peter Laurie Pew who joined the Bengal Native Infantry and later the Artillery. In 1839 he had been promoted to Major.

17 months later she was moving up the Hugli River towards Calcutta on a flood tide with the southerly wind astern when shortly before midnight on 23rd February 1799 fire in the gun room broke out and the alarm was raised. A survivor later related:

'The fire spread very rapidly and, although every exertion was made to extinguish it, within five minutes it became universal. Finding at this time that nothing could be done to save the ship everyone tried to save himself. All the spars and gratings were thrown overboard, upon which the lascars jumped. All the officers and Europeans went forward; about eighteen went on the spritsail yard, endeavoured to cut it away but the braces were cut only on one side so that one yard-arm was in the water and the other in the air. After about five minutes the main yard went with a horrible crash over the starboard gangway but in the fall one end of it was entangled with the gun so that it remained by the ship. The fire at this time was very violent. The guns, which were that afternoon double shotted, were going off in dreadful peals. We remained in this situation upon the yard about one hour and a half expecting the ship to blow up every instant. From the situation of the spritsail yards the people at the lower end were very much harassed and fatigued. By this time the Nonsuch's boats came within two hundred yards of the ship and there remained. The people when seeing the boats called to them in a most pathetic manner to save them. The Thetis's boat, with the fifth officer, came with an oar's length which they gave into our hands, and hauled on board as many as the boat could take, and then pulled off for the ship; too much credit cannot be given to this gentleman who, meeting with another of their boats, left us and again went to the ship. The conduct of a young lad, a midshipman of the Thetis who in a sloop's boat with two hands in her went close to the ship and picked the men off the wreck, and gave them to the large boats, who at this time kept at a distance. This he did until they were all taken off. The ship struck on Saugur Sand about four o'clock and continued burning till the morning.'[5]

She was totally destroyed so that even her log did not survive. Johnston escaped apparently unharmed and, there being no berth in another ship for him as midshipman, returned to England as a seaman

[5] *The Annual Register* 1798–99, p. 158.

aboard *Worcester* arriving almost a year later on 9th February 1800 to find widespread food shortages and the war in stalemate.

His experience and initiative stood him in good stead, and he joined *Neptune*[6] when, after two months' preparation, she sailed on 27th May the same year for the East. Her next voyage on 30th April 1802, a peace treaty having been signed, saw him as fourth mate until her return on 21st July 1803 when he learned that war with France had recommenced two months earlier. After some leave and avoiding the press gangs 'recruiting' for the navy he joined the *David Scott*[7] late in the year as third mate, being promoted to second mate in 1805 on her subsequent voyage. From his arrival back on 5th June 1806 until he joined *Alnwick Castle* as first mate in 1808, the war was not going well, and we have no record of his activities. The ship was similar to *Neptune* and *David Scott*, the latter being under the command of John Locke Jnr whose namesake was her principal manager/ owner. He remained with her for two voyages, the first to Madras, Penang, Malacca, Whampoa and back via Penang and St Helena. The second also showed him Manila and Macao. On these voyages the ships initially sailed in convoy to avoid attack by the French, but the convoys broke up as they proceeded (Figure 42).

According to Buckley[8] he then took command of a 'free trader vessel' of which he was owner or at least part-owner. This might have been *Sovereign* (owner John Locke) 617 tons which sailed for Coast & Bay on

---

[6]*Neptune* had been built by Wells and launched in 1796. She had three decks, was 176 feet in length and 43 feet 10 inches in breadth. She displaced 1,200 tons. The journal for her voyage of 18th March 1800 to 17th December 1801 during which time she sailed from England to Whampoa, China and back can be found in the East India records at the British Library.

[7]*David Scott*, a vessel of 1,200 tons had been built by Pitcher in Northfleet and launched in 1801. She had three decks, was 166 feet in length and 42 feet in breadth. She sailed in convoy from Plymouth on 26th February 1804 for Bombay and Madras 4th September 1804 arriving home on 10th March 1805. She remained at home until 4th March 1806 when she was off again, this time from Portsmouth. Arriving at Madras on 28 June, Penang on 15th August and Whampoa on 19th October she set sail for home via Penang and St Helena and gained 'Long Reach' on 5th June 1807.

[8]Buckley, Charles Burton. 1902. *An Anecdotal History of Old Times in Singapore*. Fraser & Neave, p. 62.

8th April 1812. Over two years later he was in command of *Ocean* which sailed from England in August 1815 and arrived in Sydney with convicts on 29th or 30th January 1816, sailing for Batavia on 16th March. He also appears in 1817 in Lloyd's Register as being in command of *Ocean*.[9] She arrived back in England, under the command of Samuel Remmington, on 2nd September 1818, possibly via Batavia or Calcutta where Johnston may have given up command and bought his half share in the small schooner *Janet Hutton* which shuttled between Calcutta, Penang and Bencoolen under the command of the joint owner, Captain Howard.

Johnston's future business partner Andrew Hay, in letters to his brother, shed light on events leading in due course to the official Establishment of A. L. Johnston and Co. Hay was a man from Lerwick in the Shetland Islands, born in 1789 and so six years his younger. Following a somewhat unfulfilling period in commercial business in Hull and Liverpool, in August 1817 he took up the offer of a passage to India from the friendly captain of the *Argo*. Arriving in the Saugar channel below Calcutta after a tedious voyage lasting five months and 11 days, with a number of letters of introduction and hopes of profitable employment, it was very quickly borne in on him that his hopes were groundless. His letters home reveal a rising sense of desperation and shortage of funds. The well-known and powerful John Palmer was, after a few months, kind enough to arrange a passage in *Auspicious* for him via Penang to Batavia, en route to a post at Semarang, Java with Deans, Scott & Co., (who were in debt to Palmer for large sums) which had been offered. John Deans himself was from the Shetlands and made Hay welcome, providing a salary of $100 per month, only half of that which his predecessor had received but taking into account the inclusion of free lodging and food. A year later Deans departed for England. The other partners, including two Scott brothers, Robert and William from Penang and a Mr Morris, immediately cancelled the lodging and food, initially without any increase in salary to compensate, later increasing it by $50. Hay was shortly afterwards dismissed and found a

---

[9] A 'licensed India ship' 567 tons-built Canada 1800, which sailed from the UK for Bombay on 25th March 1817. She returned to Portsmouth on 2nd September 1818 from Batavia (12th April 1818) and St Helena (1st July 1818). (*The Asiatic Journal and Monthly Miscellany* 1818 Vol. 6, W.H. Allen & Company, p. 445).

temporary situation. By this time he had become well known to Philip Skelton of Skelton & Co. Batavia, one of the leading British firms in Java who had set up an office in Semarang. In a letter to his brother dated 24th August 1820 Hay stated:

'I write this in haste to inform you that there seems now every probability of my soon removing to Singapore as I told you before I had some expectation of. This day's post has brought letters to Mr. Davidson from his partner Mr. Skelton intimating his having determined on the plan of sending a person to form a mercantile establishment on that new settlement [Singapore] & that Capt'n Johnston has been patched upon as the fittest person to conduct the business.

Captain Johnston with whom I am to be associated is a very worthy agreeable man a few years older than myself who was formerly a commander in the East India Extra Services and has been for three– or four–years last part trading as a merchant on his own account between England & Java and other ports in the east & his knowledge & experience in business is very well calculated for conducting such an enterprise. From Mr Skelton & the other members' intimate acquaintance with Governor Raffles and my [own] with Wm. Jack (his family surgeon ostensibly but I note really his free secretary) we may look I think for every facility being afforded us in the conducting of affairs that is in the power of the Gov't officers to bestow & more especially as I understand it to be at the particular personal instance & recommendation of Sir Stamford, himself the founder of colony, that this mercantile speculation is entered into as he is anxious to raise it into consequence by bringing in British capital & interests into play as quickly as possible.

The only obstacle which at all that stands in the way of the business being carried into execution at once is the uncertainty which still exists as to the determination of the British Government to maintain possession of the infant colony. No official communication has yet been received confirming determination & Captain Johnston, a cautious calculating man, has no idea of entering fully into the speculation [until] the official communication is actually received. There seems however to remain little doubt of its arriving shortly either upon [word missing] by that of Skelton & Co [word missing] all upon that of Sir Stamford himself for his own brother–in–law Capt'n Flint of the Navy has already been sent to Singapore to take upon him the office of Master Attendant which means director of all the shipping entering or leaving the place & which is a Government appointment of considerable local importance & Major Travers, another of his friends has been appointed Resident, that is Governor, & has gone thither to commence his duties.'

The renewal of the East India Company's charter from the British Government in 1813 had removed their commercial monopoly except for the tea trade and trade with China and expressly stated British rule over those parts of India under the Company's sway. This opened commerce to outsiders and by 1819 shipping in the area was suffering from an overdose of competition. For Johnston, being no fool, this may possibly have been one of the deciding factors in agreeing to set up in Singapore, financed to a large extent by Skelton & Co., who were much supported by Raffles himself.

Looking back after two centuries it appears that anyone investing in Singapore at that time had remarkable foresight. It is easy enough to forget that there was a very real fear that the settlement would shortly be handed over to the Dutch by the home government. The sad details of what happened to business and property valuations in Bencoolen, Sumatra after it was finally handed over to the Dutch in 1826 demonstrate just what would have been lost. Letters written by John Palmer, the Calcutta mogul, in 1820 and 1821 reveal his concerns that London did not see a vital need for the place. They were '*too busy with the antics of Queen Caroline*'[10] to give full attention to the matter and he worried that the Governor General in Calcutta would give in to constant and pressing Dutch pleas and

---

[10] Caroline of Brunswick married the Prince Regent in 1796. He could not stand the sight of her and in 1814 she moved to the Continent. In January 1820 King George III died and the Prince succeeded to the throne as George IV. Caroline wrote an open letter to the press recounting her woes and in June landed at Dover to great public rejoicing which mirrored the unpopularity of the King. Official attempts to prove her adultery failed and were withdrawn to the rapturous applause of the population. In July she attempted to force her way into Westminster Abbey for the Coronation but was turned away and died a month later.

demands. Palmer himself saw immense possibilities and had wasted no time in sending his protégé Claude Queiros[11] to Singapore initially in February 1820 and, although under no illusions as to the risks, felt the prospects outweighed them. It was only once the 1824 treaty with the Dutch had been signed in London that these fears melted away, by which time Queiros, a likeable man but untrustworthy in business, was causing him problems.

Hay sailed from Java at the end of August 1820, arriving in Singapore a few weeks ahead of Johnston who was on his way back from Calcutta, and boarded with Lieutenant Ralfe, the former gunnery officer in *Nearchus*, as Johnston had previously arranged for them both.

Johnston's experience at sea and his good reputation in Java made him a logical choice for many of the captains of ships using the port to appoint as their agent. He could understand their needs and ensure them a fair deal when trading with local native merchants. Without such an agent a Captain could very quickly find himself swindled out of his money and receive faulty goods in exchange. He could through his contacts quickly find them return cargoes and freight and undertake to sell on their behalf on a commission basis goods left behind that for some reason could not be sold before they sailed. He would handle goods consigned to him and at times back his own judgment in buying and selling using his own available funds. An example is his profitable sale to the East India Company of $474 worth of ghee for the Indian troops (29 maunds and 26 seers @ $16 per maund which weight equalled about 40 kg) as Captain Flint, acting as Storekeeper as well as Master Attendant, had run short. Another sale, in July 1821, was of a cask or pipe of rum containing several gallons for thirsty European troops or sailors.[12]

By early March 1821 Johnston had realized that a good opportunity to do business lay across the Straits in Rhio and dispatched Hay to develop this. Hay later wrote:

---

[11] Palmer's written instructions to Queiros dated 2nd January 1820 read: 'I have offered you an unequivocal proof of friendship by approving an entire confidence in your prudence and diligence, directions and activity. I look for corresponding results.'

[12] SSR L4 496

'I was sent to form an establishment for the purpose of buying up the produce of this island, gambier & pepper & collecting those products of the neighbouring countries which are brought here for sale such as tin, rattans, birds' nests, tortoise shell & other articles suitable for the China, Bengal & Java markets. I am the first European who has attempted to settle here as a merchant & I have built a fine large warehouse of planks with thatch roof (the only one used in this part of the world) where I intend to live myself as soon as it is finished. At present I inhabit a house of the same description in the midst of the Chinese camp or town, where I am surrounded by nothing but Chinese & Malays who all speak the Malay language which is our only medium of communication. The few Civil & Military officers of the Dutch Government in number only amounting to 10 or 11 Europeans, all live in a small fort on a hill (some distance from the Chinese town) the gates of which are closed every evening at ½ past 6 o'clock and there are no other Europeans or persons speaking any European language on any other part of the island so that you may suppose that I have had little society that can be called such. I have succeeded in gaining the friendship of the two Chinese Captains or heads of the Chinese settlers in the plain, with whom I do a great deal of business in the sale of opium & piece goods & the purchase of the articles above named. The immediate vicinity of Singapore affords great facilities for procuring supplies of every kind on the shortest notice & sending up the proceeds to await the arrival of the trading vessels which are continually passing by & looking in at that flourishing little settlement. In the times I have been here I have already sold goods to the amount of above 50,000 Dollars and remitted above half of it to Singapore in hard cash & the rest in produce. At present I am no more than I have always been, a clerk upon salary the amount of which I know not, leaving it entirely to the generosity & integrity of my employers (in whom I have the utmost confidence) to reward me as they think I deserve. My expenses of living &ca are paid by the concern & my salary cannot be less than I agreed for on leaving Java, 150 Dollars per month.'[13]

At the end of 1821 Hay was brought back to Singapore and replaced in Rhio by a Hanoverian named Hartmann who remained there for two and a half years when, before he could be sacked, he resigned having been

---

[13] Letter from Andrew Hay in Rhio to his brother William dated 7th July 1821.

found to be working on the side for a competitor, John Morgan, having become:

> 'Restive at last in the way that is related of Jeshurun (I think he is called in the scriptures) who is said to have "waxed fat & kicked". The fact is he has been better off than he deserved & had not sense to know that he was so, and so resigned of his own accord, much to my satisfaction.'[14]

Being the eldest of the European merchants, Johnston was called upon to take the lead amongst the few civilian Europeans. The very small police force, such as it was, was under the command of Farquhar's son–in–law F. J. Bernard. In March 1821 Johnston chaired a public meeting which had been called to discuss the Police establishment, the need to expand it and how to provide the necessary funds.[15] Apart from only eight native constables this consisted of a writer, a jailor and a sergeant. All agreed this was insufficient for the purpose and it was agreed that subscriptions be raised from the mercantile community to fund a further nine constables and one sergeant to form the Night Watch. Six months later at the Resident's request he met with the other leading merchants Guthrie, Queiros and Scott and recommended the inhabitants of Campong Glam and China Town should subscribe so that the police system could be extended to cover those areas. In all this patience and diplomacy were needed and his efforts enabled him to build up connections and contacts which served the Settlement well in later years.

His diplomacy was also tested when for three weeks in April and May he was involved in a lengthy court of enquiry[16] into the dealings of Captain Cathcart Methven, an officer of the East India Company military arm who had served under Raffles in Java. He was thought to be guilty of the charges but being still a serving officer it was decided to refer the case and evidence to the Commander–in–Chief in Calcutta. Methven promptly took ship to Calcutta to present his case, was exonerated entirely and allowed to return temporarily to Singapore where he was not well received. From the records Johnston's impartiality and good sense in the matter earned him respect.

---

[14] Letter from Andrew Hay to his brother William dated 21st May 1824. & The Bible Deuteronomy 32.15.

[15] SSR I.4 421 & Buckley, *op.cit.* p. 68.

[16] Buckley, *op cit.* p. 70.

Early in 1821 Philip Skelton died in Java, as Hay reported to his brother in his letter dated 7th July 1821:

'I have lost since leaving Java one of my best friends & a most worthy man, Philip Skelton Esq., the head of the house of that name, whom I considered as my patron & with whom I lived on my short visit to Batavia last year. He was carried off suddenly by the Batavia fever after being many years inured to the climate. He was formerly a Captain in the Company's army & was wounded at the siege of Seringapatam. There still remain John Davidson, David Fraser & Thos. Macquoid, partners of the Firm. All worthy fellows &, except the latter, well known & esteemed by me. They are Johnston's chief friends also in this part of the world.'

Thomas Macquoid became senior partner of the firm which henceforth was known as Macquoid, Davidson & Co and to which Raffles entrusted a substantial part of his savings. David A. Fraser, the third partner, had arrived at Bencoolen in November 1818 in *Providence* and went on to Batavia to join Skelton & Co. According to Travers he was *'a very superior fellow, mild and unassuming in his manners with a well-informed mind and an excellent heart.'* He had a sister with whose husband, Christopher Ridout Read, he had some years earlier been in partnership in London.[17] Read had now come to Java and it was suggested he might become involved in the Singapore business with Johnston & Hay. He

---

[17] C. R. Read (1787–1866) was, in the early years of the 19th Century in the business of ship's agent in London first in partnership with a Dutchman, John George Moojen, but they were adjudged bankrupt on 4th February 1813. His second attempt, with his brother–in–law D. A. Fraser providing the capital, also failed in 1818 and a week later he sailed as ship's husband in *Providence*, a 698 ton vessel licensed by the East India Company. She was destined for Bencoolen with supplies for Fort Marlbro' and to bring back the annual shipment of pepper. Having been made bankrupt on her return he signed on for another voyage east but appears to have left the ship in Calcutta in January 1821. Whether or not he met Raffles in Bencoolen is uncertain but unlikely. Read and his wife Amelia Fraser whom he had married on 18th May 1811 had four daughters and one son, all of whom were born before he arrived in Singapore, and one daughter born in Singapore. He retired to England in 1841 but before his death in 1866 made representations to the government on behalf of the Singapore merchants. According to Buckley (p. 155) his wife arrived in Singapore in late 1823 with a daughter aboard the 500 ton *Jamima* as did W. S. Duncan who became a clerk in A. L. Johnston & Co. for a while.

reached Singapore by September 1821 but had to go back unexpectedly to Batavia and only returned in July 1822. Later that year he went with Fraser to Calcutta to try to arrange finance from Hutton & Co. In this they were successful as can be seen from a letter written by Johnston to Thomas Hutton dated 20th April 1823, a copy of which was included in Hay's letter to his brother dated two days later.

'My dear Sir,

Your very kind letter of 25th December last, dated on board the *Bengal Merchant*, reached me the latter end of February. This will I hope find you safe with your family in Old England. Mr Read made very satisfactory arrangements with the House in Calcutta and found, as you foretold me, every disposition on the part of the partners to meet our wishes — for this friendly deposition you have my warmest thanks. The arrangements are two lacs of rupees to remain with us as capital for the purposes of local trade, chargeable annually with a (at the usual interest of 9 per cent) commission of 2½ per cent, and three lacs more to be invested in opium and piece goods, to be returned before the end of the year so that the house is at no time to be under a greater advance than five lacs. The amount [sic] to be wound up at the end of three years from the 1st of May proximo at the option of either party. We commence as partners Mr. Read, Mr. Hay & myself on the 1st May also under the firm of A. L. Johnston & Co. The interest Captain Flint was to have had, it has been thought advisable by Sir Stamford should not take place so that we shall pay him a rent merely for his premises which are very extensive and well built, and will hold about 20,000 piculs of pepper or to that extent. One very desirable object still remains to be settled for us which is a connection with a House in London to enable us through their credit to make arrangements for getting piece goods out suitable to the market direct from the manufacturers. Mr Read's brother, in a letter he has lately received from England, has informed him that Messrs Rickards & Co. he has reason to believe intend making some offer to that effect but they have not done so hitherto. Sir Stamford for whose account we have been & still have to remit largely to Messrs Fairlie Bonham & Co has kindly written them in our behalf and if you will add your influence also in the same quarter, without however being to the prejudice in any way or interfering with Napier or my worthy friend Charlie Scott it will add one more to the many obligations I feel under to you. Our remittances to Bengal will I think presently be made more favorably by shipping to England and drawing bills negotiable in Bengal than any other way. But this requires confidence on the part of the house in England as in the event of any sudden depression in the market the goods shipped although drawn against at 4/2 per Dollar may still not realize so much. To establish this confidence (he means through Hutton & Co. they being still connected with JSN [sic]) which I cannot do through Calcutta not wishing any further transactions with Messrs Smith Inglis & Co I have to solicit your good assistance. Opium sells at a fair profit and with the arrangements we have made with Sir Stamford for bills on Bengal to the extent of four lacs this year will enable us to profit by it which has not hitherto been the case.'

Although Raffles had originally decreed that European merchants' premises would be located along the beach, the lots there were unsuitable for Godowns given the shallowness of the sea offshore and the surf which beat upon the shore in the monsoon. Farquhar asked each of them for comment in writing setting out their objections and indicating their preferred sites. Johnston replied on 13th April 1822 to this request as follows:

'I have the honour to acknowledge the receipt of your letter to my address of yesterday's date requesting my opinion as to the most eligible situation in this Settlement for carrying on trade and whether I considered the lots of ground situated on the plain between the Cantonments and Campong Glam as well adapted for the purpose. In my opinion best adapted for erecting Godowns for mercantile purposes is on the banks of the River particularly the north side where the ground is firm and where wharfs may be easily constructed at a moderate expense so as to admit loaded boats alongside of them at all times of the tides. The shallowness of the beach at Campong Glam and a considerable sea which at times during the N. E. Monsoon rolls on the shore would in my opinion render it in every point of view less eligible that the others. Indeed I should consider the opposite point where the *Georgina* now lies as much preferable to Campong Glam for mercantile purposes as the water is deep close to the shore and not exposed to the sea during either monsoon.'[18]

---

[18] SSR L7 181.

Two and a half years having elapsed since his second visit, Raffles returned with his wife, on 10th October 1822, and stayed for some eight months. His clear early instructions to Farquhar to reserve all the land on the north bank of the Singapore River for Government purposes had, to a considerable extent and for very practical reasons, been ignored. Queiros, Methven and Guthrie had all obtained sites between River Street and the water on which they had built extensive godowns, as had a number of others including Chinese and Indians. Aware that not all had gone according to his plan and determined to set this to rights with his usual energy, Raffles rented part of his brother–in–law Captain Flint's house as his base and set out to remedy matters. Whether or not he had previously met Johnston cannot be traced but he would undoubtedly have known of him from others. Finding him operating from his own house at the foot of Government Hill and renting godown space as and when needed meant he would have little or no personal axe to grind over the difficult and expensive changes to be made and so needed to be made into his ally.

On 4th November Raffles therefore appointed Johnston to the new Town Committee, as well as Captain Davis, an Army officer who was Farquhar's son–in–law, and Sam Bonham, a young civil servant & friend of Lady Raffles transferred back from Sumatra. Together with leaders from the various native communities they were to make recommendations in line with his own ideas on plans for the redevelopment of the town and on allocating specific areas to the various races and dialect sub-divisions. They worked hard and, having had a plan showing their recommendations drawn by the young Lieutenant Jackson[19] who was in command of the

---

[19] Phillip Jackson, born 24th September 1802, had arrived in Singapore on 22nd January 1822 to command the detachment of Bengal Artillery in place of Lieutenant Ralfe who had departed on sick leave. John Palmer wrote from Calcutta on 3rd September 1822 to Raffles in Singapore 'My old and respectable friend Captain James Jackson has a son at Singapore, Philip Jackson in command of the Artillery. A well conducted young man. He wishes me to interest you in the youth's welfare and to suggest that you may improve his income by bestowing the charge of the magazine upon him. If this is practicable without prejudice to another or to the service I will venture to anticipate your obliging attention to the request.' Whether or not this letter had any effect Jackson was appointed Assistant Engineer on 29th October and thereafter was involved in all the many problems of change as well as drafting a map showing Raffles' plans for the town. He left Singapore in 1827.

Artillery, the committee reported its findings on 15th February 1823 and was dissolved. Raffles fully appreciated the work done and, through his secretary, wrote to Johnston:

'The Town Committee of which you were an active member, having been dissolved as from the 15th instant, the Lieutenant Governor ....desired me in a particular manner to return to you his acknowledgements and (word missing) for the ready manner in which you have assisted the views of Government and for the able advice and essential assistance which you have so handsomely and gratuitously rendered on the occasion.'

Busy with his reformation of Singapore Raffles yet found time to write to his agents in London as follows:

Singapore 26th Dec 1822

Messrs Fairlie Bonham & Co

London

Dear Sir,

Allow me to introduce to your House my particular friend Mr Alex. L. Johnston, a highly respectable merchant of Singapore & in whose character and experience I place the fullest reliance. Mr Johnston, as my agent, will make to you consignments to the extent of about £10,000 with the view of effecting a remittance of my funds to Europe and of which he will of course apprize you of the particulars. In the mean time I request to recommend the House of Mr Johnston to your particular notice in the event of your having any commercial transactions at this place. I am satisfied that in the event of your extending your speculations to this quarter you will find no establishment so respectable or in which you may more certainly confide. He is at present I believe unconnected with any House in England, and I will only add that as I am most anxious to patronize and assist his House to the utmost of my means, I shall feel indebted to you for whatever attention you may pay to this introduction.

Yours sincerely   signed T. S. Raffles[20]

---

[20] Text enclosed in Andrew Hay's letter to his brother William dated 20th April 1823.

In the archives there is a letter dated 22nd November [1822] from Johnston to Raffles' secretary reading:

> 'Sir, I have communicated your letter of yesterday's date to the merchants interested, and have been requested by them to offer their grateful acknowledgements to the Lieutenant Governor for the warm interest he has taken in establishing their characters which they consider equally honourable to him and just to themselves.'

Sadly, there is no record of just what this concerned but it may have been to inform them that he felt they met his standards for later appointment as magistrates.

Johnston was first on the list of Magistrates thereafter appointed for the quarter. Hay and Read were also listed as being considered suitable to act as such. Raffles, in contrast with the attitude of many other officials both at that time and later, thus set an example of entrusting the unofficial residents with a degree of responsibility commensurate with their position in the community, but it was of course on an unpaid basis.

His assistance and views were sought by Raffles on numerous occasions. There was the matter of a slave woman raised by the Sultan and one wonders if this was in any way connected with an early entry in his cash book reading *'Paid subscription for the release of a female European slave'*. Another case was *'As the licences for the Gaming, Arrack and the retail of Opium will expire ....I am desirous of receiving your sentiments on such alterations therein as may appear advisable to you for the future with reference to the Police.'*

Raffles intended to found a college to educate the sons of the higher order of natives and others, to afford means of instruction in the native languages to such of the Company's servants and others as might desire it and thirdly to collect the scattered literature and customs of the country and to make these available to the community through publication. Johnston was among the first subscribers to the fund set up in April 1823 to establish this Raffles Institution, later known as the Singapore Institution or just the Institution, and for many years his firm acted as Trustees for the fund. He remained involved for many years in one guise or another and made it a bequest of $3,000 in his will.

As already mentioned, Farquhar had allowed various merchants to build on or occupy land along the north bank of the Singapore River which Raffles had instructed be reserved for Government. A number of these were now ordered, with compensation being paid, to vacate their sites and move across the river where new sites were allotted to them. This was naturally most unwelcome to some but Johnston, although he had earlier been allocated a site in River Street, had not yet built his own godown and so was not affected.[21] He had bought from Lieutenant Ralfe the house at the foot of Government Hill which was in a zone reserved for the Army and in January, worried about his security of tenure, he wrote to Raffles. In the files at the British Library in London lies a copy of a letter dated 27th January 1823 from L. Nilson Hull, Acting Secretary to the Lieutenant Governor, addressed to Johnston. This acknowledged his letter of the same date on the subject of the ground *'at present occupied by your dwelling house at the foot of the Government Hill'*. It further stated that:

'The Lieutenant Governor regrets he cannot authorize the issue of any grant for the ground in question, the same being expressly reserved by Government, nor can he relieve you from the inconvenience and uncertainty to which the occupant of a building so situated must always be liable. He can only recommend to you to avoid outlay as much as possible and refer you to the Military Department for any information you may require as to the principle on which individuals are occasionally allowed to occupy ground situated in the Cantonment.'

Later in the same year, Flint and family having moved to their new house on Mount Sophia, Johnston leased and moved into their house on the south bank at the river mouth, living there until in December 1841 when he left the Settlement to return to Scotland and to which house the name *'Tanjong Tangkap'* (*'Point Catch'* in Malay) had been given by his competitors. They said he was able to put out by boat from his private landing steps and 'catch' ship's captains as they were rowed ashore from their anchored ships.

Despite moving he continued to use the house at the foot of the hill for which Raffles, despite his earlier advice, personally authorized a five-

---

[21] SSR L5 238 attachment to.

year lease just before his departure in June 1823 '*as a particular mark of consideration and with a view to the personal accommodation of Mr. Johnston*'. This was quoted in an application on 11th July 1825 by Read (his, by then, business partner) for the lease to be transferred from Johnston to himself. This stated, inter alia:

> 'During Sir Thomas Stamford Raffles' stay at this Settlement he gave a conditional grant to my partner, A. L. Johnston, of the premises then occupied by him situated at the foot of Government Hill. The Government could resume it on payment of $4,000[sic]. It is now desirable that the said premises should be occupied by me and we both agree with the transfer. At this time the house has sustained such damage from the white ants it has become necessary to take it down whereby a very considerable expense will be incurred that was not anticipated when the grant was given to Mr Johnston.'

At some subsequent date, the premises were sold as in 1832 a document '*of title*' dated 1st January 1825 [sic] from Dr John Crawfurd, who had succeeded Farquhar as Resident of Singapore, granting a nine-year lease to C. R. Read was produced by a Captain Clement Tabor. This was sent to Penang and whilst no copy of the lease could be found in Government files there Bonham knew Crawfurd's signature and recognised that the document was written in the writing of a Mr Read [sic], a Clerk at the time employed in the Resident's office. The lease was not recognised, and Tabor had only the rights '*of an occupant*'. No mention was made of any further investigation. The house was subsequently resumed by Government.[22]

Farquhar, with his long experience in Malacca, was popular alike with Europeans and natives. He was pragmatic and sensible while always under the temperamental domination of Raffles in Bencoolen. Raffles was in bad health and often '*out–station*' which meant that replies to regular correspondence could take months to come back. In addition he was a not–always–rational control freak. His return to Singapore in October 1822, plagued by severe headaches and determined that the Settlement

---

[22] SSR R3 172.

should be run exactly as he had planned, naturally led to a cooling of the relationship. Each was guilty of nepotism which today is frowned upon but in those times was quite normal. You needed people working with you whom you could trust, and who better than close relatives? Farquhar had the misfortune to be physically attacked by one Syed Yassin in March 1823 and this did not help his feelings of increasing insecurity. The relationship soon developed into near outright warfare and finally led to his dismissal as Resident by Raffles on 1st May 1823. A few days later news reached Singapore that Farquhar's earlier resignation dated 23rd October 1820 had now been accepted, and the Settlement was to be placed under Calcutta's control with Dr John Crawfurd as Resident. He arrived on 27th May and assumed charge two days later. Before his final departure from Singapore on 9th June 1823 Raffles made a further agreement with the Sultan and the Temenggong that, among other things, the entire island and those islands immediately adjacent to it should be '*at the entire disposal of the British Government*'.

At A. L. Johnston and Co. opinions differed. Read was not a particular fan of Raffles. Hay had had a serious row with Farquhar and was of the other opinion. Johnston, benefitting from Raffles' support, was diplomatic and got along well with both sides realizing the problems but recognising Raffles' ideas as essential for the future of Singapore. Whilst his name and that of Read were inscribed on the silver cup presented to Farquhar after his departure that of Hay was not. He was still smarting from Farquhar's strictly correct view, written in March 1823, that '*As to Mr. Hay he is only I believe in the situation of head assistant or Chief Clerk to Mr. Johnston, therefore can scarcely be classed among the merchants.*' and from his being subsequently ostracised by Farquhar.

Agreement was finally reached over the allocation of shares in the new firm of A. L. Johnston & Co. as Hay wrote to his brother on 25th April 1823:

'I wrote you by the *Venilia*, Free Trader for London in Jan'y and I think by some other opportunity since but am not quite certain. Having again a direct conveyance by the *Eliza*, Free Trader, I avail myself of it to inform you that it is at length concluded that a partnership takes place on the 1st May between Johnston, Read & your humble under the firm of A. L. Johnston & Co. I objected stoutly for a long while to Mr Read's having a larger share than myself considering that my length of service & acknowledged usefulness in my department was fully equal to counterbalance any advantage which he brought along with him. Nevertheless Johnston, whether from the satisfaction produced by the pecuniary arrangements Read had succeeded in making with Hutton & Co. in his last visit to Calcutta, or from a consideration for his large family (of a wife & five children, daily expected out) & being the brother-in-law of his friend Fraser, to whose firm he has been under great obligation, I know not but he positively refused to make any alteration in the terms he had decided upon, namely for himself & Read 6/16 each and for me 4/16. At the same [time] he said very handsomely that as he made me this offer from a wish to benefit me, if I thought it more to my advantage to take a salary instead, I might name any sum I thought would content me & if reasonable they would willingly agree to it. After much consideration & consultation with the few here whom I consider friendly disposed towards me, backed by the advice of those in Java, I have come to the resolution abovementioned of joining the concern as a partner.

Johnston it is true has a very heavy debt hanging over his head, both to Hutton & Co. in Calcutta & to Macquoid Davidson & Co., yet you will see from the accompanying extracts of letters which I send you for your better information what advantageous arrangements they (the former I mean) have made with him for further advances.

Of Johnston's establishment I think it may without vanity be said (as Sir Stamford you'll observe does) that as it is one of the oldest so is it of the first respectability in the place. He is the oldest man (tho' not yet forty) as well as merchant in this new Settlement & being partially bald & grey headed looks older than he is, & certainly as no individual in the place is better entitled to it from uprightness of character, there is none more universally respected than Johnston. It is rather unfortunate for those connected with him as I am, that he was not early bred to mercantile business & little conversant with the routine of a Counting House, for I find it utterly impossible to introduce into our business that due attention to method & regularity in the details which is of such vital necessity to the success of trade, and as our tempers, being neither of them the coolest in the world, are apt to clash now and then when brought in contact upon such subjects, I almost despair of ever being able to succeed unless greatly assisted by our other colleague Mr Read who is himself sufficiently regular.'

The new firm (Figure 4) got off to a reasonable start but competition increased and it is doubtful if any other merchants were making much profit. Within a year the East India Company was fitting out an immense armament against the Burman Empire which had for several years been brewing mischief. Not less than 32,000 fighting men were to be dispatched towards that country from the three presidencies. Almost all the country ships including the *Janet Hutton* were taken up by government as transports at a good rate of freight so that for a while there was scarcely a ship to be had at Singapore for the conveyance of goods. Freights had risen threefold in six months and were expected to rise still higher. Hay, who was naturally diffident in public, quite hot tempered and found it difficult to make friends, felt uncomfortable in his position. Although now a partner he was still mainly in charge of the back office, clerical work, and wrote to his brother in May 1825:

'Not that I have any wish or intention of separating myself from this connexion but I wish to be prepared in the event of its being their wish which it is not improbable it may be some day & they have it in their power to accomplish it whenever they please, there being no written articles of partnership between us. I know not why I should have these kind of misgivings of feeling about me except from the fancy I have taken that they don't like me, whether founded on any reasonable grounds or no I can't tell but I can hardly expect that a connexion can be lasting where there seems so little appearance of mutual [word illegible] for each other's interests & so little personal regard for each other as there is amongst us. The bonds appear to me to become weaker and weaker every day, till I should not be surprized if they snap at length with a very slight strain.'

He was unduly pessimistic and remained with the firm until the end of August 1829 when he set up on his own. He did however list in 1827 the properties of the partnership (Figure 5) which were:

No. 1. Dimensions 60 feet along river side & 240 feet along Market Street occupied by a brick warehouse fronting the river with dwelling house on the upper story and 11 shops or China men's houses 2 story high of planks, roofed with tiles, along Market Street & Kling Streets. The warehouse rented by a European shopkeeper at 70 Drs per month and the shops to Chinese. The whole lot giving about 200 Drs monthly, entered by Bonham and held in my own name by a regular Company's lease for 999 years.

No. 2. Dimensions 163 feet along High Street & abt 250 feet along North Bridge Road occupied by my present dwelling house, a plank bungalow roofed with attaps (a thatch composed of leaves of the palm tree) also held in my own name by a similar letter to the above.

No. 3. Dimensions 180 feet along Bridge Road & abt 240 towards Hill Street on which [word illegible] new house is building, a bricked edifice roofed with tiles. One story high only. Held by a grant in my own name from J. Crawfurd, late Resident but for which a Company's lease has not yet been obtained. This lot was purchased from the original possessor as was.

No. 4. on the opposite side about the same dimensions, purchased from the original proprietor held in my own name by the same sort of title, occupied by a small bungalow or one–story house of plank roofed with attaps. Let to a private family at $20 Drs per month.

No. 5. A small lot of ground with a Malay house upon it, dimensions abt 60 feet along North Bridge Road & abt 150 in depth. Of little or no value at present, held merely by a letter of sale from the former proprietor. No grants yet issued but little [illegible].

No. 6. the best lot of ground in Singapore for commercial purposes belonging to Captain Flint R.N. Master Attendant with two fronts to the river and the sea, occupied by A. L. Johnston, dwelling house & one warehouse/country house, the whole rented at abt 250 to 300 Drs per month.

No. 7. A lot of ground purchased lately by the Firm for $6,000 Drs with a two–story brick house upon it, the upper story a dwelling and the lower a warehouse. At present rented at 100 Drs per month for no fixed period, held on a regular Company's lease for 999 years in the name of A. L. Johnston, R. Read & A. Hay.

No. 8. A triangular formed warehouse belonging to Mr Read & held in his own name by a regular company's lease for 999 years also occupied by the Firm. Rent unknown.

No. 9. C. R. Read's dwelling house & grounds on the side spot of Govt. Hill. Originally a plank bungalow roofed with attaps, first inhabited by Johnston & me on our coming here but since sold by him to Read & now a fine large brick house two stories high — the whole however resumeable by Gov't at the expiration of 9 years at a fixed sum if they please — it being Gov't property originally, only to be [words illegible] being built on by individuals.

Correspondence between Raffles and Johnston continued both on private business and political matters. One letter dated London, January 2nd 1825, which may have been received by Johnston in about June, read, in part, as follows:

'I have received your kind letters of the 25th April last, as well as one from the House of the 16th June. The latter I have answered in a separate letter. I have also to thank you for the *tripang*, specimen of Carimon tin, &ca, which are in the course of delivery. The wretched state of my health rendered it necessary that I should abstain as much as possible from public business for some months after my arrival, and had it been otherwise, the season of the year was unfavourable to any progress, London being quite deserted. I have therefore nothing very important to communicate to you as to what is actually done respecting Singapore. There is, as you may suppose, a lively interest taken in its future welfare, and you may be assured that I am not lukewarm of the subject.'

Raffles mentioned that the directors of the Company were thinking of making Singapore a dependency of Penang which would solve the problems of the court of judicature. This was not what he had set up, yet in view of the absence of interest shown by Bengal, he was now coming round to favour it:

'Parliament will meet early in next month, and the subject will no doubt be discussed there as well as in the Court of Proprietors. Nothing will be done in a hurry and therefore it is possible letters from Singapore may arrive in time to assist our judgment. Under this possibility I urgently request your opinion by the first conveyance that offers.'

He also mentioned the absurdity of Americans not being allowed to trade at Singapore, made some disparaging remarks on Crawfurd, the Resident and added:

> 'With regard to the state of our account I have written to the House all that appears necessary, and will only add, in this place, my earnest desire that you will complete the remittances as soon as you can as I am anxious to invest my little property as early as possible.'

As foreseen in the following year, 1826, Penang, Malacca and Singapore were united as one settlement, with Robert Fullerton, appointed as the first Governor of the Incorporated Settlements of Prince of Wales' Island, Malacca and Singapore, based in Penang. Penang and Malacca were now declared to be free ports, Singapore having been so since its founding.

Flooding in town had been a major problem as was the damage done by heavy rains. In February 1827 it was proposed that drains should be constructed in town by Government at a fixed cost per 100 feet. Johnston, together with Sam Bonham and the merchants Maxwell, Syme and Scott, was appointed to a committee to check on the work carried out and decide the amount each building owner must pay. They reported in August, over 5,000 feet of drains and 110 feet of covered drains having been completed.

From this time onward Johnston's name appears occasionally in the *Singapore Chronicle* and in various Government correspondence. In September 1828 it was found that the Company ship *MacQueen* on her way to China had four chests of opium on board in clear contravention of the regulations and her captain, Walker, was called to account. It turned out that this was the fault of his new purser who had taken them as payment of a debt and had them shipped being ignorant of the rules. The chests were immediately landed and bought by Johnston who thereby reimbursed the purser and in due course sold the chests on.[23]

At some stage he must have left Singapore as he is shown as arriving back on 28th April 1829 in *Sherborne* which had come from Calcutta via Penang and Malacca but there is no indication of at which port he had boarded her nor how long he had been away.

---

[23] SSR N4 397.

The cancellation of the Presidency consisting of the three settlements and their reversion to the authority of Bengal was mandated by the Honorable Company and took effect on 31st July 1830. One of many unintended consequences was the sudden suspension of the Court of Judicature two weeks earlier resulting in any debt of more than 32 Spanish Dollars being irrecoverable through legal process. Amounts up to this figure were dealt with by the Court of Requests which continued to operate.

The Court of Directors in London had been aware of the need to have changes made in the recent Charter of Justice and admitted this in a letter dated 7th April 1829, but no government official was keen to risk his career by chasing them up and Bonham had no intention of so doing. The absence of the Court was mainly to be attributed to the functions of its judges having been vested in the officers of the Company's government, contingent upon their possessing the titles of Governor and Resident Councillor, which titles now disappeared and the absence of a Recorder since the departure of the last incumbent in September 1829. This had been an arrangement unpopular in its nature throughout and not considered by many as best fitted for providing impartial justice, the officers concerned not having been trained in legal matters and the Recorder having had little experience in India. Native traders had swiftly taken advantage of this lack and European merchants knew all too well the diminution of confidence and the heavy losses many had sustained. There had been no forewarning of the suspension and found the community totally unprepared to stem the current of misfortunes which followed in its train.

In September 1831, with no remedial action by Government apparently in progress, a committee consisting of Guthrie, Boustead, James Fraser, J. D. Shaw and Diggles of Syme & Co wrote to James Loch who was Acting Registrar of the non–functioning Court at Penang asking for his views:

'as to the particular form and constitution of a Court best adapted to provide for the proper, impartial and uninterrupted administration of justice at Singapore and the probable costs which might be incurred by the establishment of such a Court. On receipt of his reply they called a public meeting "to discuss the best means to procure the re-establishment of a Court of Justice at Singapore".'

The meeting which took place on Saturday 8th October 1831 was attended by almost all the European merchants but very few from the native communities. Johnston was unanimously elected Chairman. It was resolved to submit a petition to the House of Commons through the President of the Board of Control.

The titles of Government officials were subsequently changed. Ibbetson was now Governor and Bonham Resident Councillor in Singapore. The first court for two years was opened on 7th May 1832. Johnston was balloted to be on the Grand Jury and elected as Chairman. One case of murder had been held over from the previous court and two prisoners had died in police custody. Once the criminal cases had been dealt with Johnston, as Chairman gave the Jury's Presentment on the state of affairs. Of particular interest to him was the unsafe state of the bridge, given that he owned a large property beside it on the south bank of the river. Also of concern was the physical state of the Native Poor House and Infirmary, an attap shed which was funded by the entire takings of the Pork Farm. Income greatly exceeded expenditure and there were ample funds to construct a proper building which should be done forthwith.[24]

Government officials appointed by the East India Company did not consider it any part of their duty normally to be involved directly in the day-to-day management of affairs of the town. This task was left to those appointed as unpaid magistrates or justices of the peace, Johnston being, both in age and in standing in the community, the senior and most respected. His great contribution to the development of Singapore has been vastly underestimated. The discharge of responsibilities so important in the running of the town and in smoothing relations between the racial groups cannot be undervalued. Acting as Sitting Magistrate in the Police Office, as he was doing in June 1831, to record the complaint of a local Chinese merchant over piracy, took up many hours, often at times inconvenient for himself and his business. Overseeing the conduct of the small police contingent responsible for keeping the peace, punishing those who broke it, acting as mediator in the commercial disagreements of others, property tax assessment and all the hundred and one matters which needed frequent attention should give him a status in Singapore's history only slightly less

---

[24] *Singapore Chronicle* 17th May 1832.

than that of Farquhar or Raffles who could not have achieved their successes without such help.

His business was in serving the needs of visiting vessels, more than 47 in the year 1836, but he also acted as banker to many including Raffles and Farquhar, and initially as executor of Captain Flint's estate. The firm acted on occasion as property agents, insurance agents, auctioneers and mail forwarders.

Occasional mention of Johnston's name in the *Singapore Chronicle* and elsewhere tells us that he was in Singapore in May 1833 and January 1834. Although not a Roman Catholic he responded to an appeal in December 1832 for funds to build a small church which, after his retirement, was felt to be too small and later replaced by the Cathedral of the Good Shepherd. Not content with this he also contributed in 1834 to the fund to build the first St Andrew's Church and was a member of that church committee until mid–1837. He witnessed marriages on 15th July 1834, and that of the American missionary Ira Tracy on 15th January 1835. He may have then made a short visit to China as a Johnstone [sic] arrived back in Singapore from Canton on 26th April in *Red Rover.* In further support of this supposition, according to a letter in Jardine Matheson's archive and written in May that year, their principal book–keeper Thomas Chay Beale was leaving to become a partner in A. L. Johnston & Co. Singapore. There is no evidence that this actually occurred, but it may be that Beale acted as the company's agent in Shanghai where he later lived until his death in 1857. Two days after his return Johnston undoubtedly left Singapore for Calcutta aboard *Water Witch*, arriving back in the same vessel on 8th June.

The clipper *Sylph* was a regular if fleeting visitor to Singapore on her voyages from Calcutta to Canton with cargoes of opium, and on her return journeys. She was a copy of a famous American privateer and could beat to windward against monsoons in the South China Sea. Her speed enabled her to outrun the pirates who infested not only the coast of China but also the straits near Singapore. Built in Calcutta she was at this time owned three eighths by Rustomjee Cowasjee, one eighth by her Captain Wallace, and the rest by others. In 1834 she had made three round voyages from Calcutta to China and called in at Singapore on 29th January 1835 on her fourth. Sailing the next day she had the misfortune to encounter a strong southward tide when off the northern shore of Bintang Island and was swept onto a shoal where she was held fast. On the news reaching Singapore the East India Company's sloop of war, *Clive*, was dispatched to help and over the next few days the cargo including 960 chests of opium was brought back to Singapore (Figure 6). The ship herself was guarded by the Dutch and just over a year later she had been re-floated and towed to Singapore for repair.[25] Captain Hawkins of the *Clive* arranged for A. L. Johnston & Co to ship the chests to Canton and for the proceeds of sale to be remitted to the Indian Government Treasury. This was done and it led to lengthy disputes both in Calcutta and in Canton between the insurers, Captain Hawkins, Captain Wallace of the *Sylph* and the sellers of the chests. This may have been a reason for Johnston's visit to both these cities. Later in 1836 he received from the insurers in Calcutta a large silver cup to be forwarded to Rhio and presented to Mr de Groot, the Resident, by way of thanks for his help in guarding the wreck and so preserving her and her cargo from pirates.[26]

Early in 1835 Jardine Matheson & Co had ordered a '*wood paddle steamer*' to be built for them in Aberdeen, Scotland. The plan was for her to run between Macao, Lin Tin where the opium holding ships were anchored and the Whampoa port up the Pearl River below Canton. No permission could be obtained from the Chinese for her to proceed upriver and on New Year's Day 1836 a group of Europeans attempted to take her up to Whampoa but were stopped when one of the forts at the Bogue fired on her. Three of those on board went by boat to persuade those ashore to stop and invite the Admiral to come on board which he did, with 100 or so attendants. Although he agreed the vessel was not armed, his orders were specific that the *"fire ship"* was to be stopped and so, once he had gone ashore, the ship turned back towards Lin Tin.

It was now suggested that *Jardine*, as she was named, might be just the ship to deal with the pirates operating with impunity in the waters around Singapore and on 22nd February A. L. Johnston & Co., as agents

---

[25] *Sylph's* repairs in Singapore cost Rs 20,000 before she was able to sail back to Calcutta where she was re-coppered at a cost of Rs 5,500 and sold by the insurers back to Rustomjee Cowasjee for Rs 50,000. Captain Wallace was reassigned to Cowasjee's newest ship. *Sylph* had many further experiences during her career.

[26] *Singapore Chronicle* 24th September 1836.

for the owners, advertised the new steam vessel (expected shortly) for sale (Figure 7). Arriving a week later she was offered to Government to whom the terms were not acceptable. The editor of the *Singapore Free Press* lauded her suitability weekly and the idea of forming a company to own and run her was floated, but to no avail.

On 6th May she set off on a day's picnic with high hopes and a party of local merchants, presumably including Johnston himself, who had paid for the privilege of seeing how she performed at sea. The wood loaded, used for fuel, was too much and too heavy. A good part was swiftly jettisoned. She set off again but before long had run ashore on a mud bank from which the crew extricated her with difficulty. Currents around the outer islands being strong and against her, she made less progress than expected until some recently repaired piece of machinery broke and left her powerless. One davit securing her only boat also broke leaving the bow trailing in the sea. Sails were then set, with difficulty due to the absence of clue lines and other ropes. Wines, spirits and food were far from missing and in great demand. The arrival of two local yachts to rescue them found them a merry crowd in no great haste to get home.

Repairs were put in hand by Stephen Hallpike at his shipyard on the banks of the river and three weeks or so later she set off for Malacca early one evening. Before long she ran aground but was got off and then steamed intermittently up the coast, being abreast of Muar at breakfast time. It was then noticed that steam was coming out of the forward hatch from the engine room, but the steam became smoke. The Captain tried to stop the engine but failed, and in due course it stopped of its own accord after a good deal of water had been pumped in. The boiler remained intact and Hallpike who was on board managed to raise steam and the vessel limped on to Malacca, anchoring well offshore. The party returned to Singapore by other means and *Jardine* having unshipped the paddles and paddle boxes sailed back to Singapore. Any sale now being out of the question the owner arrived from Macao and in September she departed for China with a cargo of rattans and black pepper, arriving there safely a few days later.

Johnston was around in January and February 1836 when he chaired meetings expressing grave concern that the East India authorities were proposing to institute duties on imports and exports, thus imperilling

Singapore's free port status. Although the proceeds of the taxes would be used to fight piracy the fact that Rhio, across the Straits, was now a free port meant that the trade carried out in Singapore would certainly migrate there, with most undesirable consequences. Several months later he received news from London that the proposal had not been and would not be approved, much to the relief of merchants in Singapore.

Johnston witnessed a marriage on 15th September 1836. He was also mentioned in February 1837 when he chaired a meeting which led to the formation of a chamber of commerce and in September 1837 as being a member of the Grand Jury. He was elected the first Chairman of the Chamber of Commerce but at the next annual general meeting, held in July 1838, his name does not appear as chairman or as a member elected to the committee. After September 1837, no reference to his name appears in the Singapore newspapers until August 1839 but the appointment of J. C. Drysdale and Robert Jack to sign *per pro* the firm with effect from the 13th December 1837 implies that he was leaving or had just left Singapore. Maria Balestier, wife of the United States Consul, mentions in a letter dated 17th August 1838 that he had *'been absent in China for many months'* and so this omission was presumably due to his being away from Singapore for an extended period. It is of interest that Mrs Balestier's letter also indicates that he could speak French as *'none of the persons left in his counting house could speak French'* and as a result Captain La Place of the *Artemise* used the services of her husband who did.[27]

Johnston's mother, Elizabeth Laurie, died at Rerwick Park, Kirkudbright on 13th August 1838 surrounded, according to the inscription on her tombstone, by her children, grandchildren and great grandchildren. Given Maria Balestier's comment it seems he was unlikely to have been present. The date of his arrival in Canton is not known but he was named as being at a farewell dinner given to William Jardine before Jardine's

---

[27] Hale, R. E. 2016. *The Balestiers.* Marshal Cavendish Editions, Singapore. p. 99.

departure on 22nd January 1839, preceding a time of turbulence and difficulty for all the foreigners at Canton.[28]

On 26th February 1839 he was a signatory in Canton to a petition to
his namesake A. R. Johnston, HM Deputy Superintendent, deploring the
strangulation in front of the factories of a Chinese who had been accused
by the authorities of smuggling opium.[29] In protest all the foreign *'hongs'*
refused to continue to fly their national flags and asked that the 18 gun
corvette HMS *Larne* should remain to protect them rather than sail for
India as planned. The following month the Chinese Commissioner Lin
who had been sent by the Emperor to suppress the trade ordered that all
the opium then in ships in the river was to be handed over and, in the
meantime, suspended the issue of passports for those who wished to leave
or to move outside the confines of the factories. Captain Elliot, the Chief
Superintendent, returned to Canton from Macao and hoisted the Union
Jack. All the Chinese servants and tradesmen in the factories left. Despite
more provocation, without consulting his countrymen, he arranged for all
the opium in British ships to be surrendered. Many thousand chests, some
owned by the merchants and more on consignment, were handed over but
due to new demands from the Chinese this was temporarily stopped. In
mid–May the Chinese became more threatening and in view of their military preparations Elliot warned foreigners that Canton was no longer
somewhere they could stay with safety or honour. By the end of May the
foreign community in Canton was down to a few Americans, six British
and not a single Parsee. In June, the opium handed over was destroyed.
Outward bound cargoes of tea had been dispatched, inbound cargoes of
Indian cotton pre-sold and the normal trading season was effectively over.

Johnston, one assumes, left with the others in May if not before, and
sailed for Singapore. Back in his house at the mouth of the river he once
again resumed his place as leader of the business community, becoming as
before much involved in its affairs and on 9th August 1839 made a proposal

---

[28] Hunter, W.C. 1911. *The Fan Kwae at Canton before Treaty Days, 1825–1844*, Kegan Paul
Trench & Co London, p. 83 gives the date in November 1838. In *China Trade and Empire*
by Alain Le Pichon p. 350 it is given as 22nd January 1839 as William Jardine had had to
delay his departure by over a month. He left Canton on 26th January and sailed in *Bolton*
from Macao on 31st January. The vessel called at Singapore on 7th February.
[29] *China Repository* March 1839.

for a free school.[30] That he was back in the chair at the Chamber of Commerce is shown by his letter of 23rd September addressed to Governor Bonham complaining of the actions of a Dutch naval vessel arresting four trading prahus from Singapore almost within sight of the harbour.[31] Whether or not he remained chairman the following year we do not know but he was again chairman when writing in October 1841[32] in response to a query from the Governor seeking specific examples of British ships bringing woollen and cotton goods to Dutch ports and being charged extra duty as these had originated east of the Cape of Good Hope. Such duty had been specified in an edict of 1834 but repealed by Holland in 1839.

Known for his hospitality, he put up many ship's captains and their wives at Tanjong Tangkap during their visits to the port. Some may have been true guests. Others paid for their accommodation. Mrs Clara Elliot, wife of the Chief Superintendent in China, stayed in his house for some months after her arrival from Macao in March 1840 and reported in a letter to her sister–in–law:

> 'Since my arrival here I have been living with a merchant of the name of Johnston, *a very old man.* [He was then 57, and she 34]. He is good and hospitable but his house is mercantile and dirty. I remain with him from prudential motives (of the purse). As the time lengthens I find it irksome and shall probably take a small place of my own.'

She had several small children, was a pleasant and lively person, a creole from Haiti in the West Indies where her English father had been Consul General.

On 22nd June 1840, 30 lots of land at Bras Basah Road were sold by the Government on building leases. All were comparatively small lots, but Johnston bought by far the largest. This was an uncleared lot in area one acre, two rods and 28 perches at an annual quit rent of $24. The cost was $100.[33]

---

[30] *Singapore Free Press* 29th August 1839.
[31] *Singapore Free Press* 26th September 1839.
[32] *Singapore Free Press* 21st October 1841.
[33] SSR AA11 page unnumbered.

Johnston's decision to retire to Scotland appears, at least to the Chinese community, to have been a surprise. J. C. Drysdale was appointed a partner with effect from 1ˢᵗ January 1841 and Read's son had joined. Johnston sailed on 20ᵗʰ December 1841 aboard *Charles Grant* en route to Bombay, his fellow passengers being Alexander Guthrie and William Spottiswoode. On 1st February all three took passage in the steamer *Berenice* from Bombay to Suez, crossed the desert to Alexandria and boarded *Oriental* for Falmouth and Southampton, arriving towards the end of March.

In a letter to her sister, Maria Balestier wrote:

'Mr Balestier was at a dinner party last evening given to three of the gentlemen of the Settlement who are about retiring from Singapore. It is quite a serious loss to the place for Mr Johnsons [sic] is the oldest white man and came with Sir Stamford Raffles to the island at the [illegible] he took possession of it so that he is quite the patriarch of it and his decision is the law to the natives whose disputes have been always referred to him and he has had a similar influence on the white inhabitants. He paid us the compliment of coming out to breakfast on Friday morning and I parted from him with a heart ache. He has been absent from Great Britain twenty–two years. How changed everything will be to him. He says if he does not find himself better in health he shall come back to his old friends.'[34]

Even allowing for the compliments normal on such occasions, the farewell address from 38 Chinese merchants and their collection of $1,000 towards a piece of silver plate for him, the genuine feelings expressed ring true:

'You are one whose own character is regulated by the laws of moral rectitude and whose conduct towards others is marked by mildness and gentleness'..... 'If any of the Chinese merchants of Singapore was involved in distress or was falsely accused by others, the affair however difficult to arrange, was with the utmost confidence laid before you for consideration, in full dependence on your ability to make everything plain and simple; and the result was that a mighty affair was reduced in dimensions to a small affair, and a small affair became nothing.'

[34] Letter from Maria Balestier to her sister dated 15ᵗʰ December 1841.

Several other Chinese merchants joined together in raising $500 for a splendid gold snuff box and the Arab merchants had subscribed a similar sum. An article in the *Singapore Free Press* of 5th August 1847 mentioned that the funds subscribed had been *'invested in a very chaste and handsome service of plate'*.[35] It seems strange that at the time there was nothing more in the press than a short paragraph that he was leaving. He remained a partner until, having withdrawn his capital, his interest in the firm ceased on 31st August 1847.[36]

It seems very possible that the firm had run into difficulties of some sort. At the end of December 1841 his partner C. R. Read also retired and it was thereafter managed for many years by his son W. H. Read. W. H. then aged 21 had only arrived in town three months earlier on 12th September. In the absence of some explanation perhaps in a surviving private letter or memoir we may never know the reasons. Read was later in difficulty in England as, on 8th January 1858 with an office at Moorgate Street Chambers and living at 32 Ladbroke Square, Bayswater he assigned his estate to his son W. H. Read of 6 Putney Hill, Putney and Singapore together with Lewis Dunbar Brodie Mackey of London for the benefit of his creditors.[37]

The house on the Singapore River deteriorated and in 1848, rotten and riddled with termites, was pulled down. The firm subsequently took up newly reclaimed land on the other side of Battery Road on which their offices were later built. It may have been due to C. R. Read's purchase of the triangular lot, No. 8 on Hay's list, that they were able to extend the site. A much later proposal to widen Battery Road would involve them in the loss of 15 feet along the edge of the property and in 1861 they sought clarification as they wished to rebuild.

Johnston died on 19th February 1850 at Bluehill, Kircudbright, Scotland in the house of his unmarried elder sister Jane. The news reached

---

[35]The service consisted of a complete tea and coffee service, spoons and silver forks for four dozen persons, a handsome tea urn, corner and beef-steak dishes, dessert knives and forks, a set of very superb trays with an inscription on the largest, liquor and cruet stand which had all been manufactured by Messrs Marshall, George Street, Edinburgh.

[36] *Singapore Free Press* 1st July 1853.

[37] *London Gazette.*

Singapore by the February mail and the *Singapore Free Press* carried a long obituary, part of which read as follows:

'In almost every public transaction connected with the affairs or interests of Singapore, Mr Johnston took a prominent part, and did his utmost to carry out measures for the general good, no matter with whom originating, for there was not the slightest taint of jealously or narrow mindedness in his disposition. He exerted his influence with the public authorities, which was always great, in behalf of every good work. The precedence which was readily accorded to him on all public occasions, testified alike to the respect and esteem with which he was regarded, and to the kindness of his manners and disposition. He was indeed eminently urbane and social, and no less a high spirited gentleman, than a bland and courteous neighbour and associate; and if he sometimes displayed that quickness and ardour of temper, that *perfervidum ingenium* [very ardent temper] which is said to be characteristic of his countrymen, no one could be more willing to forget all cause of difference. He was liberal and hospitable in the extreme, nor was any one more ready to attend to the claims of distress, and those appeals to benevolence which are of no unfrequent [sic] occurrence in British colonies.'

His character could not be summed up in better terms than in the emphatic language of one of his oldest friends and associates *'to know him was to know an honest man and a warm friend.'*[38]

Although there are today members of a family who believe they are descended from Johnston there do not appear to be any records of a marriage or of his having children either within or without wedlock. It is possible that he married during one of his periods of leave from the East India Company service and that his wife died, perhaps leaving a child but this is pure surmise.

In his will dated 11th December 1841 Johnston, apart from a $3,000 bequest to the Singapore Institution, left his entire estate to his two sisters, Mrs Burnet and Jane Johnston. His executors in Singapore were W. H. Read, J. C. Drysdale and Robert Bain all three of whom when the will was

---

[38] *Singapore Free Press* 19th April 1850.

executed were living at the house at *'Tanjong Tangkap'*. Drysdale had been made partner at the beginning of January 1841 and when he retired from the firm in 1847 was replaced as partner by Bain.

On 8th June 1854 at midday, two properties belonging to the estate of Alexander Laurie Johnston were sold by Public Auction. These were a bungalow[39] with a compound area of 31,600 sq. feet, on the banks of the Rochor River (perhaps shown at the left in Figure 8), and nine brick-built shops in Selegie Road with a ground area of 12,200 sq. feet.

An article in *The Straits Times* dated 18th April 1959 titled 'The Singapore Esplanade' by a singularly inaccurate H. T. Sutton relates in some detail a supposed public quarrel between Johnston and the new Governor Colonel Butterworth:

'Colonel Butterworth, the new Governor, and Alexander Johnston, the town's elder citizen, were fighting out a battle of prestige — to the death. And Singapore watched the contest as it unfolded, with bated breath. Every evening as the sun began to throw shadows across the Padang and the cool breeze off the sea made the promenade stroll just a little more briskly, a splendid, shiny, exquisitely appointed brougham drawn by a pair of beautifully groomed horses would pass through the gates of Government House taking Governor Butterworth for his evening drive along the Esplanade.

At just about the same time, a similar carriage, in some ways even more exquisitely appointed, left the house of Alexander Johnston, conveying that rich and influential merchant to the same fashionable promenade.

It was an occasion for decorously raised hats (toppers most of them) by the Europeans and gracefully inclined heads by the Chinese, Malays and Indians (for already in 1843 Asian wealth had overtaken European and was much in evidence). As the carriages passed and their occupants acknowledged mutual recognition, the crux of the snobbery (which it undoubtedly was) came in the urgent desire of everyone concerned to be recognised by their superiors — and given respectful acknowledgement by their inferiors.

---

[39] This *'newly finished'* bungalow had been advertised on 1st October 1841 to be let and appears to have remained empty until early 1844.

The point at issue, being fought tenaciously to the great delight of Singapore, who was the superior, the Governor or A. L. Johnston?

Who should raise his hat first — Colonel Butterworth or the first Chairman of the Chamber of Commerce? Who was senior, the Queen's representative — or the man who was at Singapore with Stamford Raffles, with a hand in every development to the town since it emerged from the jungle?

It was a matter of great interest. And as, each evening, the two most expensive carriages in Singapore passed one another along the Esplanade drive, their two middle–aged occupants with heads turned away in determined ignorance of the other's passing — Singapore giggled and waited for the next instalment.'

All grist to a journalist's mill but a complete fiction, as Johnston had retired to Scotland, leaving Singapore on 21st December 1841, whereas Butterworth did not arrive in Singapore until August 1843.

The firm continued in existence until the 1890s and the Johnston name was continued in the main landing pier, Johnston's Pier. This was first completed in March 1856 and survived after many restorations until 1933 when it was superseded by Clifford Pier further along Collyer Quay. The opening of the new pier was boycotted by much of the business community who objected to the loss of the Johnston name but were overruled by the Governor of the day.

Chapter 2

A. L. Johnston's Recollections in 1848 (based on the Author's Research)

Arrival in Singapore. Other Merchants.

My bones ache. Although Singapore was damp enough, the raw damp of Scotland in winter brings on my rheumatism. Sitting of an evening in front of a peat fire with my sister beside me, listening to the click of her knitting needles or the sound of her spinning wheel while outside a winter's gale threatens to blow down the chimney, my memory returns to the years spent in Singapore. While Jane has of course patiently listened to my repeated stories and reminiscences, neighbours who have never ventured more than a few miles from Bluehill will listen politely for a while and then revert to discussing local events and personalities. I cannot get out and about much nowadays and, although my memory is not what it was and my eyes find candlelight too dim to read, it seems sensible to write down something of what I remember happening in those early days of Singapore and of the people I knew, relying partly on the records brought back with me. Possibly in years to come some of the children or grand-children of my other sister Jean will find the tale interesting. Letters received from the Settlement tell me it has grown strongly in the seven years since I returned to Scotland and I would doubtless find many changes were I to go back. That relentless hot humid climate which we found so trying I now remember with some affection when, as now, warming my feet in front of the fire. The low cloud, thunder, lightning, the twisting of coconut palms like shaken mops, the thrashing branches of jungle trees followed by a sudden downpour of rain moving like a grey curtain across the Cantonment Plain, the blazing sun that followed, the pungent smells, the stench, the babble of local dialects, the mud following rain and the dust in the sunshine, good fellowship, ...

I should begin.

Aged 35 in 1818, I had been roaming that part of the world since I was 12, had had some success in my career at sea but, for the past year or two, it had seemed an increasingly attractive notion to settle down ashore. I knew from personal experience most of the ports in the Indies, the markets, and had some idea of the trade which was carried on between them. The decision to be made was which place would be the best (and most lucrative) for me to choose. Ports in Java had earlier offered possibilities. Now, however, despite persuasive arguments from my optimistic friend Philip Skelton to join him in Batavia, the Dutch being back in charge and determined to make life as difficult as possible for the erstwhile British occupiers, these were losing their appeal by the day.

It was only late in 1819 that Skelton determined, with the active encouragement and support of Raffles, to recruit a person to establish a presence in Singapore and after discussion with his partners suggested I should be that person. He would also send as my clerk a Shetland Islander named Hay who had been not long in Java and had fallen out with his erstwhile employers Deans Scott & Co but of whom he had formed a high opinion.

The authorities in Penang had been constantly working to prevent the establishment and growth of Singapore and done everything they could to hinder its development, even, in May 1819, refusing to send troops for its protection and instead suggesting that the settlement should be evacuated in the face of Dutch threats. They feared its success would render Penang of less importance and following discussions there I believed them to be correct in their assessment, conceiving that Singapore had a good future. As will be shown we were all right. My main concern was whether or not the British Government would retain its new territory or allow it to be taken over by the Dutch, but I was eventually persuaded by Skelton to take that risk. After all it was mostly his own money he was putting in.

Marchioness of Wellesley, the ship in which I was a passenger from Batavia, anchored in the roads of Singapore just over a mile from shore. The view was of a coastline with a number of low hills thickly covered with trees. As I was rowed towards it, I could see a number of wooden houses with attap roofs. We landed on the beach near a police post which faced the mouth of the river at the seaward end of the one street, High Street. This stretched for a mile to the foot of Government Hill with the Cantonment Plain nearby to the right now cleared of the scrub with which it had been covered. Apart from four public buildings of Penang Deal which had been completed, all other buildings were of flimsy materials. Although bricks and chunam were easily available people were reluctant to use them, given the uncertainty of our being able to retain the Settlement. When one lands the river is on one's left, the mouth partially blocked by rocks, and once out of sight turns right up into a wide loop where the boats of the *Orang Laut* may be seen. Beyond the far bank was a muddy swamp with mangroves whilst nearer the sea lay a low hill which I felt would make a good site for a dwelling house. Not far up the near bank the Temenggong's village was situated around a clump of tall coconut palms which must have been planted when he arrived in 1811. The overall impression was of a muddy creek not visible from the sea making an ideal hiding place for the piratical activities which all upper–class Malays feel is their rightful business. I later heard that Farquhar had had to have collected and buried at sea quantities of skulls and human bones which lay thickly on the beach when he arrived with Raffles, a testimony to the activities of the Temenggong's men and others. The Chinese Campong, almost all of the houses being built on stilts over the mud, stretched for half a mile on the south bank of the river across which some 35 wherries plied their trade to and fro. Looking to the right from the landing place, beyond the Cantonment, lay a small bridge across the Freshwater Stream leading to the Bugguese Campong which was about the same size as the Chinese. I was told that an uneven road four miles long had been laid out round the base of Government Hill which was being cleared of vegetation ready for a house to be built at the summit. No house was actually built until early January 1823 when Raffles and his wife, with his sister and Captain Flint (of whom more anon) moved in.

Howard, who, with myself, owned the *Janet Hutton,* had plans to commence business in Singapore in partnership with Allen, an acquaintance of his. He had applied a year earlier, successfully, for allocation of a plot of ground. One facing the sea had been granted on the understanding that they would build on it within six months and that one of them would occupy the godown. So far, they had not done so, and it had not yet been reallocated to anyone else. I came with letters of introduction and called on Lieutenant Colonel Farquhar, the recently promoted officer administering the Settlement, officially called the Resident, who wholeheartedly suggested I install myself as a merchant. He was about 10 years older than I and served under the authority of Sir Stamford Raffles, the Lieutenant Governor of Bencoolen on the West coast of Sumatra. This was a challenging task given the great difficulty of communication with Bencoolen and Raffles' inclination to micro–manage despite absences up country in Sumatra and elsewhere. Singapore was growing rapidly, and he was short–staffed. I also got on well with Captain Travers, an Irishman who, with his wife and child, had arrived from Bencoolen in April with orders from Raffles to take over from Farquhar. I gathered that although there had been some differences of opinion the handover was now to take place on 1st September.

Travers told me that the population was estimated to have been six thousand at the end of May. Whilst this could have been an over-estimate there was without doubt a large number of people crammed into a motley collection of huts, mainly Malay style buildings of planks, attap and matting; those of the few Europeans being of marginally higher quality.

Europeans were few. Apart from officers from the 20th Regiment Bengal Native Infantry, from the Bengal Artillery and a few civil servants of The Honorable East India Company the others would not have been at most more than 20.

I met a Captain Cathcart Methven whose service at Bencoolen had, according to Travers, not been without serious problems, and was, in theory, en route back to Bencoolen after sick leave. He was thinking of resigning his commission in the Company's service to become a full-time merchant. John Morgan, a former lawyer's clerk and East India Company mariner had just arrived from Batavia where, with his brother Alexander, he ran a retail business. I did not talk much to him. Both these two I perceived were no different from many Chinese and Chuliahs in their determination to make as much money as quickly as humanly possible and, I feared, with little regard for ethical dealing. Singapore at the time was a place to make money fast and then go home rich — or not, as the case might be.

The swift expansion of the traffic of the port was far greater than anyone had first expected. Prahus and junks large and small, up to 40 at any one time from all around the region, could be seen offshore. This was thanks not only to the Settlement's geographical position, its being open to all and without duties, and the fact that the Dutch were increasing taxes throughout their islands but also, in my view, to the fact that Farquhar had for many years been Resident and Commandant in Malacca where he was deservedly popular and respected. This reputation led to many of those who were living there deciding to escape the harsh clutches of the Dutch, now back in control and doing their best to prevent any such move. They came to Singapore to join others from the region, some respectable and some decidedly not, and carry on their many trades and businesses. Farquhar's mild manner, upright and correct conduct allied with his informality when not on duty as he took his daily walk with his dog, resulted in his continued popularity except among some of his few underlings and a merchant or two who resented his tendency to favour his son and two sons-in-law over themselves. When in Java during the British occupation, I was told, he had been felt to be lacking in drive which mattered not as he was there supported by an assistant who made up for this weakness. In Singapore he had been helped by a Lieutenant Crossley, Raffles' former secretary, who was *'hard headed'* and who *'to his good abilities joined a bluntness more than usual even among the English'* but this position had been abolished by orders from Calcutta at the end of 1819. A number of other cuts in the establishment had been imposed and he was now under considerable stress.

Square-rigged vessels arrived, as did native craft from all over the islands. There was evidently scope for a trustworthy agent ashore who could assist the commanders of commercial vessels visiting the port to sell their cargoes and find them goods to take onwards. Commission on such deals was recognized to be 5 per cent, attractive enough to a Scotsman.

I also recognised a need to guard against the already evident greed and importunities of the new Master Attendant, Captain Flint. He was about my age, a well–covered man who had had many financial difficulties and used his family connection with Sir Stamford Raffles to his great advantage. The job having been reserved for him by Raffles, he displaced Francis Bernard, Farquhar's son–in–law, who had been filling the post pending his arrival. It was perhaps fortunate that Bernard could thereafter be put in charge of the skeleton police force as Assistant in the Police Office and use to the full his knowledge of local languages.

General opinion in Calcutta was that the Company would not be allowed to retain Singapore. Commissioners had been appointed in Europe by both sides to discuss the question and nobody had confidence that the decision would go our way, given the apparent indifference of the ministers in London. It was believed that in a few months an official order would come to hand the island over to the Dutch, leading to ruin for many, particularly those who would, by then, have laid out good sums of money to develop godowns and so on. The local population was extremely concerned and both the Sultan and the Temenggong had sent official letters to Farquhar hoping he would lay the rumours to rest, thus putting him in a most difficult situation as he knew no more than anyone else. Perhaps, to be fair and justify his reluctance to handover to Travers, he felt that, given his status, if he left at this stage it would be interpreted wrongly by them.

We did not know then what was happening in London. George Canning, President of the Board of Control which oversaw The Honorable East India Company, was in charge of the discussions which concerned Singapore as well as the various Dutch trading posts on the mainland of India and the future of Penang, Bencoolen and Malacca. He had in July given indication that Singapore could be possibly exchanged for the island of Banca which, fortunately for us, was not taken up by the Dutch. Further negotiations were, with mutual agreement, postponed while awaiting a letter from the Governor General in Calcutta, the arrival of which would take months. Canning then left England for three months to avoid having to vote in parliament on the Queen's divorce and many more months passed without action. The Dutch, who were facing their own financial and other problems in the Indies, were in no hurry to pursue solutions.

After considerable thought, I agreed with Skelton to settle with Singapore as my base and sailed first to Calcutta to make some necessary preparations and contacts, arriving at the end of August. My arrangements were relatively quickly made and in early November 1820 I was back in Singapore to set about business.

On my return I found that, to my surprise and great disappointment, Travers was still not in charge of the Settlement. On the very day, 1ˢᵗ September, on which Farquhar had undertaken to step aside, the cutter *Frolic* had arrived from Bencoolen with Captain Flint's wife and son on board. Also on board was Captain William Mackenzie, who was said to have some ability allied with a most consummate good opinion of himself and whose brother later became Secretary to Government in Calcutta. Raffles, supposedly thinking that Travers was now installed and knowing that he wanted to return to Europe after a year in the job, had decided to send Mackenzie to Bengal via Singapore bearing dispatches, return to Bencoolen and then take over from Travers in September 1821. This complicated matters further. Farquhar remained adamant. He would not hand over to anyone until directly instructed to do so by the Governor General. On 1ˢᵗ October Mackenzie sailed on to Calcutta in *Investigator* in some doubt as to his own eventual fate. He reappeared briefly in June 1821 en route to Bencoolen and when that settlement was to be returned to the Dutch was appointed Resident in Malacca for about a year, taking over from the Dutch governor. After retiring he died in 1842.

With his wife Mary (who was pregnant) and their baby son, Travers had been staying in Farquhar's compound but had moved out as they were no longer on speaking terms. He had then accepted the offer of accommodation from their old friend, Lieutenant Ralfe, the Engineer Officer in charge of Ordnance, whose house (which I later bought) on the lower slopes of Government Hill looked over to the newly laid out High Street. Travers considered going up to Calcutta to lay his case before the Supreme Government which would have been expensive and, if the Settlement were eventually to be handed over, something of a waste of time. In letters from friends there he learned of strong rumours that the salary and allowances of the Resident were likely to be reduced and feared that, even were he to take over, these would be insufficient to cover expenses.

Frolic had brought news of a private trader ship, *Minerva*, which, was expected to come up from Batavia and then sail direct for Europe. Travers determined to take passage in her. As the days passed with no sign of her, I suggested that they should take one of two Indiamen, knowing both Captains as reliable and good seamen, which were expected to call in shortly on their voyages to China. He could then travel to Europe on their return voyage which would not involve a call here. Although it would be a lengthy and roundabout route there seemed to be no alternative. On 17th November *Minerva* at last made her appearance and, although she looked dirty, good spacious accommodation was available. Travers paid £300 passage money for the family and two servants to Cape Town where they should arrive before Mary was due to have her second baby. The ship was intended to sail on 1st December but was not quite ready and on the same day another ship arrived with letters from Raffles confirming that the Governor General had approved Travers' appointment and giving him further instructions on his future administration. Travers had Ralfe take these to Farquhar and ask him to hand over, being ready to give up his voyage. Farquhar declined. We discussed the position. Uncertainty, perplexity and annoyance were the main emotions. In the end Travers decided to leave as planned and embarked with his wife and child. They were seen off by Captain and Mrs Flint and, there being a fair breeze, many friends followed in small boats as far as they were able.[1] Only Farquhar was happy to see them go.

Travers had during his wait in Singapore acted as Military Paymaster, assisted by R. P. Reed, a writer who had been first employed by Raffles in 1817, and S. G. Bonham, a young writer. Although it had not yet been

---

[1] Journal of T. O. Travers. Memoirs of the Raffles Museum. p. 153–6.

officially advised to Raffles, Farquhar had told Reed that he could take over from Travers and had written to Bencoolen for approval. Being a regular churchgoer and there being at this stage no church in Singapore, Farquhar allowed religious services to be held in one of the buildings in his compound and expected all Europeans to attend regularly. Reed did not do so and, when reprimanded and instructed to attend under a Garrison Order, pointed out that he was a civilian and so was entirely within his rights not to do so. Farquhar thereupon cancelled his appointment, reasoning that he was not suitable to hold it and gave the job to his own son-in-law Captain Davis. The case was referred to Raffles.[2] He sided entirely with Reed and admonished Farquhar strongly. Communication problems ensured that this, although written in March 1820, did not reach Singapore until August when Reed was re-employed as translator of official documents.[3]

Bonham, who had also been helping out, at 17 years old thought he was better qualified than Davis to do the job and wrote a personal letter of complaint to Raffles. This did not get him the job although in January 1821, perhaps as a result, he received instructions to go to Bencoolen and on via Tappanooly to Nattal as assistant to John Prince, the Resident. Nattal and Tappanooly were *'pepper'* ports on the west coast of Sumatra.

Reed was later, early in 1823, instructed by Raffles to proceed and take the place Bonham had earlier filled.[4] He sailed in *Janet Hutton* and sadly died at Nattal in December the same year.

And then of course there was Queiros who came to Singapore initially in February 1820 with his wife and child when he obtained through Farquhar allocation of what was probably the best site for a godown near the mouth of the river next to Ferry Point. He later returned to Calcutta and Java, coming back with me in the *Wellesley* in June. He had arrived with no idea where they would live but plenty of funds from his *éminence*

---

[2] SSR L4 138-141 October 1820.
[3] Raffles' letter of 22nd March 1822 received in Singapore on 17th Aug 1822. See SSR L8 181-4 for Farquhar's reply in protest.
[4] SSR L17 473.

grise John Palmer of Calcutta who was whispered to be his father.[5] Socially a pleasant man to meet and shake hands with (as long as you counted your fingers afterwards), he was a sore trial to Palmer. He offered a good price for Acting Assistant Surgeon Prendergast's house, $750 if I remember correctly, and very quickly fell out with Farquhar. When he suggested to me at the end of the year that we might form a *"joint connection"* I made my excuses although I continued to assist the captains of Palmer's vessels whenever needed.

Our European merchant numbers had increased since my visit in July. D. S. Napier, a young Scot from Edinburgh had turned up in Singapore in September the previous year with recommendations from Calcutta expecting to be taken on to the staff at Bencoolen. Farquhar liked the look of him and offered him the job of Assistant in the Police Department at a salary of $150 a month, subject to approval from Raffles. When in mid–April 1820 a letter in reply to the proposal was received which did not approve his employment, Farquhar refused to pay him his outstanding salary. Napier sent off a private letter of complaint to Raffles and left for Calcutta via Penang a week or two later, only returning in November to set up as a merchant in partnership with Charles Scott, the son of one of Penang's leading businessmen. In due course Raffles censured Farquhar and approved the payment but there was little love lost.

Queiros, Napier, Scott, Morgan and myself were all given a joint Christmas task by Farquhar on 22nd December[6] to provide him with details of business done at Singapore during the year as well as a general view of trade and what this might become should the Settlement be permanently fixed under the British flag, as the Government had only begun compiling statistics in May. This involved a good deal of guesswork, for obvious reasons. The figures produced were sent off to Bencoolen and no more was heard on the subject.

---

[5] Letter from John Palmer to Claude Queiros dated 1st February 1820 before the latter had left India. For the full text of this letter please see p. 264–265.
[6] SSR L4 236-7.

Chapter 3

Troublemakers. New Partners.
Chinese Merchants. Coinage.

There was no bridge over the river when Raffles first arrived and before he left in July 1819 at the end of his second visit, he had given instructions for one to be built where the river narrows, upstream from the site of the Temenggong's village. In 1821 we still had none even though the materials had already been assembled and were gently rotting away in the Government godown. This, I was given to understand, was because there were now strict instructions to spend only the minimum on public works, given the uncertainty that we could retain possession of the Settlement. In fact the absence of a bridge was of no great consequence as any number of small *orang laut* boats served as ferries. In 1823 a temporary wooden bridge with a drawbridge in the middle to allow boats to pass under it was constructed and as often happens, became more permanent than expected. It was 240 feet long and 18 wide and before long was in urgent need of repair, in which state it remained for many years despite occasional attempts by Government and others to patch it up.

The drawbridge was designed so that ships' boats going upriver to draw water from the freshwater spring at the side of Government Hill could pass freely. So–called freshwater for public use was obtained through a large number of wells dug all over the town to tap the water table just below the surface. This tended to be slightly contaminated by salt and was not felt suitable for visiting ships, particularly in view of the work involved in drawing the water. Thus the spring was used and a small reservoir or pond which it supplied was built. Repairs were much needed by late 1823 and the capacity to supply what was required declined. As a result of a major drought in Java in 1824 the company ships *Thames* and *Marquis of Huntly* had both been supplied with green stagnant muddy water at Anjer on their passage through the Sunda Strait. Within a few days half the crew were suffering severe bowel complaints and both ships put into Singapore to replace the water they already had and take on sufficient quantities to last them on their passages up the South China Sea. This took time and in the meantime *Marquis Camden*, *General Harris* and *Lord Melville* as well as other vessels had to await their turns. It was then determined to build an aqueduct and further enlarge the reservoir so that any sized fleet should be able to draw water within a reasonable time.[1]

The arrival of the first junk from Amoy, China in February 1821 was welcomed by all as the possible forerunner of many others. It was customary and, as we only found out later, a requirement of the port regulations, that Nakhodahs (Captains) of native boats should pay courtesy calls on the Temenggong and Sultan after they had registered at the Master Attendant's office. At such visits, as was customary throughout the eastern seas, presents were offered by the visitor although according to official regulations these were not mandatory. The Nakhodah of the junk was unaware of the requirement and a few days later was sent for by the Sultan and, whether because the $20 offered was not considered enough or because he had not come earlier, was arrested and put in the stocks by the Sultan's men.

The news travelled fast, and we were worried that in the future a European captain might be so treated. Within the day Scott, Morgan, Christie,[2] Guthrie (who had only just arrived in Singapore), Andrew Hay and I wrote to Farquhar asking for action, given the possible damage to our good reputation for free trade. In the true style of the *'heaven born'* officials of the East India Company he replied by return, roundly castigating us not only for writing a joint letter but also for interfering in matters

---

[1] *Oriental Herald & Journal of General Literature* 1825, p. 305.
[2] Peter Christie arrived in 1820 and worked for a short period for Morgan before setting up on his own. He is thought to have left Singapore in 1824.

connected with politics. We were not prepared to accept this, and although we found that some of the news brought to us had been incorrect, pointed out that it was the fault of Government insisting that native Nakhodahs must pay a courtesy call on the Sultan. We also suggested that the Nakhodah should be given some compensation. Later we found out that his interpreter, sensing trouble, had left the Sultan's compound and rushed to Tan Che Sang, effectively the head man for the Hokkien community, who at once advised Farquhar what had happened. Bernard, Farquhar's son–in–law and now head of the Police, was sent to Campong Glam to demand the prisoner's immediate release, which was carried out, the detention having lasted four hours. Thus he had been freed before Farquhar received our letter.

We had no judicial court in Singapore in those days and when disputes occurred between merchants an arbitration panel would be set up whose decision, by common agreement, had the effect of law. As mentioned, I had hardly had time to settle in before I was asked in November 1820 with others to arbitrate on a trade dispute between Syed Jassin of Lingin and Captain Methven. We found against Methven. He was an officer in the Bengal Native Infantry who had been serving in Bencoolen where he got into some unspecified trouble before falling ill and being sent to Penang on sick certificate. Having regained his health he arrived in Singapore in March 1820 and asked to be taken on the books until he could get back to Bencoolen. Finding what he thought were good commercial opportunities and knowing that as an officer he was not permitted to trade, he applied in May to the Commander–in–Chief in India for permission to resign his commission. Fully certain that this would be granted, without waiting for the reply which would take some months, he started lending out the funds he had had sent from Calcutta. He was able to obtain high interest rates due to the general shortage of ready money among local traders and quickly acquired a reputation for underhand dealing and the dislike, in particular, of John Morgan who did not appreciate a competitor as unethical as himself. It was thus with some surprise that Methven received in November a letter from the Adjutant General in India advising the Commander–in–Chief's recommendation that he should withdraw his resignation in view of the doubts held on the future of the Settlement. This he did, the same day, also requesting time to unwind all his outstanding business affairs and remit the funds back to Bengal, but apart from this to stop trading.

Despite his undertaking, Methven could not resist doing business when it offered. Two merchants and their follower came from Trengganu to sell him gold dust. When the deal was agreed he delayed payment on the grounds he had no cash and proposed to sell them opium instead. Not only did this turn out not to be Company Opium but a dispute arose over the quantity of the gold dust. The other merchants supported the case of the Trengganu men and, if he refused to comply, undertook to bear the loss themselves so as to preserve the reputation of Singapore as a good place to do business. In any small community there is often a degree of backbiting and spite and the cantankerous Morgan stirred up the merchants' distrust. Captain Seppings, who had commanded the local detachment of the Bengal Native Infantry since the Settlement began, felt that although Methven was not under his command his actions were injurious to the Army's reputation and told him, in no uncertain terms, to behave himself. His social life becoming unbearable, Methven asked Farquhar to call a court of enquiry into the allegations and Captain Davis,[3] Lieutenant Ralfe and Lieutenant George Bonham were appointed to officiate. This took up an inordinate amount of time from 14th April to 4th May, the court sitting from 10am to 3pm daily. I had to attend as an *'evidence'* as did other merchants, both European and native. In the end it was determined that, although all knew of his misconduct and guilt, as he was still a serving officer the case should be referred to the military authorities in India. The papers were forwarded, and Methven left in the same ship for Calcutta to defend himself. He was successful in doing so and was exonerated of all charges by the Commander–in–Chief who in July[4] allowed him

---

[3] Charles Edward Davis, a Lieutenant in the 29th Regiment Bengal Native Infantry, arrived in Singapore from Calcutta late in 1819 having been granted compassionate leave to attend to personal matters. It seems he came to request the hand of Farquhar's youngest daughter Catherine Dorothy who at that time was in Calcutta. Farquhar agreed and held open for him the position of Cantonment Adjutant. The marriage is believed to have taken place after the girl's arrival on 30th May 1820. He was later promoted Captain and remained in Singapore until April 1827. Also see SSR L5 142 showing that Lt George Bonham had been appointed, and not S. G. Bonham.

[4] SSR L5 296 Letter to Farquhar dated 7th July 1821.

to return to Singapore to wind up his affairs and then go to Europe on furlough. Seppings, poor fellow, was roundly castigated by the Calcutta authorities and replaced shortly afterwards by a Captain Murray.

Meanwhile Morgan, a troublemaker, leaving the day–to–day business to his brother Alexander who had arrived from Batavia, sailed for Bangkok. He had been appointed by the President of the Board at Prince of Wales Island, with the sanction of the Supreme Government, to proceed to Bangkok to sound out the views of the Court of Siam and to collect precise and authentic information on current conditions there. He carried a letter from Farquhar addressed to the Siamese King which was intended to open doors. This did not succeed and the voyage to both Siam and Trengganu was a failure, both commercially and otherwise, returning to Singapore in October. In due course, having padded his accounts with mercantile commissions, interest, house rent et cetera he was awarded an extra $1,200 for his services and reimbursed by the Government in Penang to the tune of over $4,500.[5]

Alexander Guthrie had arrived in January from Cape Town where he had been working for a Captain Harrington, in whose ship *Ganges,* Ibbetson (later our Governor) and Raffles had come out to Penang in 1805, and who had retired from the Hon'ble Company's marine service in 1813. Guthrie, a farmer's son from Brechin in Angus was a little over 10 years younger than I and his two years with Harrington had taught him a good deal. He was at first able to rent a brick godown from Dunn, a naturalist who, having been employed in Java and Banca, was sent by Raffles to Singapore bringing nutmeg and clove plants. Quite soon after he had moved his cargo of trade goods into it, Dunn, leaving for Batavia as his position had been revoked by Farquhar for reasons of economy, sold it to some Armenian traders from Malacca, Aristarkies Sarkies and Arratoon Sarkies, and he had to move out at the end of the one year's lease. He was offered a site at East Beach but turned this down and was fortunate to be able to take up a vacant lot of ground on the north side of High Street opposite the Temenggong's pagar and build his own godown.

---

[5] SSR A16 628-633

By July 1821[6] most of us had applied to Farquhar to be allotted ground along the riverbank on which to build godowns although only Methven had so far actually completed one. Land along East Beach towards Campong Glam had also been surveyed and almost all of the 22 lots allocated although this site was not suitable for business purposes, the beach suffering from rough surf which made the landing of goods difficult. Guthrie, Napier, Mackenzie & I wrote to Farquhar at his request in April 1822 giving our opinions as to the best and only place to build godowns.[7] My lot at Campong Glam, No 3, transferred to me from Macquoid in Batavia, remained unoccupied as were almost all the others. By now I was living at the foot of Government Hill in a house which at that stage still belonged to Ralfe from whom I later bought it.

I think it was at about this time, September 1821, when C. R. Read joined me initially as writer but very soon had unexpectedly to go to Batavia. He only returned in July 1822[8] and with Hay became a partner in the firm when we reorganised in May 1823. Four years younger than I, he had been in the business of shipping agent ashore in London and twice had failed. The second winding up came in 1818, when he had been in partnership with his brother–in–law, D. A. Fraser who was now in business in Batavia. As ship's husband he had then made two voyages in *Providence*, a ship licensed by the East India Company.[9] On the second voyage he left the ship and made his own way to Singapore via Batavia.

Our European merchant numbers grew slowly. Graham Mackenzie arrived early in 1821, John Purvis from Macao a year later and J. A. Maxwell now spent most of his time in the Settlement rather than at Batavia. Christie gave up the struggle and sold his godown to Mackenzie. Dunn had left. G. D. Coleman, a young Irish architect, came down from Calcutta in June 1822 in the expectation of meeting Raffles, but had to wait four months until the latter's arrival in October.

At this time there were two leading Chinese merchants in the Settlement. Tan Che Sang, or Che Sang as we knew him, being in his late

---

[6] SSR L5 237 plus attachments
[7] SSR L7 181
[8] SSR L9 45. His letter applying for ground in July 1822.
[9] Lloyds Register of Shipping, 7th June 1818.

50s was a good deal older than any of us. He had emigrated from Fujian province in China at the age of 15 in 1778 and over the years, first in Rhio, then Penang and lastly Malacca, had made a fortune before transferring his activities to Singapore in 1819. By this time he had two large and three small shops in River Street and had bid successfully for the arrack farm giving him the sole right to manufacture and sell arrack in Singapore, through three other shops. He later had a godown on the riverside above the bridge.[10] He had a brick kiln up the Kallang River, was probably head of the local Hokkien *hoey* and was a tough, ruthless and canny operator whose interests were widely spread.[11] By the end of his life he had become completely bald.[12] He was agent for many of the Chinese junks and one of his sons, Baba He, worked for me for a while as my agent in buying goods for export on which he undoubtedly made good profits. In the summer of 1834 there was quite a sensation on account of his daughter being run away with by the Rajah of Singapore. She conformed to his Muslim faith and became his wife but did not become reconciled with her father.[13] Being too fond of gambling in his youth, he had cut off the top joint of one finger to cure himself of the habit. This action failed to do so, and he gambled until his death in April 1835 which was followed by a funeral, the like of which had not been seen in Singapore before.

When disputes broke out among the Hokkien community Che Sang was able to deal with them albeit not always in ways of which we approved. We magistrates had an emergency meeting in about 1831 I think, when an affair excited considerable attention in the Settlement. This concerned a poor deranged woman who broke a large quantity of earthenware and crockery exposed for sale at the front of a shop in Teluk Ayer Street. The elderly Chinese owner was naturally furious and with the assistance of two of his employees struck the woman and pushed her into the drain. Her family was wealthy and felt they had been insulted. They insisted that the matter be referred to Che Sang for arbitration but he, before agreeing, went to Bonham to get his approval, having first gone

---

[10] *Singapore Free Press*, 6th January 1841.

[11] *Singapore Chronicle*, 5th May 1834.

[12] Letter from Maria Balestier to her sister dated 10th April 1835.

[13] ibid.

and slapped the face of the elderly Chinese. Bonham, without considering the matter deeply, gave his approval. Che Sang then condemned the three Chinese to undergo a dozen lashes each with a rattan cane which he inflicted personally and in public shortly afterwards. It was rumoured that both Che Sang and the mad woman's son–in–law had an old grudge against the shop owner and so used this occasion to gratify their feud. The case came to public notice in the *Singapore Chronicle* which described Che Sang as having risen from the dregs of the population, no one quite knew how, and whose character was in line with his origins.[14]

The other was Choa Chong Long coming from a wealthy Hokkien family in Malacca. He too arrived in Singapore in 1819 and having plenty of funds was able to do well. He became the opium *'farmer'*, bidding the highest rent payable to Government for the right to convert the raw drug into the refined article so popular among all classes of Chinese at the time and to sell it to them through four shops. He acquired much property and, being an outgoing person, to celebrate his 44th birthday in 1831 gave a dinner party to which I remember we were all invited. He sailed, aged 50, for Macao in 1838 where, to our dismay, he was murdered. He had by then had had a house built along Beach Road although he never occupied it. After his death it was used for a short while as a theatre and later sold. Amateur dramatics were a very popular activity among our small community at one time but not everyone approved. On one particular occasion, when no ladies were present, the evening got out of hand and the editor of the *Singapore Chronicle* wrote that the performance could have been much better had several of the performers kept sober.[15]

Another new arrival, Lee Ha Ki (also known as Li Hu Ke) sold off goods for Methven, had the key to his godown and traded successfully on his own account.[16] For most of us his claim to fame was the dinner he gave at the house on the hill above Chinatown in mid–June 1824 to which the entire European community were invited and which was a memorable success (at least for those who did not overindulge in champagne) despite the entirely Chinese food which was strange to many of the 50 or so guests

---

[14] *Singapore Chronicle*, 3rd March 1831.
[15] *Singapore Chronicle*, 2nd February 1834.
[16] SSR L5 106,109,135,136.

attending. I find it is always best on such occasions to try the dishes before asking of what ingredients they are made. Later descriptions of the raw materials for the dishes served were imaginative to say the least and appeared in print the next year in an account in the Oriental Herald published in London.[17]

Large numbers of Cantonese, Teochew and Hakka as well as Hokkien Chinese merchants, brokers, coolies and tradesmen continued to flood into the Settlement. Their attap huts sprang up along the coastline, along the south side of the river and inland, in fact wherever space could be found. Although not yet the largest ethnic community, Malays still holding that distinction, the Chinese were undoubtedly far the most important in commercial terms.

It was in September 1821, as far as I recall, that regulations were promulgated concerning wholesale dealings in opium. None other than that officially exported from the Company's sales in India might be imported, and any smuggled or foreign grown was prohibited. Duty to be paid was 6 per cent which, if I am not wrong, could be reclaimed when it was exported. I occasionally was sent opium to be sold on a commission basis and, if in doubt as to its origin, was very careful to point out these doubts to potential buyers.

One of the challenges in doing business in Singapore and elsewhere in the region was the variety of coinage in use and the very great quantity of spurious money circulating. This was mainly brought in day by day from other ports and places and every description of coin passed current in the bazar. Without an experienced *shroff* to examine the coins offered, a merchant could be a considerable loser for much of the coin had to be rejected as forged or chopped.

Those who have never left Scotland can have no concept of the situation. In India under the Honorable Company the standard coin had been and still is the rupee, cast in silver, known as the Sicca Rupee and divided into 16 annas, each anna being 12 pice. Sicca was a standard measurement of weight for many articles and originally had indicated the weight of silver in the coin. By the 1820s the actual value of the rupee varied from port to port and the official books of account were kept in an imaginary

---

[17] *Oriental Herald and Journal of General Literature*, Feb 1825, p. 290.

currency called the *'Current Rupee'*. The value assigned to actual coins, depending on their origin and quality, was reduced by a variable percentage (known as Batta) when being entered into the books. The Government used Sicca rupees on a day–to–day basis while the Military used the Sonat rupee worth slightly less. Most of us European merchants used the Spanish Dollar (Figure 9) as our unit of account. This was, and still is, a silver coin minted by Spain with the head of their king or queen on one side. We all kept certain mint condition dollars to use when weighing gold, two such coins weighing the same as a buncal of gold dust or one twentieth of a catty. Of catties there were two types with a slight difference in weight, so merchants had to be alert. The Spanish Dollar was in Singapore officially subdivided into 27 fanams and each fanam into 10 doits. The Sicca rupee was stated to be worth so many fanams, but the numbers differed from port to port and city to city. Madras was still unofficially using Star Pagodas which were of gold, divided into 42 fanams, each fanam being divided into 80 cash. You will understand just how confusing all this could be, particularly to the captains of visiting ships who also had to cope with measurements of weight strange to them such as maunds (82 lbs) and taels. The tael was made up of 16 mace and one mace was the weight of 24 scarlet beans, from a tree the seeds of which did not vary in weight.

The Resident, Colonel Farquhar had by now brought down from Malacca his long–term Eurasian mistress Nonia Clement, his unmarried daughter Elizabeth and one son, Andrew, who started business on his own. There can be little doubt that, as I have already stated, the commercial success of the Settlement was almost entirely due to his able leadership and the way he acted, whenever possible, in the interests of the community despite the need to refer too much to Raffles in Fort Marlbro' at Bencoolen, Sumatra. Communication with that port was intermittent at best and letters could take months in transit. He was not helped by the determination of the authorities to spend as little as possible on Singapore, given the doubts that it could be retained. It always amazed me that the Government staff establishment in Bencoolen was 10 times that of Singapore and the work which existed for them to do was far less than a tenth of that needed in our Settlement. He was very conscious of his official position and reacted strongly if he felt this had been in any way denigrated by merchants who, despite their necessary importance in the scheme of things, he considered, as did many others of the Supreme Government administration, definitely second class when compared to themselves and the military.

He had a number of critics, John Morgan for one, who accused him of trading and other misdemeanours, but the most dangerous and difficult to counter was Captain William Flint, Master Attendant and Storekeeper.[18] Flint, a few years younger than Farquhar had been in command of HMS *Teignmouth* prior to the invasion of Java and had married Raffles' favourite sister Mary Anne in Malacca in 1811 before setting sail. In Java he was appointed to several lucrative positions by Raffles although his appointment by the Governor General as Prize Agent for the Honorable Company was disputed and he spent much time and money seeking compensation in Calcutta and London. This was, in the end, denied by the Honorable Company's directors. Being then *'on the beach'* and on half pay, with his wife and small son he next, at Raffles' invitation, joined him in Bencoolen and shortly thereafter sailed for Singapore where Raffles had reserved for him both land and the appointment of Master Attendant and Storekeeper. Arriving in Singapore in April 1820 he dislodged Bernard, Farquhar's son–in–law, who was doing the job on a temporary basis and proceeded to build himself a two–storey house opposite Ferry Point. The official approval for him to occupy the site was granted in October.

Because of his naval rank Flint considered himself senior to Farquhar and quickly made this clear in a number of ways calculated to irritate, while at the same time finding means to increase his own income. The Temenggong complained that his own small boats were now being charged port clearance fees and this was stopped following a brisk correspondence.[19] Reduced fees, half of which were now paid to the Temenggong, continued to pay for Flint's office stationery &ca. His store-keeping was not up to naval standards and the European troops refused on occasion to accept the salt beef he provided. Even worse for them was that the stores twice ran out of rum (which ill wind gave me the opportunity to sell some to the Company). As time went on, he famously refused to work

---

[18] Born 17th October 1781. Died 3rd October 1828.
[19] SSR L4 301 dated 19th March 1821.

outside the official working hours of from 10 am to 3 pm (which some years later in, I think, 1828 were changed to 10 am to 5 pm).[20] On one even better known occasion he refused to accept certain stores from the military *"because he would have to receive them from the hands of a sergeant rather than an officer"*. He demanded more clerks, was in the habit of flying a King's Ensign[21] over his office and refused visiting ships permission to fly pennants in the harbour as this was contrary to Admiralty instructions. This affront to Farquhar's dignity required further action and Flint was told in no uncertain terms not only had his naval rank no validity in the Settlement but that he was merely Master Attendant (harbour master) and Storekeeper. Being a small community such gossip raced from person to person and even the terms of official correspondence were rarely kept entirely secret. Every official or commercial letter was copied several times and entered into the records by means of a *"letter book"* by writers or clerks employed for the purpose and leaks did occur.

It was known by July 1822 that Raffles proposed to revisit Singapore and several applications for land were put aside pending his arrival. Nobody I knew foresaw the whirlwind tornado which was about to descend upon us and cause immense distress and loss in many quarters.

---

[20] SSR N4 184 dated 22nd April 1828.
[21] A White Ensign.

Chapter 4

Raffles' Reorganisation. Property Matters. Farquhar's Problems.

As I was saying, the storm was about to break over us, unprepared as we were. Raffles, the Lieutenant Governor, arrived on 10th October 1822, a date never to be forgotten. He had had a fast passage of 23 days from Bencoolen and brought with him his wife, her younger brother Nilson Hull who acted as his secretary, Dr James Lumsdaine, Captain Francis Salmond and young Sam Bonham from his post in Nattal.

Salmond who had been Master Attendant at Bencoolen since 1810, had been sent to Palembang by the Lieutenant Governor in 1818 to persuade Sultan Ahmed to accept British control. On arrival he was arrested by the Dutch and later returned by them from Batavia by sea. A very close personal friend of the Lieutenant Governor, he came on the voyage mainly to recruit his health. Not succeeding, he died back in Bencoolen in late 1823.[1] Dr James Lumsdaine, a Eurasian who had been Assistant Surgeon and Surgeon at Bencoolen since before the turn of the century, was also a longstanding botanist friend. Bonham, now just 19, was brought along as an assistant.

It later became clear that not having seen the Settlement for over three years and altho' pleased with its growth and success, the Lieutenant

---

[1] Salmond died 23rd November 1823.

Governor considered this success to be a dire threat to his claim to be the founder. His vision for the whole of Sumatra to come under British influence had come to naught; he had many denigrators and a reputation for taking matters into his own hands; here was a Settlement which he conceived owed its existence solely to him yet whose growth could be, and was, justly attributed to Farquhar. He was not well and knew that if he remained in 'India' much longer he would not survive. The time in which to act was short but he had no option if he was to be remembered for this one successful project. He set about it with gusto, trampling on sensitivities and causing much heartbreak and concern.

Given his plans for remaking the Settlement, it was not suitable to base himself with Farquhar and, in the absence of other accommodation, he warmly accepted his sister's invitation and stayed with the Flints in their planked, attap–roofed house as paying guests ($150 per month), occupying the upper story of four bedrooms and a centre hall until other arrangements could be made. This gave Flint the immediate opportunity to give his own version of events and, by way of a slow drip–feed of anecdotes, express anti–Farquhar sentiments to his brother–in–law while his immediate investigations were taking place.

Flint took full advantage and arranged with the Lieutenant Governor that his official reports of arrivals, departures, imports and exports might now be passed direct to him rather than through Farquhar, who did not realise this for several months. Once he did so he complained bitterly, to no great effect.

Immediately on arrival, the Lieutenant Governor saw for the first time that the land on the plain and North bank of the river for which he had given clear instructions was to be retained for military or Government purposes only, was now occupied by merchants both European and native who had built godowns and houses, some of masonry and some of plank and attap. He ignored the fact that there were at the time no other suitable sites and that he had been advised of this the previous year. Nothing must now stand in the way of his improved master plan in which the various races were to be kept well apart from each other. Chinese and Malay huts had sprung up wherever possible, many on stilts over muddy mangrove swamps. Noting that all the merchants had been given notice when receiving occupation certificates that the ground was liable to be taken back by Government and that they merely had a lease with no termination date, he saw no reason not to repossess them without compensation. Within a week he had appointed a committee of three to consider and report on his plan which now included building godowns for Europeans on the southwest riverbank. The three were Dr Lumsdaine, Captain Salmond and N. Wallich, a friend of his who was Superintendent of the Botanical Gardens in Calcutta and had arrived in September on a short visit for health reasons. Despite having no previous knowledge of Singapore, they all agreed, after taking local advice, that the new site was healthy but would have to be drained and protected by an embankment to prevent flooding at spring tides.

Shortly after their appointment, the Lieutenant Governor issued a dictatorial proclamation, on 29th October if I am not wrong, warning those with buildings of masonry on portions of ground on the north bank and elsewhere, reserved exclusively for public purposes, of their proposed future removal and forbidding any further construction whatever. The proclamation specifically exempted for the time being officers' bungalows (as was mine having been built by Ralfe) which remained under Cantonment regulations. I was appointed to a new Town Committee a week later with Davis (Cantonment Adjutant, Farquhar's son–in–law) and Sam Bonham, to which we added, as necessary, representatives from the various racial communities, and which was the recipient of lengthy, clearly thought out but extremely detailed instructions. I was now dragged into the planning and early execution thereof. Beset by an uproar of complaint from merchants on all sides and from all communities who feared the present arrangements and business would be disrupted, with losses to all which they could ill afford, I too had my doubts. We worked from dawn to dusk with Montgomerie the Surgeon as Secretary. Altho' I had sympathy for Farquhar it was evident to all of us that he would before long be replaced and meanwhile had no effective authority, all questions being referred to the Lieutenant Governor. As the oldest European merchant I conceived it my duty to assist as far as practicable and spread oil on troubled waters whenever possible. Plenty was needed.

I happened around that time to be building a small outhouse and an undated note was delivered to me which I have retained until today:

'My dear Sir,

I am sorry to observe that you are going on with a brick building in a very objectionable part of your compound and that I am compelled to stop your progress in it. If you and Captain Thompson will favour us with your company to dinner on Friday, I shall explain more fully.

Yours sincerely
T. S. Raffles.'

We accepted, and he did.

In mid–November Dr John Crawfurd with his wife and baby arrived on their way back to Calcutta from his unsuccessful official mission to Siam and Cochin China. We had met him the previous year when he arrived en route to Siam aboard *John Adam* in mid-January and remained for just over a month.[2] A dour Scot who was known personally to the Lieutenant Governor from Penang and Java days, he this time stayed a week. Private discussions were held, private decisions taken, and a private recommendation sent to Calcutta. A few months later he was appointed to succeed Farquhar. His opinion of the Siamese Government was not favourable. Venal, corrupt, jealous and distrustful of Europeans, extortionist and insincere were among the adjectives he used. His four-month sojourn in Bangkok had been a sore trial as much of the negotiation covered the Sultan of Kedah who at the time was sheltering in Penang from the Siamese troops of Ligor. His dealings were complicated by the discovery that Captain MacDonnell of the ship carrying the mission, *John Adam,* had, contrary to all orders, been trading with the Siamese officials whilst negotiations were going on.

Instructions from Calcutta, issued the previous year forbidding any but the most urgent and vital expenditure, were now ignored and no expense was to be spared. Coleman, the young Irish architect from Calcutta, who had been waiting for this moment for four months, was required to produce plans for a temporary house on Government Hill and

---

[2] SSR L7 153 dated 9th March 1822.

a garrison church. Construction of the former with 10 rooms and a spacious hall was completed in the first week of January and the Lieutenant Governor, his wife and the Flint family moved up the hill. Coleman's garrison church was never built although Jackson had to estimate the cost of (a) the church and (b) the steeple and we had to wait many years for St Andrew's to be constructed. The fish market was to be removed from the site where it had grown up to a new one at Teluk Ayer, Davis and Bonham being appointed to make recommendations.

Day by day new instructions or peremptory demands for information came down to us. Salmond and Flint were required to make a study of the mouth of the river. They reported, as expected, that while Queiros' godown and wharf among other buildings on the north bank had caused the channel to silt up, removal of these would allow it to return to its normal course. The bar at the mouth prevented fully laden boats crossing it at low water but it could be dredged and the line of rocks partially blocking the entrance should be removed.

The Lieutenant Governor had already decided that, as all Chinese were to be removed to the campong on the south bank, a bridge over the river with roads on each bank leading to it was essential. Young Lieutenant Jackson,[3] in charge of the Artillery detachment and powder magazine and just appointed Assistant Engineer by him, was detailed off to design this. Tenders were called and were rejected as too expensive, alternative arrangements being made shortly afterwards with two Chinese contractors and a guarantee from Scott, the bridge to be completed in four months.[4]

We were quizzed on local currencies, rates of exchange and any problems we had as merchants. Details of those who had been allowed to build on the north bank or had bought from those who had, and why, were sought. From Ferry Point these were, in order along River Street as far as I can recall, Queiros, Methven, Napier & Scott, A. Farquhar, Mackenzie, Morgan and Guthrie but it was not just Europeans. Che Sang had two large and three small shops, Naraina Pillai one (or had until it was burned down that month), Francisco de Pastania one and so on up to the Temenggong's pagar. I myself had one lot not yet built on, as I was renting

---

[3] See Chapter 1, Note 20.
[4] SSR L11 151-2, 13th December 1822.

some storage space from Methven whose godown was the most fireproof of all (Figure 10).

In December, the Lieutenant Governor had another round of devastating headaches but, nothing daunted, and determined to ensure his place in history should Singapore be retained, his campaign continued with increased tempo and severity. Over 100 Chinese small shopkeepers petitioned Farquhar to intervene. 130 buildings housing many families were to be demolished without compensation and they had nowhere to move to.[5] Others made the same complaint and Farquhar tried to reason with the great man, stating that if he did not modify his plans and offer some compensation, the Chinese would start to leave, and his great success story would be abandoned. Our committee was told to deal with this. Such mass petitions were not to be entertained. Guthrie was, I think the first individual to confirm to the Lieutenant Governor in writing that when he was granted leave to build a house and godown it was clearly stated that were the ground to be repossessed compensation would be granted. Others including Morgan, Napier, MacKenzie, Queiros and Bernard echoed this; at length and often so did Marquard, acting as agent for Methven who had been required by the Lieutenant Governor to leave the Settlement and in November 1823 died after being thrown from his horse on parade, thereby probably saving him from shameful exposure and public disgrace.

Permits for the privilege to occupy lots for European commercial godowns on the south west bank upstream of Flint's were to be auctioned on 1st January 1823. The terms and conditions of occupancy were stated to be advised later by the Supreme Government. Chinese who were already on the site having previously had to move from the Cantonment plain were now to be moved on again to sites in Teluk Ayer put up for sale but would not have to pay for them. Reasonable moving expenses would be paid. We were told that this, with the assistance of the police, *'should be accomplished within a few weeks if it was effected with that zeal and determination which should characterise the execution of all orders issued by Government.'* Implementation is easy for those who do not have to carry it out.

---

[5] SSR L6 25-6 plus attachment dated 4th December 1822.

A list of the parties who had been allotted the 24 lots of ground on the East beach, with dates, was required and whether the parties had now settled or were likely to settle in Singapore. The lots would be put up for sale and the current occupiers be allowed to bid for them. Also details were demanded of the various hills in the immediate vicinity of town and the terms on which they had been allotted to individuals. Valuations of various properties were required, fast. Sandy Point was to be cleared of huts, planted with coconuts to provide shade as well as prevent erosion by the sea, and prepared as a site for a marine yard. Flint was also to tidy up the public landing place at Ferry Point and move his boat office to a part of Methven's godown to be rented for the purpose.

The Temenggong had, as allowed under the treaty, granted land for gardens and plantations within the town limits. Land outside had also been allocated, both before and after the treaty to various parties but mainly to Chinese coming from the large Hokkien community at Rhio who were engaged in growing gambier and had followed the Temenggong after his arrival in 1811.

The Army was roped in to assist after a prisoner escaped from jail the security of which needed strengthening. Lieutenant George Bonham was delegated to survey and complete a new road to New Harbour (later known as Selat Road) for which he was to be paid Rs 150 per month for four months.[6] This George Bonham was the elder half-brother of S. G. Bonham and had served in Singapore since shortly after the founding. The fact that both men were named George created some confusion and S. G. became known unofficially as Sam. A young man, not yet 20, he had evidently caught the Lieutenant Governor's eye and had earlier earned Farquhar's written thanks for his assistance. He was and is quite short, with a snub nose, a stutter and a lisp but worked hard, cheerfully and with enthusiasm on our committee, seeing problems as challenges to be solved rather than roadblocks. He was now appointed Assistant to the Resident with effect from 1st January and specifically directed to act as future Registrar for the Land Registry to be set up, to act in the Judicial Department and additionally to act in any way as directed by the Resident. As all who were in occupation of land had, under pain of requisition, to

---

[6] SSR L17 625 dated 31st May 1823.

register their claim before 1ˢᵗ February he could look forward to a very busy period.

The various hills in or outside the town, apart from Government Hill, were sought after by many as a house built on one, although not greatly higher than the town, caught what breeze was blowing. Farquhar had with the Temenggong's tacit approval, appropriated to himself Bukit Cawah.[7] Bukit Selegie was held by Flint. Both had been partially cleared at Government expense and later in 1823 Selegie was renamed Mount Sophia after Lady Raffles when the Flints moved there. The Teluk Ayer hills to the south, seriatim, were one occupied by Scott, one allocated to J. J. Erskine, a civil servant from Penang who had departed on retirement, and one allocated to John Palmer on one of his two visits from Calcutta in 1821 where a Chinese temple and a bungalow had been built. Captain Pearl of the *Indiana* had purchased a hill with the Temenggong's consent from some Chinese gambier planters. Ryan and Guthrie had acquired small hills, and Bernard land at Blakang Mati and Kallang. Salmond applied for a hill to the west of Government Hill overlooking the Chuliah brick kilns.

As if he did not already have enough to do as he was drawing up a plan for our committee showing what was contemplated, Jackson was in the first week of January commanded to survey all the hills. He was also to put a fence (high and robust enough to keep in the deer which Wallich had been asked to send from Calcutta) round the new Botanical and Experimental Garden without delay, to clear and drain the whole of the Rochor Plain from the back of the lots along the beach which were about to be sold, to mark out and form a 50–foot wide high road leading from the site earmarked for the bridge to Rochor River and to mark out other roads planned. He was forthwith to clear the ground marked out for the proposed church and to remove all the huts of the stonecutters, an activity now to be banned there.[8] He was short of carts and bullocks, all but two of the bullocks brought in from Penang having died.[9] No more were readily available and the manual removal of the hill behind the south west bank of the river was causing a great shortage of coolie labour.

---

[7] Bukit Cawah was later renamed Mount Emily.
[8] SSR L13 58 dated 30ᵗʰ January 1823.
[9] SSR L13 75 dated 5ᵗʰ February 1823.

Bernard was brusquely desired to take down all the remaining huts on the south bank between Flint's and the new road beyond the old fish market in the course of a morning, the occupants being given 24 hours' notice of this. He was also to get full details of all those living in the ground now allocated for the Botanical Garden and the compensation which would need to be paid, and to provide full details regarding the Police.

By mid–January 1823, the relationship between the Lieutenant Governor and Farquhar had, according to local gossip, seemed to have reached its nadir. Flint had previously taken over from Davis the quantity of tiles he had refused to do the year before and, without counting them, signed a receipt. He now discovered that some were unusable or broken and demanded that Farquhar make up the loss. Farquhar quite rightly complained to the Lieutenant Governor that, having signed the receipt, Flint was liable. Despite this he was peremptorily overruled and ordered to pay. At about the same time the Lieutenant Governor for some reason took a violent dislike to Bernard and described him publicly as merely a Head Constable. This insult, implying that Bernard was not of the officer class, drew a lengthy response from Farquhar that the man was by birth and upbringing as good as or better than any person present in the Settlement, a clear reference to the Lieutenant Governor's origins and those of Lady Raffles. Whatever faults Bernard had, and they were many, there was certainly nobody else in the Settlement who could have undertaken the oversight of the Police and the Police Magistrates Office, given his experience of local people, customs and languages.[10] In the end, although the Lieutenant Governor did apologise, the resentment festered.

The matter of Acting Assistant Surgeon Prendergast then arose. This poor man had come in 1819 with the troops as Sub–Assistant Surgeon and had for some time, prior to Montgomerie's arrival, been the only medical man in Singapore. The Lieutenant Governor had promoted him to Acting Assistant Surgeon, raising his social standing and allowing him into general society as a gentleman on the same footing as military officers. He had sold his bungalow to Queiros in 1820 (at a nice profit) to house the Queiros family and later had another site in the Cantonment. A dedicated medical man, he looked after all our medical needs as well as those of as

---

[10] SSR L13 43 and three succeeding pages dated 24th January 1823.

much of the local population as he could handle, was popular and respected. Montgomerie, who although younger was senior to him in rank, split the duties. Prendergast had to take leave to go to Madras in the summer of 1822. He had returned and after a few months, due to unspecified family problems there, had a breakdown and applied for four months leave to go back. This was granted. After his departure it was announced by the Lieutenant Governor that he had been dismissed from his post, demoted to his previous rank and that the ground he occupied was to be allocated to one Thomas King, a newly arrived ship's captain. No explanation was given or forthcoming even after Farquhar, bravely and on behalf of and reflecting the views of many in the Settlement, protested most vigorously but to no avail. I wonder what happened to Prendergast in the end?[11] Although the blatant injustice gave rise to much discontent the Lieutenant Governor's ill health at the time may have had a bearing on the matter.

The next confrontation occurred shortly afterwards when the Lieutenant Governor took issue with Farquhar and Bernard for clearing land initially at Government's, then lately at their own, expense at Bukit Cawah and elsewhere for a plantation, garden or country retreat. He found this unacceptable until Farquhar pointed out that Flint, under new regulations the second [sic] most important individual on the island, had a larger tract of land at Bukit Selegie which was also outside the limits, between Bukit Cawah and the town. Its position and height meant that it was far more valuable than his property. He regretted being forced to make unpleasant comparisons but had no choice.

Back in early 1821 Morgan had applied for an allocation of ground to which Farquhar was unable to agree. Others were given ground and, feeling discriminated against, he set his mind to get his revenge. Farquhar had needed to bring in some funds to set up his elder son Andrew in business. This could be done either by buying in Calcutta bills of exchange drawn on Singapore or alternatively, as was often done, by instructing an agent to use the funds there to buy produce and ship it to Singapore. On arrival the goods would be sold, and the funds become available. The risk was that the selling price would be less than the buying, thus experiencing a

---

[11] SSR L13 34 a seven-page letter dated 22nd January 1823.

loss on the deal. In Farquhar's case nine chests of opium were purchased, marked WF and consigned to Bernard, his son–in–law. All went well, the opium sold, and the funds were paid to me to be held available as and when required. A 10 per cent profit had been made on the deal and this gave Morgan the opportunity to charge Farquhar with trading. I am sure this was not his intention, but he had acted without thought in allowing his agents to ship opium. There were various other allegations re rice exports. At times when rice was in short supply in Singapore its export was forbidden without special permission and Bernard had been allowed to sell a few hundred bags to Rhio where there was an even worse shortage. I was given permission to do likewise. This was highlighted as favouritism. Somebody was alleged to have been seen paying, at the Resident's compound, money owed to Queiros, leading to an accusation he was acting on behalf of Queiros, contrary to all regulations. Farquhar denied this altho' he admitted Queiros had left funds with him when he left for a visit to Bengal, which weakened his defence.

Farquhar in May 1822 had advised the Lieutenant Governor in Bencoolen of the charge. No reply was made until after his arrival back in Singapore in October when Morgan was told to apologise. Despite it being indicated by his brother Alexander Morgan that he would do so on his return from abroad no written apology was ever forthcoming. Farquhar was meanwhile given a dressing down while Morgan later managed to persuade the Lieutenant Governor that he was justified in his remarks and was subsequently named among those merchants considered suitable to serve as magistrate.

By the middle of February it was clear that the rearrangement of campongs would take a very considerable time and expense. We, the Committee, had had to plead many cases of misfortune or where the person to be moved did not have the means even to pay that expense, let alone acquire a new site. Some who had found new sites across the river could not yet move to them because either there was a shortage of labour to put up new houses or the previous occupants had not been able to move out. I particularly felt for those who, with the best will in the world, wanted to abide by the new rules but for valid reasons could not do so. It was a relief when on 15th February the Committee was formally disbanded with the gratitude of the Lieutenant Governor written to me officially through his secretary acknowledging the time and effort spent and with thanks for the *'ready manner in which I had assisted the views of Government and for the able advice and essential assistance which I had so handsomely and gratuitously rendered on the occasion.'*

Sam Bonham was now to be even busier as he was appointed Registrar, in charge of registering all the nearly 600 new grants of land approved by the Lieutenant Governor. This task would however be mitigated by being allowed to charge an official commission payable to himself personally of 2 per cent. He, Jackson and Bernard were to be responsible for the continuing implementation of the moves.

In the initial instructions given to our Committee the Malay population, being mainly fishermen, were expected to move out of town along the coast to the east. The Temenggong and his followers, now many hundred strong, were expected to move upriver some miles which in the event they showed no inclination to do. They could not be allowed to remain in their choice site on the north bank of the river and after much discussion let themselves be persuaded that land along the shore of New Harbour, [at the foot of what was later named Mount Faber], would suit them well. The Temenggong's (and the Sultan's) necessities were more than keeping pace with the liberality of Government and within three months or so, in mid–March, the Temenggong, hoping for increased allowances, signified his acceptance of some 200 acres there in lieu of the ground on the riverbank. This was officially granted accompanied by a requirement that his whole campong move over to the new site within 10 days. This was clearly impracticable and because of a rush to build new huts there the price of new attap rose vertically, but in due course the move was achieved.

It was, I think, in February 1823 that the Lieutenant Governor stirred up another hornet's nest which, had it not been dealt with, could have called down on him the disapprobation of the Supreme Government. Captain James Pearl, Captain of the *Indiana* and whom he had known since chartering that ship in January 1819 to take him southwards to Singapore and back to Penang had, over a period from May to October 1822, bought from various Chinese gambier planters' ground on the slopes of what he had called Mount Stamford.[12] These purchases had at the time been approved by the Temenggong and registered with the Police Office with Farquhar's knowledge. He had also, with the private approval of the Lieutenant Governor, taken over and cleared at his own expense some waste land adjoining that purchased. The Lieutenant Governor now asked for details of the ground and purchases which, when received, he pronounced totally irregular and refused to recognise the claim. The same day Farquhar was instructed, to his great embarrassment, to proceed without delay accompanied by police to take possession of the dwelling house, grounds, goods and servants. This was followed by Pearl's blistering protest challenging (correctly as the ground was not within town limits) the legality of whole affair and threatening, if it was not reconsidered, to obtain redress by laying an official protest before the Supreme Government in Calcutta. A meeting between the Lieutenant Governor and Pearl failed to resolve the matter and two days later he lodged an official notarised protest which among other things pointed out that he was not less entitled to the protection of the law than the Chinese or other settlers and doubted that the Lieutenant Governor would have been authorised to deprive the former Chinese cultivators of their rights. A further meeting took place. The Lieutenant Governor gave way and Bonham, who had acted as the Notary, was persuaded to replace the original protest with a watered–down version omitting various sensitive phrases which reflected badly on

---

[12] Born 1790, James Pearl was commissioned as a Lieutenant in the Navy on 21st December 1808. It appears that at the end of the Napoleonic Wars many officers found themselves without employment and were allowed to serve afloat in merchant ships or foreign navies, forfeiting their half pay during their absence but restored on their return. Pearl came to Asia in 1816. *Indiana* was a new ship built in Calcutta in 1818 and had a crew of 4 Europeans and 50 lascars. He became her captain and took Raffles to Singapore from Penang in 1819. On a second voyage he brought a cargo of bricks from Penang and sold them well. In 1821 he bought Mount Stamford (later Pearl's Hill) with the Temenggong's permission from four Chinese gambier planters. In 1822 while sailing north near Banca he saved the lives of 190 Chinese passengers in a junk from Amoy which sank nearby. He fell out with Raffles when the latter tried to annul his purchase of Mount Stamford. In 1828 this was sold to Government by his agents. He returned to the Navy in about 1824. He and his wife settled in Newfoundland in 1829. He was knighted but died on 13th January 1840.

the Lieutenant Governor while Pearl regained his property which in due course was renamed Pearl's Hill.

It was earlier the same year that Pearl had been sailing from Batavia to Sinkawan in Borneo and shortly after dawn, on approaching the small rocky uninhabited Gasper Island in the strait of the same name between Billiton and Bangka, his lookout spotted some apparent rocks not marked on his chart. Closer inspection revealed the sea covered in floating wreckage — boxes, bundles of umbrellas, planks, flotsam and jetsam — most of which had at least one person clinging to them. He hove to, lowered the two boats and set about rescuing as many as possible despite difficulty with wind and sea. A few hours later a strong squall caused the ship to drift to leeward, anchors were let go and the boats attached to the ship by long ropes in case they too should drift away. By noon they had pulled from the sea 95 weak and exhausted unfortunates, most of whom had no clothes. The weather at first moderating, they were able before dusk to rescue another 45 persons but after dark the wind, blowing violently from the northwest, caused heavy seas. One of the rescued was a young Chinese from Batavia who spoke some Malay and through him they learned that all were passengers or crew of the *Tek Sing,* a 150 foot long, 30 foot wide 900–ton junk which had sailed from Amoy three weeks earlier with cargo, crew and 1,600 passengers. She had struck the Belvedere Shoal 14 miles away and capsized before sinking in deep water. Early next morning the wind moderated once more allowing them to take all remaining survivors off the island and also 27 men, survivors of 47 on a raft. They were short of water and food for so many but sailed on to Borneo arriving at the mouth of the Pontianak River a week later. 180 Chinese rescued were landed there and 10 remained on board until the ship returned to Batavia.[13]

Pearl, who was a few years younger than I, had been a lieutenant in the navy. Following his service in HMS *York* and the end of the war with the French he had been laid off as had so many others of his contemporaries, there being not sufficient ships in service to employ them despite the war with the United States which followed. He found his way east and as already mentioned became captain of *Indiana* making a considerable sum

---

[13] *Asiatic Journal,* December 1822.

of money when he sold the cargo of bricks he had carried down from
Penang as ballast. He had also carried the Lieutenant Governor back to
Bencoolen after his second visit to Singapore when he ran aground in the
Straits of Rhio. This meant a brief stay at the Dutch port. It seems this was
not held against him as very early the following year he took him and the
Flints from Calcutta to Bencoolen via Tappanooly. Three years later having had his property seized by the orders of the Lieutenant Governor
which, after his furious true naval style reaction, was returned to him he
left the Settlement. In 1835 we read in the *Singapore Free Press* that he
had been presented to the Queen and had also received a gold medal from
the Dutch for his having rescued the Chinese in 1822.[14] I heard gossip
years later that he had been knighted and is now in Newfoundland but that
is only rumour.

Cases of '*amok*' among the Malay population were infrequent. A case
which occurred about this time initially gave us great concern. One
evening after dark the news of an attack on Farquhar spread like wildfire,
possibly indicating an uprising by the Temenggong's people. This was
later quickly found to be false in so far as an uprising was concerned but
the '*amok*' was all too real. An Arab, Syed Yassin from Pahang owed a
large sum to Syed Omar bin Ali Al Juneid, one of the Settlement's earliest
Arab settlers. The case had that morning come to the Resident's court and
the verdict was for Yassin to pay up, give full security or go to jail. This
he considered an insult to a descendant of the Prophet, albeit that the debt
was to another descendant, and in his mind called for revenge. From the
court he was taken to the police office near the river mouth and, unbeliev-
ably, was not searched for arms. A few hours later he asked Bernard for
permission to go to see Syed Omar to try and negotiate. This was granted
and off he went, guarded by a Hindu police peon. Omar lived on High
Street opposite Guthrie and as Yassin rushed in Omar, seeing him, fled out
of the back and ran to Farquhar's compound to raise the alarm. Meanwhile
the peon, alarmed that his prisoner had disappeared, called loudly for him,
whereupon Yassin reappeared, stabbed him dead with his kris and ran
back inside to hide under the *balei*. Farquhar, with his son Andrew, Davis
his son–in–law and some sepoys, hurried to Omar's house to see what was

---

[14] *Singapore Free Press*, 22nd October 1835.

going on, calling for Yassin to come out. He sprang out and stabbed Farquhar who collapsed from loss of blood and was carried across the road to Guthrie's house. More sepoys with guns were fetched from the Lines and took up position in front of the Temenggong's pagar just as the Lieutenant Governor arrived in his carriage having been told Farquhar was dead. Meanwhile the sepoys had made short work of Yassin whose body, by now unrecognisable, was dragged into the centre of the Plain. Dr Montgomerie let it be known that Farquhar's wound was fortunately not mortal, but such an attack had to be seen to be dealt with severely. Next morning a public meeting was held, with the Sultan and Temenggong in attendance and the corpse, now enclosed in an iron cage, was sent round the town in a buffalo cart and thereafter hung from a mast at Tanjong Malang as a warning to others. Some days later the Sultan in the name of the Malay population asked for a pardon and was allowed to bury the rotting corpse at the site. An unintended consequence was that the place, to this day, has become a place of pilgrimage as Syed Yassin had killed a kafir (non-believer) and wounded a Nazarene.

Not so long after this the Lieutenant Governor advised Maxwell, Napier and myself as current Magistrates that, there being currently a shortage of labourers, he was of opinion that all prisoners sentenced to hard labour should be put to work for the public good under Jackson on the new roads being laid out. Guarded by one or more police peons they would work in the forenoon from 6 to 11 and resume from 2 till 6.[15] At the same time by another letter we were required to proceed to mark out a spot where the public jail would be constructed. The *'spot'* lying under the hill was at the time occupied by Chong Long and by a Malay government writer. Both would have to vacate the land and as no grant of it had yet been made to them no mention was made of compensation. In the meantime as he considered the present jail to be a very objectionable place, he called our attention to the need to provide more acceptable accommodation for the prisoners pending the completion of the permanent building.[16]

---

[15] SSR L17 501 dated 28th April 1823.
[16] SSR L17 502-3 dated 28th April 1823.

The Lieutenant Governor's sympathy for Farquhar personally, if it in fact ever existed after the attack, did not manifest itself in his official dealings or in his reaction to Farquhar's various requests on his own behalf or those of his family. Bernard's well documented request for financial recognition of many tasks undertaken apart from his official position and the fact that his private property had been used for police purposes was turned down flat. He was instructed to move out of his bungalow and offices with the least delay possible. Davis, as Cantonment Staff Officer had, despite postal matters being part of Flint's responsibilities, prior to Ryan's appointment as Postmaster to take effect on 1st February,[17] had the whole trouble of making up the General Letter Packets and the assorting and distributing of all letters which were received from ships in Post office packets. This fell upon him to perform without his having drawn any allowance whatever for his trouble. A squabble arose between Napier and Farquhar's son Andrew over a strip of ground between their two godowns. Napier and his wife were on particularly good terms socially with the Flints and Lady Raffles who referred to them as *"the Naps"* and looked on them favourably. The case was only finally settled in Farquhar's favour after Crawfurd had taken over as Resident.

As I heard later from private sources in Calcutta the Lieutenant Governor continued his longstanding campaign of sly denigration and clandestine misrepresentation of Farquhar, complaining among other matters that he did not wear his military uniform on all occasions and referring this to the attention of the Commander–in–Chief.[18] On 1st May the Lieutenant Governor took over all duties of the Resident, who was left with being merely in charge of the troops.

Farquhar himself heard through friends the unexpected news that, as published in the Calcutta press in March, he was shortly to be replaced by Dr John Crawfurd. The Lieutenant Governor, lying, denied any knowledge of this until the arrival a few days later on 23rd May of an official letter. He immediately removed Farquhar from command of the troops, replacing him with Captain Murray.

---

[17] SSR L17 271-2 dated 22nd January 1823.
[18] SSR L15 60 dated 25th April 1823.

The official reason for his replacement was given as acceptance of his October 1820 letter of resignation, his two subsequent letters applying to cancel it having not been forwarded to Calcutta by the Lieutenant Governor. Another twist to the tale was that from 1ˢᵗ June 1823 Singapore was to report direct to the Supreme Government in Calcutta rather than through the medium of Bencoolen. He had been obliged to carry on a precarious communication with that remote and disadvantageously situated place and which had served only to retard, obstruct and render abortive those measures most necessary to be pursued in the Settlement.

Farquhar's privately-financed compound with its bungalows and numerous other buildings had served not only as his residence but also as Treasury, church, offices, accommodation for visitors and much else besides. As this was the only available compound which afforded sufficient accommodation for the Resident, he was asked to vacate on Crawfurd's arrival all those portions hitherto used for public purposes and personally to move to his other small bungalow on the beach. The compound being on Cantonment land belonging to Government there would be no objection to paying him the present value of the buildings. He pointed out he had a big family, and this would not be possible. He considered, based on original cost, the present value of the buildings to be some four thousand dollars and offered to sell. This offer was considered unacceptable and temporary accommodation had to be found for Crawfurd who arrived on 28ᵗʰ May with his young 20–year–old wife and assumed the position of Resident on 29ᵗʰ May.[19]

It seemed that the Lieutenant Governor at first deemed the bungalow on Government Hill to be his own property which he was sharing with the Flints. Crawfurd was given a rent allowance of $150 per month which, if I am not wrong may have been paid into the former's account, but by mid–July he had nearly rebuilt the house.[20]

The Lieutenant Governor, just prior to his sailing, came to an informal agreement with the Sultan and Temenggong whereby they were to receive higher allowances. These were partly in consideration for their agreement that, with the exception of their own campongs, all of Singapore and its

---

[19] SSR L19 112 dated 28ᵗʰ June 1823.
[20] Crawfurd letter to Morrison dated 12ᵗʰ July 1823. *Malixun hui yi lu* by Eliza Gillis 1839.

adjacent islands was to be at the entire disposal of the British Government, In addition they were to lose the right to a share of the port duties and certain monopolies. Having left this for Crawfurd to finalise, which was achieved just over a year later, he departed on 9th June aboard *Hero of Malown* for Bencoolen with his wife, secretary and young nephew, the son of Captain Flint, and was seen by us no more (Figure 41).

Figure 1: A. L. Johnston. Print by D. J. Pound from a painting by George Chinnery painted during ALJ's visit to Macao. National Portrait Gallery, London.

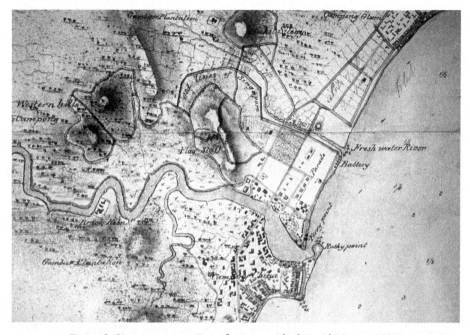

Figure 2: Singapore town. Part of a map marked 'Rec'd 18 June 1825'
in the British Library London.

Figure 3: Deptford, England, where *Earl Fitzwilliam* was built in 1786.
Private Collection.

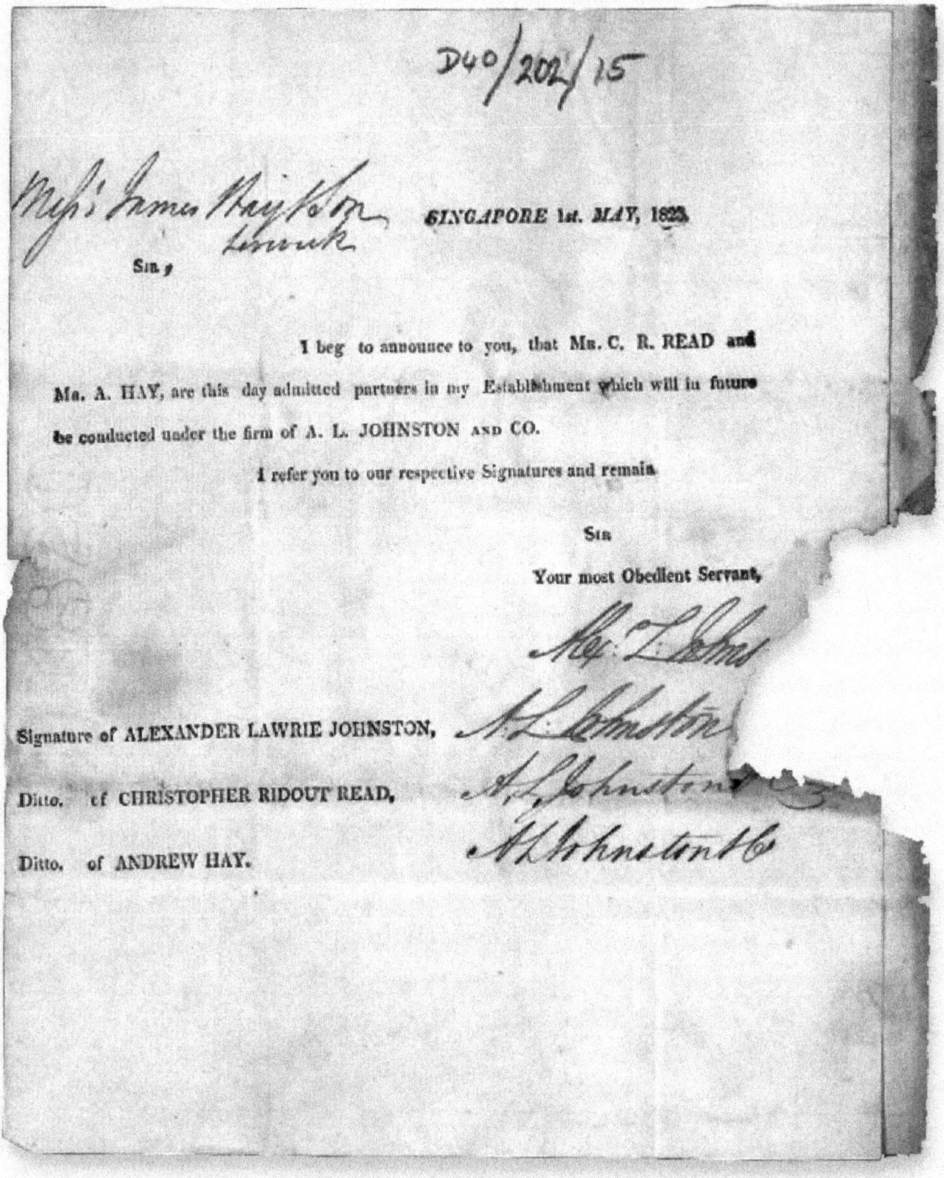

D40/202/15

Mess.rs James Hay & Son
Leruck

Sir,

SINGAPORE 1st. MAY, 1823.

I beg to announce to you, that Mr. C. R. READ and Mr. A. HAY, are this day admitted partners in my Establishment which will in future be conducted under the firm of A. L. JOHNSTON AND CO.

I refer you to our respective Signatures and remain

Sir

Your most Obedient Servant,

Signature of ALEXANDER LAWRIE JOHNSTON,

Ditto. of CHRISTOPHER RIDOUT READ,

Ditto. of ANDREW HAY.

Figure 4: The circular announcing the formation of the firm A. L. Johnston & Co.

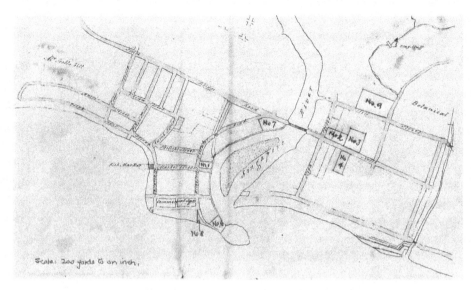

Figure 5: Map hand-drawn by Andrew Hay showing the properties held by A. L. Johnston &
Co. in 1827, with lots highlighted as the original markings are too faint to show up.

Figure 6: Sloop *Clive* salvaging opium clipper *Sylph* off Batam Island, by W. J. Huggins.
Source: National Maritime Museum, Greenwich, London.

FOR SALE,

THE NEW STEAM-VESSEL
JARDINE,
(daily expected).

Substantially built at Aberdeen in 1835. The Engine is by *J. Duffus & Co.* on the most approved principles, and is adapted for Wood or Coals. The Vessel measures about 115 Tons, builder's, or about 56 Tons Steam measurement, works 48 Horse-power and is considered to be one of the fastest Steam Vessels hitherto built. She will be delivered to the purchaser in thorough order.

Apply to
A. L. JOHNSTON & CO.
Singapore, 22nd. Feby. 1836.

Figure 7: Excerpt from *Singapore Free Press*, advertising the Jardine.
Source: *Singapore Free Press*, 1836.

Figure 8: 1846 Kampong Rochor by J. T. Thomson
Courtesy of the Hocken Collections, University of Otago.
Source: John Thomson 1846

Figure 9: Silver dollar of Charles IV of Spain 1806.

Figure 10: Print taken from a painting by Francois-Edmond Paris of the French frigate *La Favorite* which called in at Singapore from 18th to 25th August 1830. This shows not only the drawbridge over the river but also on the right Methven's godown which was still used by Government at the time. Courtesy of the National Museum of Singapore, National Heritage Board.

Figure 11: August 1830 Singapore with Boat Quay godowns on the left. Courtesy of the National Museum of Singapore, National Heritage Board.

Figure 12: Dr John Crawfurd, much later in life. National Portrait Gallery, London.

Figure 13: Dutch Guilder 1786.

Figure 14: Ruins of the Canton Factories after the Fire.
China trade painting – Public domain, via Wikimedia Commons.

Figure 15: HEIC ship Repulse in East India Dock 25 September 1839.
© National Maritime Museum, Greenwich, London.

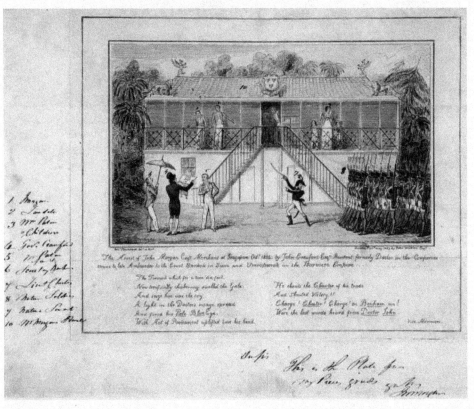

Figure 16: The Peter Wilkins print of Cruickshank's sketch with Morgan's identification of the participants. Courtesy of the National Museum of Singapore, National Heritage Board.

AMHERSTIA NOBILIS WALL

Figure 17: Orchid Tree or Pride of Burma (Amherstia nobilis Wallich.)
flowering branch with separate fruit and sectioned ovary.
Chromolithograph by P. Depannemaeker, c. 1885, after B. Hoola van Nooten.
Source: Wellcome Collection. Attribution 4.0 International (CC BY 4.0).

Figure 18: Robert Fullerton (1773 – 1831). St Marylebone Parish Church, London.

Figure 19: An example of one of C. R. Read's tokens,
his name being inscribed below the cockerel figure.

Figure 20: Wood engraving by Heinrich Leutemann of Coleman's surveying party under attack by a tiger. Courtesy of the National Museum of Singapore, National Heritage Board.

Figure 21: The former Keng Teck Whay building, 150 Teluk Ayer Street.
© Frank Chiew

Figure 22: Alexander L. Johnston and friends at Tanjong Tangkap, Singapore.
© Frank Chiew

Chapter 5

Impressions of John Crawfurd. Fundraising. Problems with Property Sales. Chinese Junks.

First impressions of our new Resident, Crawfurd (Figure 12), revealed a very different character to those to whom we had become accustomed. A surgeon by profession, he had served in Penang for four years before joining the invasion of Java where he served as Resident Governor at Jogjakarta. He had a good knowledge of local languages. Most recently he had been sent on an official embassy to Siam without great success and then on to Cochin China. Two years older than the Lieutenant Governor and younger than Farquhar he was no extrovert. Taking over a Settlement of which he had little direct knowledge, he took a cautious approach and despite having been given detailed and explicit instructions by the Lieutenant Governor before his departure, viewed these with an enquiring and independent mind. His immediate concerns were to deal with the question of Government stores, how the over 200 troops were fed and the currency of the Settlement.

Within six weeks he had disposed of all remaining Government stores by auction, releasing the stores clerk to assist him in his own office and auctioned six–month renewable leases on the Government godowns.

Food supplies for the troops were provided by the military commissariat and usually supplied direct from Bengal although local prices either equalled that cost or were cheaper. It had been required by the Supreme

Government that the troops in Singapore be paid a cash allowance in lieu and buy food locally for themselves, their followers and children at an exclusive bazar to be established in the Cantonment. Invitations to local merchants to participate had generated no response whatever as those who would buy at the bazar were comparatively few and the alternative general market was easily accessible, thus the business prospects were not good. Despite his best efforts the troops could not be persuaded that this was in their interest. They would be paid on the basis of food prices in Calcutta whereas in Singapore at the proposed exclusive bazar prices were expected to be double. The principal commodities concerned were rice, dhal[1] and ghee,[2] all of which had to be imported wholesale at high cost. He calculated that a private Sepoy currently earning 11 rupees should, if the proposed system was to be imposed, receive an increase of around 5 rupees. Some had feared that relying on local supplies might lead to the risk of scarcity, but all three commodities were imported on a large scale from many surrounding countries other than Bengal and he was of opinion that the risk could be discounted. Government should cease sending down provisions on its own account as this could disrupt the local market. Pending approval from the Supreme Government he had engaged with a contractor, John Purvis, to supply the usual ration of Moonghy rice, best buffalo ghee and urrear dhal of equal quality for six months more cheaply than under the previous system.[3]

10 days after the departure of the Lieutenant Governor all we merchants were invited to come up to the Residency House on the hill to discuss the currency of the colony. This was a most worthwhile exercise as Crawfurd took detailed note of our concerns and by mid–July made recommendations to Calcutta. He recognised that as far back as 1819 a serious mistake had been made by approving the acceptance of all Indian rupees other than Sicca rupees, Java rupees and guilders at the rate of 225 per silver Spanish Dollar, resulting as business improved in a discount of between 8 and 12 per cent. Naturally, the silver Spanish Dollars were exported, followed by the Indian Rupees while Java rupees flowed in,

---

[1] Dhal is the name given in India to dried pulses such as lentils, peas and beans.
[2] Ghee is a type of clarified butter used throughout India.
[3] SSR L19 99 dated 21st June 1823.

followed by Guilders. The Spanish Dollar premium had now risen to 18 to 20 per cent and distinction was made between '*hard*' dollars and '*currency*' dollars resulting in goods being invoiced at that premium. The Batavia government had now fixed the rate of exchange locally at 220 guilders to 100 dollars. The Supreme Government had now ordered a rate of 2 Sicca rupees to the Spanish Dollar which made sense in Bengal. Silver Spanish Dollars were the real currency of all, universally understood and the standard against which every other coin was estimated and by which every commodity was valued.

To create order out of chaos he had decreed that only hard Spanish Dollars would be received into and disbursed from the Treasury and that all accounts should be kept in that currency. For the present, Guilders would be valued at 260 to 100 Spanish Dollars.[4] Bills drawn on Calcutta by which funds could be remitted had hitherto been awarded under sealed tender resulting in large amounts accruing to certain individuals. He was now putting up for open auction sets of bills on Calcutta of Rs 1,000 each which led to a more representative spread. To us this was indeed a welcome move. Our concerns raised later that the Collector in Calcutta was not aware of the difference between currency dollars in Singapore and hard dollars and so calculated higher duty based on the latter were taken up and resolved.

The small change then in general use consisted of silver pieces which were fractions of the Dutch Guilder (Figure 13), of very inferior-standard silver and much worn but passing at least 70 per cent above the intrinsic value of the metal they contained. He therefore recommended the introduction of local coins of similar silver fractions of the Spanish Dollar and of copper coins of one and of one–half cents which could only be used for amounts up to one dollar. These would be minted in Calcutta. This suggestion was fully supported by us all, although they could not immediately be produced by the mint. It was I believe from January 1824 that certain other small coins were officially provisionally allowed for amounts up to $5 and the official values published. We did benefit after it was known that Bencoolen would be handed over to the Dutch by the delivery to us of ten

---

[4] SSR L19 124 dated 8th July 1823.

tons of copper coinage originally ordered for circulation in Sumatra, but which could also be issued in Singapore.

Before leaving Singapore, the Lieutenant Governor had advised the Supreme Government that the only public works of importance that were in progress were the construction of the new bridge and the new Sepoy Lines. Crawfurd swiftly discovered this untruth and moved to review all projects. The only ones he could stop in to were a road across the island and the clearing of St John's Island and Sandy Point. Completion of the road from Teluk Ayer across the marsh to connect with the bridge was essential, it being constructed two feet above the level of the spring tides, of clay covered with one foot of red earth. The new fish market and police station were sufficiently advanced to continue to completion. Those who had purchased lots on the South bank of the river in the previous January were much concerned that some of the public works there had been suspended and wrote requesting that they be recommenced in accordance with the undertakings they had been given. Crawfurd could not find any written undertakings but after consulting Bonham and Jackson agreed unhesitatingly that there was indeed an obligation on Government to complete the bridge across the river, the road leading from it, an embankment along the face of the river as far as the first creek and a practicable road leading from the river face and from the bridge to the warehouses on the seafront. He did not, however, find that any pledge had been given regarding the further removal and levelling of the hill in Commercial Square.[5] This latter had been commenced under the personal supervision of the Lieutenant Governor late in 1822 or early in 1823 by removing the boulders and earth and using these to reclaim a part of the swamp.

To raise funds for Government expenditure it had been the practice to put out to tender monopolies for the local processing and retail sales of opium, sale of pork, sale of arrack, pawn-broking, and also gambling or gaming as we called it. This last had been suspended by the Lieutenant Governor during his stay as he considered it an immoral encouragement for the local Chinese to gamble. Crawfurd disapproved of such monopolies and instead issued a certain number of short-term licences for each branch of revenue which were auctioned off to responsible individuals

---

[5] SSR L19 124-5 dated 10th July 1823.

against security. European and American spirits with the exception of gin were free of control. It was not long before gaming licences had to be reinstituted due to corruption in the police and his realisation that a passion for gaming pervaded all ranks of Chinese and Malays to a most extraordinary extent, which passion, as far as the Government was concerned, was incurable. Although regarded as a vice by Europeans, Chinese regarded it as an amusement and recreation to which even the most industrious of them were accustomed to resort. Total prohibition would result in clandestine gambling. He therefore felt it best to restrict it unless for ready money, and through licenced house fees to raise funds. In addition although much gunpowder was imported it was found to his alarm that at least five residents were manufacturing it locally within the town and so this had, for safety reasons, to be controlled by licence and moved a safe distance away.

The most important festival for all Chinese is probably the arrival of the New Year according to the lunar calendar. This does not coincide with our New Year but normally falls in January or February. The celebrations last for 15 days, and while business comes to a standstill, its place is taken by feasting, gambling and general rejoicing. Before the festival prices of meat, fish and almost all provisions rise by 20 or 30 per cent. The chief amusement on such occasions is gambling, the taste for it being universal among all classes at all times and large sums of money are won and lost. Quarrels at the gambling tables are however rare and during the festival in 1825 no disputes or riots warranting the interference of the police occurred.

He now turned his attention to Captain Flint whose protector was gone. To the duties of Master Attendant had been added magisterial responsibilities and with this Crawfurd did not agree. He proposed to the Supreme Government an updated set of Port Regulations which effectively blocked the Master Attendant's opportunities to increase his income. Flint was no longer to be Storekeeper and the newly appointed Postmaster was now to report to the Resident. He had used his position to monopolise and gain from the *'wooding, watering and ballasting'* of visiting ships which did not use their own boats. The maximum allowable charges for these were now stated and he was to take an oath not to undertake any commercial pursuits whatever. The charging of port clearance fees for small boats was to be discontinued and thus the former practice of using these as a perquisite to buy his stationery was stopped.[6]

---

[6] SSR L19 218-222 dated 4th September 1823 reading as follows:

1. 'I have the honour to acknowledge the receipt of the observations with which you have favoured me in your letter of the 1st inst. on the new provisional Port Regulations & the recent revision of the Master Attendant's establishment. The few following remarks in reply will, I trust, be satisfactory, pending the decision of the Hon'ble the Governor General in Council.

2. In answer to the general objection contained in the second paragraph of your letter it will be sufficient to state in explanation of the changes which have been made that, besides complying with my instructions, it was discovered on mature and deliberate enquiry that the execution of the late Port Regulations did not comport with its letter or spirit; but on the contrary that its real effect had been to throw a very complete monopoly into the hands of the Master Attendant as far as the wooding, watering & ballasting of ships are concerned, that such a monopoly could not have been in the contemplation of the Hon'ble the Lieut. Govr. of Fort Marlbro'. I have his own solemn assurance & it is scarcely necessary to remind you that this pledge was repeated before yourself in the presence of every European in the Settlement. At all events I am quite certain that the practice which gave occasion to the change which became necessary could not be but injurious to the interests of this port — that it is at variance with the whole principles on which the Settlement was founded — & that I should not on my part be performing my duty did I not denounce it to the Supreme Government as unsound & contrary to every principle of good government.

3. In answer to the 4th paragraph of your letter touching the abolition of your magisterial function it will not escape you that the exercise of the power of giving & inflicting corporal punishment upon your competitors in the business of wooding, watering & ballasting ships & furnishing cargo boats, a class of men who in your capacity of Master Attendant fell naturally under your control & regulation, could not be continued with justice or advantage either to their interests or those of the public.

4. In reply to the 5th paragraph I trust you will consider it on reflection no hardship to take the usual form of oath which on a public principle is prescribed to every civil servant of the Government holding any situation of trust of confidence & which on the present occasion is equally required of the Resident, his assistant & yourself.

5. In regard to the abolition of the Port Clearance fees considered as a perquisite of the Master Attendant which is the principal subject of the 6th paragraph of your letter I have the honour to bring to your notice that the principle on which these were levied has been already disapproved of by the Supreme Government; a circumstance which I make no doubt whatever escaped the observation of the Hon'ble the Lieut Governor of Fort Marlbro' when he enacted that clause of the late regulations which has reference to them. Annexed you will find a copy of the document in question. In relation to the

Flint's first action on learning the news was to indent for a large supply of stationery from the Resident's office and was upset to be told this would only be fulfilled when supplies permitted. Following his long list of complaints which were effectively nullified one by one in Crawfurd's response he demanded an increase of $200 in his $300 salary. This demand was not recommended to Calcutta. He never gave up trying and shortly before leaving on sick certificate in 1828 took a five per cent

---

Port Clearance fees in general I may further observe that however light they may be in amount it can scarcely be reasonable to expect that when the Government itself has abstained from levying every species of duty on the trade of the port it should countenance an impost for the avowed purpose of a perquisite to one of its officers.

6. In reply to the 9th paragraph I beg to state that the person whom I have designated as Chinese & Siamese writer is the well-known linguist Siami and that it is for him the salary of 50 dollars is intended, as it is now understood that this is the sum which has been hitherto drawn on his account. The boatswain's merits & length of services were unknown to me when I revised the establishment nor am I yet entirely satisfied that a crew of 15 lascars and two tindals will not prove adequate to the performance of every necessary duty. It is within my own knowledge that they are not called upon on an average once in 24 hours to board a ship and that they are occasionally from five to eight days without any occupation of this nature whatever. To return however to the case of the boatswain, whether his services be necessary or not, I feel convinced that the Indian Government, who are always ready to listen to the claims of their meritorious servants of whatever rank, will be happy to take his services into consideration & I have to request therefore that you will have the goodness to forward to me, for the information of the Governor General in Council a statement of their length and nature. [Paras 7 to 9 related to minor crewing matters and are omitted]

10. Touching the loss of emolument which you may have legitimately sustained by the new arrangement, as I feel assured that it is not in the contemplation of the Supreme Government to deprive you of the full and fair reward of your services, I request you will have the goodness to transmit to me a statement of your losses that I may have the pleasure of submitting them to the liberal consideration of the Hon'ble the Governor General in Council.

11. In conclusion it is scarcely necessary for me to observe that the regulations which I have found it my duty to pass, are entirely of a provisional nature; that they will be immediately laid before the Supreme Govt. and that the rules of the service admit of your submitting to the Hon'ble the Governor General in Council a temperate & respectful remonstrance against them should they appear to you to militate either against your own personal interests or those of the public.'

commission on the sale of a boat but was promptly ordered by Penang to pay it to Government.[7]

During the course of the investigation complaints had been raised regarding the imperfect manner in which the tonnage or measurement of the cargo boats belonging to the port had been hitherto determined. This had caused much inconvenience and I was requested to form a Committee with Maxwell and Napier to look into the complaints and make such permanent arrangements as might be equitable to the owners of the boats and also ensure the community against loss or imposition.

In an attempt to clarify another situation new regulations were published in June 1823 concerning the clearing of land. Requests for location tickets giving permission to do so were to be accompanied by details and measurements of the site in acres or fathoms [1 fathom equals 6 feet]. If not cleared and cultivated on the expiry of two years such sites would be resumed by Government and all expenses incurred forfeited. Once the future of the Settlement was decided in our favour a grant defining the ownership and the capital sum needed or quit rent would be granted. Those currently clearing land were requested to apply for location tickets.

The way in which the Lieutenant Governor had handled land sales in the last six months of his visit had led to almost insuperable problems. Lots were bid up in the unfortunate expectation that only a quit rent of 10 per cent would be payable each year rather than that plus the sum bid. Not realising this Crawfurd arranged the auction of various lots of ground on the Bridge Road on 1st July. These lots, 18 ft by 75 ft, were to be built on, according to an official plan, with masonry or good planks, and to have a verandah of six feet facing the street. Should they not be developed within one year they would be resumed by Government and re-sold. All the lots sold, as did the lots for single story masonry houses on the seaside of Teluk Ayer Street, but the amounts bid were far in excess of a reasonable value. Worried about this he called for several discussions with purchasers of these, the commercial lots on the south east bank of the river and of other lots from June which he now annulled should the purchasers on reflection so desire. He admitted that he had not realised the effect the reorganisation of the Settlement on residents' finances. From its nature the Settlement was filled with needy native adventurers and speculators and their capacity for making good their contracts, be it for property purchased or licenses bid, had been considerably impaired by the heavy outlay of capital, estimated at $150,000 for individuals, incident to the recent changes. In future auctions by public outcry deposits or immediate security would be required to attempt to avoid such problems.[8]

Trade with the region continued to expand despite the Dutch in Malacca waiving most duties in an attempt to woo back those who had left and to attract new residents. Some 25 junks had come during the year from Cochin China bringing mainly rice which was a prohibited export and taking back opium which was a prohibited import. The rewards were good if the crews were not caught, and death if they were.

China's junks, particularly those from Amoy, had traded with this part of the world for centuries. In former times the trade with Java (Banten and Batavia) was large except when interrupted by either economic events or political restrictions in both places. This had shrunk almost to nothing by the end of the last century. There was also regular trade with the Sultanate of Johore, the junks, up to five or six a year, seeking to buy tin.

Those junks which first arrived on our shores soon after the Settlement was founded came both from Canton and Amoy. Those from Canton were known as *'Red-headed'* as the bows on each side of which a large eye is painted were coloured red, and those from Amoy as *'Green-headed'* for the same reason. Taking from between 20 and 40 days on the voyage they would set off with the onset of the North East monsoon initially keeping close to the coast until Hainan, avoiding the Paracels and joining the coast of Cochin China before crossing over to the Malay Peninsula and turning to starboard at Cape Ramunia, a haunt of pirates, to reach Singapore in the first few weeks of the year. The largest junks of up to 800 tons did not come to us but those that did were in the 250–400–ton range carrying cargoes worth 30–60,000 Spanish Dollars. On arrival they would anchor a mile or two offshore and quickly be surrounded by sampans and small boats carrying local Chinese merchants anxious to be the first to see musters of the cargo brought and find out the quantities. Much of this was

---

[8] SSR L19 200 dated 23rd August 1823 and 266–271 dated 15th September 1823.

destined for the emigrant Chinese community spread all over the archipelago, the raw silk, nankeens, tea and camphor would be of interest to us European merchants for export westwards. All the cargo invariably passed through the hands of the Chinese merchants before anything reached us. The passengers are of two kinds, merchants who rent cabins from the crew and emigrants or coolies whom one could say had mortgaged themselves to pay their passage in the hope of making good overseas. These poor souls have no food or drink other than what they themselves bring aboard and are forced to sleep where they can find a space on deck. Overcrowding is usual. I remember a day when two large junks arrived from Canton and one from Amoy with some one thousand two hundred immigrants between them.[9] Whilst they were ferried ashore it occurred to me that our population was thereby increased by 10 per cent. This percentage would have fallen over the next few days as the majority were then crowded into the *sampan pucats* and prahus heading to Rhio and other destinations. Such arrivals, known as *sin kehs* were in principle good for the settlement but as years went on, we had an increasing problem in the streets of sick, penniless coolies with nowhere to go and no funds to keep them. At the end of 1828 I with Sam Bonham, Read and others, when asked to comment on the new regulations for Singapore, suggested a regulation to control paupers although we did not suggest just how this could be done. Their numbers infesting the streets had become a serious nuisance. Many were disabled by leprosy or other disfiguring diseases and could not work. Despite some coming from Rhio the greater number came in the Chinese junks bringing numbers of destitutes. Opulent Chinese took these off the hands of the commanders of the junks by paying so much as would redeem them out of pawn, upon an engagement that in consideration of their release they would work for their benefit for a certain time. Where the coolies retained their health, their masters had reason to be satisfied but where their health broke down, they were often unfeelingly cast off as so much useless lumber and this was the main source of beggars in the Settlement.[10] The junks return to China by the same route as they arrived once the South East monsoon starts to blow, usually in late May or later.

---

[9] *Singapore Chronicle*, 1st February 1827.
[10] SSR N4 516 dated 28th November 1828.

By then each one would have acquired new masts in place of the old and kept the latter to be sold on their home-coming.

In addition to these big junks there were of course many which were smaller. I recall going aboard one of medium size soon after she arrived from the north. She was about 80 feet in length, 22 feet beam and about 18 feet out of the water forward, dropping in a gentle curve to about four feet amidships and rising again at the poop to 25 feet. She had three masts, the central one being the mainmast made of one single piece of timber. Water was stored in several holds being drawn up by bucket through hatches in the deck. The stove for cooking was on this one deck beside the mainmast. Astern were several small cabins, some of bamboo, for the officers and merchants and exactly in the middle of these was a platform from which she was steered, and a small altar. The rudder, to us very over-sized, was not attached to the vessel but hung with ropes when at sea and is drawn up alongside the hull when in harbour. Lumbering and cumbrous in the extreme, as they cannot tack or sail other than before the wind, they hoist their sails and effectively let themselves drift as the wind blows them.[11]

Junks, some 30 or 40 a year in the early stages, of a 100–200 tons, known as *topes,* came to us regularly from Cochin China bringing mainly rice and salt. They were mostly owned and operated by emigrant Chinese. Return cargo always included cloth, a chest or two of opium and sundries. Since the penalty there for its possession is death, one may suppose that either the law is not well enforced or that bribery will open prison doors. Each year two, or sometimes more, ships of about 500 tons owned by the King of Cochin China and with junior mandarins as supra cargoes would arrive in January bringing large quantities of sugar as well as some lead and copper. Built in very rough fashion with huge sterns and exceedingly thick sides, they were modelled somewhat on the lines of a French vessel wrecked on their shores half a century ago which may account for the middle deck being pierced for guns. They would depart in late April or May taking away with them woollens and glassware.

---

[11] China Trade to Batavia during the days of the VOC. Leonard Blusse in Archipel 18, pp. 195–213, 1979.

Trading with Siam was no easy business although Morgans Hunter & Co had some trade with the country. Some small junks brought down cargoes of sugar as did the King's own ship in later years. This was bought and exported to Europe. We were not permitted to deal in arms with the Siamese. In September 1823 a small schooner, the *Marianna*, en route to Bangkok, under English colours and owned by an Englishman arrived from Amsterdam where she had loaded 9,000 French and German muskets. By clearing out from Holland, she avoided infringing the Hon'ble Company's charter, which limited the navigation to or from British ports to vessels of not less than 350 tons. If arms could thus be supplied to Siam the question arose as to why we ourselves were prohibited from doing so.

In November 1822, a catastrophic fire had broken out one evening at Canton in China. It started in the west of the town and for two days spread remorselessly, consuming swathes of houses, then the foreign factories and spreading for a mile and a half along the riverbank (Figure 14). The Company's losses were very great. When we received the news, the Lieutenant Governor, thinking that all stocks of pepper previously held by the Company there would have been lost in the fire, deemed it advisable to enter into a contract to purchase at $12 per picul on account of the Hon'ble Company some 7,000 piculs originating mainly from Sumatra but also from Rhio, Lingin and Kelantan and arranged for us to store this on his behalf until freight was available in their ships en route to China.[12] When the Company's ship *Repulse* (Figure 15) arrived from Tappanooly in mid–September, it was found that she only had cargo space for about half the stored quantity and, as our storage contract expired at the end of the month, I asked Crawfurd for instructions, presenting our account at the same time. There was not the least probability of any other of the Company's ships taking the remaining pepper on. Its public sale, to save further loss, would therefore become a matter of expediency, should no favourable opportunity offer of forwarding it to China before the end of the month.[13]

The one other possible ship had no space for additional cargo. Crawfurd had no alternative other than to sell it off. The sale called for

[12] SSR L20 No 32 dated 4th July 1823.
[13] SSR L19 228 dated 10th September 1823.

sealed tenders, so we bid, and won, over 2,400 piculs at 10 ½. Guthrie took 200. The remainder went to auction and Morgan took it all at 9 ¾. In due course we sold it all off profitably to some Americans.

Repulse was also carrying six chests of camphor which, following the Lieutenant Governor's written instructions, Crawfurd offered for sale to her Captain personally. He was prepared to pay substantially more than we and so we lost that business.[14] Almost at the same time *Eliza* arrived from Bencoolen with over a thousand bags of new coffee for us.

Reliable reports reached us of a fleet of Illanun pirates from Sulu off the coast of Pahang, ransacking and laying waste the islands in the vicinity as well as several villages which acknowledged the sovereignty of the Sultan and Temenggong. The coasting trade was in the meantime inter-rupted and several boats and persons belonging to Singapore had been captured. Three large war boats about 50 feet long, mounting one long gun on the bow and some swivels, crewed by about 100 men each had been seen three days earlier between Sedili and Endau on the east coast of Johore. This induced Crawfurd to charter for 15 days the fast–sailing ketch *Boa Fortuna* with four 12 pounder carronades to go in pursuit. Captain Murray detailed Lieutenant Jackson who could speak Malay to take command of the detachment of infantry and artillery troops he put on board and off they sailed, returning later without (rather as I had expected) having found any trace of the pirates.

The want of any official judicial court other than that of the Resident and the magistrates was on occasion to cause a problem. Before Crawfurd had been with us a month a Balinese man murdered his Chinese mistress in broad daylight and when apprehended made a full confession, sup-ported by the accounts of witnesses. Whilst there was no doubt of the homicide, there was no legal tribunal in the Settlement where he could be brought to trial. Not being a subject of the Sultan or Temenggong nor of any of our possessions in India to which he could be sent, he had to be kept in jail until instructions came from Calcutta.[15]

Most of the European residents lived in houses on the Cantonment Plain next to the Sepoy Lines. My own was one such and I had been given

---

[14] SSR L19 230 dated 13th September 1823.
[15] SSR L19 133-5 dated 15th July 1823.

a special lease by the Lieutenant Governor before his departure in recognition of the help I had given during a difficult period. It was for my own residence but as my partner Read's wife, child and her sister Miss Fraser were expected to arrive shortly it made sense for me to move, leaving the house for them. As this might invalidate the lease, I applied for permission to Crawfurd who, to my relief, agreed. Being in a military area rules applied not only to the residents, military or otherwise but also to those receiving public pay such as native doctors, writers, syces, bildars [diggers], grass cutters, domestic servants or others who were to be subject to Court Martial if they misbehaved. Any person found selling spirits or drugs to the troops would be seized and brought to trial. Any disorderly person or Chinese, Malay, Bengali, Chuliah or Portuguese passing within the limits of the Cantonment at unreasonable hours without a lantern or torch and being unable to give an account of themselves would be seized and confined. No kris-carrying person other than the Sultan, the Temenggong and their attendants were permitted to enter at night. No procession might pass through without prior permission from the Officer Commanding the Troops. Lastly the number of cattle permitted to wander at large during the night had become such a public nuisance that a pound was being constructed into which any strays found would be put. A charge of 8 annas per day would be charged. If this were not paid and the animal reclaimed within four days, it would be sold to clear the expense.

Murray was concerned at this time that due to illness &ca taking its toll the number of troops at his disposal was insufficient to carry out the tasks allotted to them and he repeated his request to Calcutta that an additional company of sepoys plus two European officers might be sent to add to their strength.

Farquhar who, following his brutal dismissal had been granted six months leave from the Army, had brought his letter books up to date, had his accounts approved and written to Calcutta letters of complaint about his treatment by Raffles, now started to make preparations to leave for home. The last few months had been an extremely difficult time for him although, at least, he had the satisfaction of receiving a copy of an official letter from Adam, the Acting Governor General, Calcutta addressed to the Lieutenant Governor whose former protector Hastings, the Governor

General had been recalled to Britain. This castigated Raffles in no uncertain terms for the way he had behaved to Farquhar, which must have been only very cold comfort to the latter.

When we learned that our respected former Resident was leaving most of us felt we should at the very least subscribe to a farewell gift which would reflect his private worth, uniform kindness and his hospitality as well as our own feelings of respect and gratitude for his unswerving commitment to the good of the Settlement. Not all agreed, notable exceptions being John Morgan, Andrew Hay and D. S. Napier all of whom had had their disputes with him and retained long memories of supposed insults, and of course Captain Flint. The others, including Crawfurd and several Armenians, contributed to a piece of plate costing the equivalent of 3,000 Sicca Rupees which was ordered for him from a firm in London. The other racial communities vied with each other in extolling his virtues. Tan Che Sang and Li Hu Ke (Lee Ha Ki) on behalf of the Chinese requested Crawfurd's permission to present him with a gold cup and in the end commissioned a silver epergne to be sent to him in Britain. Not only was he leaving a part of the world where he had spent nearly thirty years but also Nonia Clement, his mistress who had born his first child, Esther in 1796, followed by Elizabeth, Catherine, Andrew and Arthur. Esther had married Bernard in 1818 and produced Farquhar's first grandchild *"Sri Singapura"* in Singapore a year later. Catherine had married Captain Davis, the Cantonment Adjutant and Andrew, still single, was at this stage a merchant. He died a few years later in Batavia.[16] The other two grown up children were in Calcutta.

A vast crowd assembled to bid Farquhar farewell when he sailed on 28th December accompanied by two of his grandchildren, Bernard's daughter and Davis' son, for Malacca, Penang and Calcutta to defend himself against charges made by Raffles justifying his dismissal and then on to Britain, battles with the directors of the Hon'ble Company, marriage to a young girl in Scotland and production of six more children. Living near Perth he died some few years back.

---

[16] He married Elizabeth Robinson in 1827 who, after his death, married his executor James Scott Clark.

Chapter 6

1824 Floods. John Morgan. Rhio

1824 opened with near disaster. I remember it well. A very strong wind blew from the east on 18th January and the surf thundered on the beach. The tide rose two feet above the highest spring tide so far recorded and flowed over the recently built embankment on the right bank of the river flooding the streets of the Chinese town and giving much employment to anyone who owned a sampan. People moved what goods they could to their upper floors, the rest being badly damaged. My own outhouses and godown were not spared, the former mostly collapsing. My house, rented from Flint in its own compound fenced off from Battery Road (then a mere unnamed path) survived unscathed but my wall and steps on the riverside suffered considerable damage.

A short while after this, together with nine others, in the absence of an official coroner, I was asked to investigate the death of Captain John Hale of the brig *Philotax* and one of his crew who had died in a sad accident. The two had been examining the lower hull of their brig, beached out at Sandy Point. They had dug away the sand on one side of the vessel to do this. It was not sufficiently buttressed, and the brig suddenly rolled over on top of them. It was a sad affair. There were no suspicious circumstances, and we gave a verdict of accidental death.

A second disaster, fortunately merely social, occurred when Crawfurd and his wife held a dinner for some 50 Europeans and their ladies on 6th February. It was held at the then unfashionable time of 7 pm. Dinner was normally eaten about 4pm and one would go out for a drive or walk afterwards before dark. There was plenty to eat, less to drink and the wine ran out. Conversation did not flow, there were no bursts of cheerfulness or jollity, the timing was bad and the speeches worse. Guests were reluctant to speak out and they seemed to have no interests in common. He may have had diplomatic qualities, but these apparently did not extend to those he felt were his inferiors and he lacked the common touch of either Farquhar or Raffles. It was some time after this dinner that news reached us, by way of the American brig *Leander* which had come from Batavia, of the tragic loss of the *Fame* which was to take Raffles and his family home. All Raffles' magnificent collections were on board and had been lost. To our relief we understood the family had not yet boarded the ship and so was safe. It was only later that we heard that they had in fact been on board, our distress being mitigated by the fact that no lives had been lost and the Flints' young son Charles was safe despite their having been for 24 hours adrift in an open boat.

Although the Lieutenant Governor had appointed me and others in teams of three to act as magistrates for three months each this did not work well as it interfered substantially with our varied business needs. Before his departure he had changed the system and appointed 12 of us for the period of one year to deal with minor crimes and the Resident's Court to deal with others. Any two of us could sit when required and this allowed us some leeway. Unlike Penang we had no judge, trained lawyer or Court of Justice in the Settlement. This was needed particularly to deal with troublesome Europeans such as John Morgan. The behaviour of this man, after the departure of the Lieutenant Governor, continued to worsen. He took a delight in baiting Crawfurd, in undermining the Government and putting himself in opposition to all law and control to such an extent that Crawfurd instructed Sam Bonham (now Assistant Resident) to arrest him and send him off to Calcutta where he would be amenable to the authority of regular law and at the disposal of the Governor–General in Council. This was on the basis that he did not have a licence from the Court of Directors or certificate from the Chief Secretary to reside in India. The arrest was made, and Morgan confined in the Guard House prior to being sent to Bengal. A number of people intervened on his behalf, not because they supported him but rather due to the fact that many also lacked such written authority and feared that, if they incurred the wrath of the authorities, they too could be expelled. Crawfurd was persuaded to accept a grovelling apology and a promise to reform. Morgan was released and left us not long afterwards to attempt his revenge. The firm was left under the control of Messrs Robert Hunter and William Paton and went out of business in 1827. Their property in Commercial Square was auctioned off. Hunter continued in business in partnership with Alex Watt, but they failed in 1830.[1] Presumably at the request and expense of Morgan a sketch of the arrest was later drawn by Isaac Robert Cruikshank, the brother of the well-known artist and caricaturist George Cruikshank, in London from which prints were made and circulated (Figure 16).

Morgan was not the only one to fall foul of Crawfurd. In August and September 1824 he had written to Calcutta complaining of the behaviour and the abusive language Captain Pearl had addressed to Bonham and of the behaviour of John Francis who ran a tavern. He was not happy with the reply received which exonerated both individuals and allowed them to continue to reside in Singapore.

In the early days my business, apart from selling goods on commission was, as already stated, to a large extent looking after the requirements of visiting ships and their crews. I knew well from my own experience the sort of things needed and was able to supply them, adding a commission. Hay, soon after he joined me, had opened for us an agency at Rhio and himself spent a few months across the strait. The agency was a collecting point for the gambier grown on nearby islands by some of the estimated few thousand Chinese living there and was then taken across to Singapore for shipment to Batavia and other ports. It was also able to service the few American ships that anchored at Bulang Bay a few miles away. When the Anglo–American Treaty of 1815 had been signed listing all the British–controlled ports at which their ships could trade Singapore had not been founded and so was not included. This omission led to the absurd situation of allowing them to visit our port but not trade there. So they contracted their sales and purchases and then had to anchor south across the straits in Dutch waters to load or unload the cargo which was sent across. After Hay returned the agency was left under the charge of Captain Ong Ban Hok, a

---

[1] *Singapore Chronicle* dated 17th January 1828, New firm w.e.f. 1st January 1828 Failed 16th December 1830.

Rhio resident supported by a young man, Hartmann, who later proved to
have been acting under cover for my competitor, Morgan, and was sacked.
I replaced him on a salaried basis with W. S. Duncan who, like Hay, was
a Shetlander from Lerwick and who had arrived in Singapore the previous
November in the same ship as Read's wife and daughter. We were not at
all pleased that Hay had apparently arranged for him to come out without
first mentioning it to me. He was however here and so at Hay's request I
took him on, initially as an unpaid writer to learn the business and the
Malay language, and he was of great help in 'sailing' the various vessels
which came to us. He boarded with Hay who, on his return from Rhio, had
built a bungalow on a piece of waste marshy ground in the Cantonment
next to the then Sepoy Lines which he had earlier bought. Under the
Lieutenant Governor's regime this fell within the limits set out for the new
experimental spice garden and he was waging an unsuccessful campaign
for compensation. He had by now also acquired a small hill along the new
path to Tanjong Pagar which he was having cleared of scrub and later built
himself a bungalow along High Street.

The former Lieutenant Governor Raffles himself deplored the prohibition on American ships trading with Singapore and in a letter to me from
London dated 2nd January 1825 wrote:

> 'On the subject of the clause in the treaty which restricts Americans from
> visiting Singapore, nothing can be more ridiculous. I have conferred with
> the American Minister and our own authorities on the subject, and I hope
> I shall succeed in removing this bar to your commerce.'

In this he failed, and the objective was only achieved in 1836. As I was
holding funds for him, he asked in the same letter to *'complete the remittances as soon as you can as I am anxious to invest my little property as
early as possible.'* He continued, rather ingenuously, that:

> 'the overflow of capital in this country has occasioned a degree of
> gambling that some steady people think will end in something like
> the South Sea Bubble. Independent of the foreign loans, which are to
> an enormous extent, there is an association for almost every possible
> speculation that can be conceived, and vast sums of money have been
> made by the rise in the value of shares.'

Local competition was fierce. I took great care of '*my*' captains and insisted that while in port they should stay at my house where I could make sure they were not tempted away by competitors. It made sense to give them all the help possible. Years later Mr Balestier, the newly arrived United States Consul designate, lamented that his friend Captain Hall of the American ship *Canova* had appointed me rather than himself as his agent. Hall felt under great obligation to me for the friendship he had experienced when he had been in Singapore some years before under perilous circumstances. If I am not mistaken, he must have referred to his arrival in *Padang* from Manila in March 1828 when I was able to assist him and supply his cargo once he had safely anchored at Rhio across the strait.[2]

Goods were consigned by overseas merchants to us in Singapore for local sale and on the proceeds of which commission was charged. The advantage was that if one's reputation for honesty and business acumen was good then a large capital was not needed. We handled shipments of pepper, tin, sugar, gambier and much else besides, had sent to us gunahs, sannahs, cumas, gunny bags, saltpetre, iron, household furniture and a considerable quantity of opium. Early on I was consigned Malwa opium from Batavia but, as this was not a product of the Company, I could only get special permission to land it provided I undertook to re-export it and not to sell it locally. I remember *Valetta* arriving from Calcutta en route to China with two consignments of Patna opium totalling 25 chests for our firm but we noted that the consignor had invoiced them at a higher price than those he consigned to Dents at Canton. At about the same time *Janet Hutton* arrived from Calcutta with a cargo of goods for the local market and chests of opium. Howard and I had decided to sell her in Calcutta as her upper works suffered from dry rot and there was little good to be done by a vessel of her size in those times. Instructions from our consignors could not always be followed to the letter. In one case one consignment of 35 chests of Patna opium was received which was to be sold on receipt for what it would fetch. Read and I ignored this as it would have completely disrupted the local market. The scene when the owner arrived from Canton and found no sale had taken place is best forgotten.

---

[2] Arrived 27th March 1828 and sailed to Rhio on 2nd April.

The question of the future of the Settlement continued to exercise our minds. Rumours percolated down to us that Anglo–Dutch talks had been broken off and the news of Canning's resignation reached us in January 1822. To Hastings in Calcutta, with whom he had had much acrimonious correspondence, that was good news, but Hastings was keen to resign his position as Governor General, being afraid that his many enemies at home might get him sacked. News then arrived that he was to be replaced in India by Canning. While the latter was preparing to sail Castlereagh, the Foreign Secretary, committed suicide and Canning replaced him, resigning his appointment as Governor General. He now had many more urgent matters on hand and the question of the Dutch factories in India and Sumatra, financial penalties to be paid by the Dutch and the Singapore question were left unattended until negotiations restarted in London just before Christmas 1823. A series of 11 meetings followed and on 17th March 1824 a treaty was signed under which Malacca, Singapore and the former Dutch factories in India would come under British control, while Bencoolen and the outstations in Sumatra would be taken over by the Dutch who would pay Britain £100,000. Areas west and south of an imaginary line drawn down the Malacca Straits, turning eastwards to divide Singapore from Rhio, would be the Dutch sphere of influence and the Malayan Peninsula British. The line stopped before Borneo was reached, leading to later disputes. The Treaty was ratified by the House of Commons on 17th June 1824 although the first we in Singapore learned of it was from a report in a newspaper from Java received late in September.

It did not take long after the departure of the Lieutenant Governor for the Sultan and Temenggong to endeavour to wheedle more advantages out of the new Resident. While the Lieutenant Governor was with us a British flag was, with his permission, raised by them in Johore to guard against an attack by their opponents from Rhio. They were later instructed to take it down. In November, the same year when the Dutch were reported not only as having installed the Sultan's brother as Sultan of Johore but to have planted their flag some 20 miles up the Johore River, it was found that our flag still flew. The Temenggong was asking for action which Crawfurd declined[3] and threatened to send some sepoys to lower the flag

---

[3] SSR L19 317 dated 18th November 1823.

if they did not comply with the earlier order. Next came a long letter alleging that we had withdrawn our protection from them in defiance of treaty obligations. There were no such obligations. Another long–simmering problem arose with the question of how slavery needed to be defined. They regarded all their own people, two thirds of whom were women, as their slaves which was totally against the Settlements' regulations. The Temenggong asked for yet further funds to cover the removal of his followers to Teluk Blangah and to retain his existing site on the riverbank, which could not be permitted. Crawfurd recommended action to Calcutta. His suggestion was approved, and a draft of a suitable new treaty sent to him. The Sultan and to a lesser extent the Temenggong had, under our protection, experienced a vastly improved quality of life and now expected yet better. Negotiations were protracted and finally on 2nd August 1824, before we had received any news of the treaty with the Dutch, Crawfurd won through and a new treaty was signed ceding the sovereignty and property of Singapore and islands within 10 miles of its coast to the Hon'ble East India Company. They would retain some autonomy over their people in their personal property at Campong Glam and Teluk Blangah. All earlier treaties and agreements were nullified. To demonstrate British control Crawford, Jackson and some others a year later sailed round the island anticlockwise, visiting Pulau Tekong in the east and both Rabbit and Coney Islands which are the westernmost of those belonging to us. It took them the best part of 10 days to complete the voyage. The Temenggong died four months after this and was succeeded by his 15–year–old son Ibrahim.[4]

---

[4] *Asiatic Journal*, August 1826 p 230. per *Singapore Chronicle*. Abdulrahman Sarima Raja Died 8th December 1825 aged 45.

Chapter 7

Education. Effects of Loss of Bencoolen. New Government. Sam Bonham.

If I am not wrong, it was in January 1823 that the Lieutenant Governor was of opinion that the sons of the Sultan and the Temenggong should be sent to Calcutta for proper education, but this notion was rejected out of hand by both fathers. This refusal, on religious grounds, led to his proposal to set up instead a local college to educate the children of the higher–class Malays and Chinese, as well as to teach local languages to the European residents and, reflecting his own interests, to collect documents relevant to local traditions and history. The timely arrival of Rev Morrison from Canton raised the possibility of moving to Singapore his recently founded Anglo–Chinese College at Malacca. Because the Dutch were in possession of the territory this idea came to naught. The Lieutenant Governor selected a site for the college, the Institution, and endowed it with several large lots of ground which could be leased out, the rent from which would provide running expenses. We had a meeting three months later when Morrison came back to take things further. Jackson was tasked with designing the new building, Maxwell to be Secretary of the Committee and ourselves to be Treasurer. Donations were sought, a substantial sum raised and promised (neither Morgan nor Queiros contributed) and a foundation stone was laid by the Lieutenant Governor before he left us. Sad to say Crawfurd felt the project to be overambitious and although Jackson proceeded, if not rapidly, at least uninterruptedly with accumulating and preparing of materials the walls were not constructed for some time. Morrison, who had returned to England after the death of his wife, reappeared in 1826 en route to Macao and stayed two weeks with the Flints at Mount Sophia.[1] He brought with him 6,000 ounces of silver which he passed to me, part of which went to pay for the hill he had earlier purchased at his own expense, and the house for missionaries built on it. The clearance of the large trees on the Institution site took far longer than had been expected. Four years later we offered the unfinished school building to Government for sale or rent for other purposes but this was refused and so it languished incomplete and increasingly dilapidated, becoming known as Jackson's Ruin.

One consequence was the arrival in 1825 of a 13–year–old American, William C. Hunter, who had been sent out from New York to Canton to study the Chinese language. In Canton it proved impossible to engage a suitable teacher and so, having heard of the proposed establishment of the Institution in Singapore, his mentor Mr Covert sent him down in April with introductions to the Resident and others, and *'consigned to Messrs A. L. Johnston & Co.'* Covert's information was of course inaccurate. The large two–storeyed brick building stood unfinished without doors or window shutters, a ghost of a house. It was unlikely to start taking in pupils in the near future. Thus after two months stay with Mr and Mrs Read, her sister Miss Fraser and their little children in the bungalow on the slopes of Government Hill where he was made to feel truly at home[2] we sent him off in a small native brig to the Anglo–Chinese College at Malacca where he remained until the end of 1826. In later years he resided in Macao and Canton under the well–known American firm of Russell & Co.

The threat of fire was always very real given that most buildings were of wood and attap, huddled closely together and dependent on wells for water. Some 90 buildings were destroyed in a fire which broke out in December in a house in Cross Street. It was after dark and in less than an hour all the houses between it and the sea were in flames. We were fortunate that the wind was blowing from the northeast and so we were able to

[1] Gillis, E. 1839. *Malixun hui yi lu*, p. 356.
[2] Hunter, W. C. 2020. *The "Fan Kwae" at Canton*, Outlook, Germany, p. 9 and Hunter, W. C. 1885. *Bits of Old China*, K Paul Trench & Co., p. 234

prevent the fire spreading to Market Street and the Square. Most of the European community assisted, including the captain and officers of the brig *Rhio* but regrettably no help was given by the Chinese or other native communities. Some Chinese did come to watch and stood gazing with looking glasses in their hands, which they held up towards the flames to propitiate the gods and avoid further calamity.[3]

Our European community was growing apace. William Spottiswoode and the Connollys arrived in their brig *Guide*. Connolly stayed and Spottiswoode later commanded and traded in the *Mary Ann*. Syme & Co was formed and many others followed suit. These included the Portuguese naval surgeon Jose d'Almeida who was about my age and who, when he had passed through Singapore earlier, liked the prospects and left money with Bernard to build him a house in Campong Glam. When this was ready, he moved down from Macao with his wife and the first few of a large brood of children — 20 in all in the end I think — and set up in business at the western end of Commercial Square. These arrivals were reinforced by officials and civil servants from Bencoolen which was to be handed over to the Dutch officially on 1st April 1825. The actual handover only took place later when they found the time and the troops to do so. They were in financial difficulty and also fighting numerous minor battles with local sultans who felt disinclined to be taken over. The Company's ship *Repulse* evacuated a large party of residents to Singapore in June including Garling, Patullo, and Perreau (none of whom stayed long) as well as local employees from Bencoolen families of longstanding such as Burrows and Leicester who were found government employment. Others went to Penang and Malacca. It was not until the following year, 1826, that John Prince was able to close the books as instructed, head for Penang prior to taking over Crawfurd's position in Singapore and leave the territory to the tender mercies of the Dutch. Trade was at a standstill; property had fallen at least 80 per cent in value but much could not be sold as there were no buyers. The convicts from mainland India and stores were sent to us and to Penang and the troops with their officers back to Bengal. Bencoolen had always been a drain on the profits of the East India

---

[3] *Asiatic Journal*, August 1826, p. 229.

Company but for those who had made their livelihood in the territory the handover was a death blow.

Immigrants from China had been arriving each year when the North East monsoon blew the junks down the South China Sea. Poverty, starvation, local politics as well as rumours of money to be made in the south were all causes of this movement of people. A passage with food provided cost six Spanish Dollars which some were able to pay in advance and so be free on arrival to take up whatever work they could find. Others were bound in advance to agents who paid the fare for them when they reached Singapore and deducted this plus commission in instalments from their wages. I remember a large junk arriving from the Canton region in February 1825 carrying nearly 900 immigrants plus other cargo. She anchored in the roads and within minutes was surrounded by just about every small sampan or boat in the place, bargaining to carry the passengers ashore and, once a price was agreed, landing them at the nearest point on the beach an overloaded vessel could reach. Having suffered a very uncomfortable and cramped passage these new arrivals, or *sin keh* as they were known, presented a most dismal spectacle, few having anything except the clothes on their backs and many having not even enough to cover themselves fully. Within a few days a third had departed for Rhio and a tenth for elsewhere. The next morning a second and larger junk arrived with over 1,000 immigrants. She anchored much farther out in the roads and was soon surrounded by boats of every size and description in which they disembarked. As ballast both junks brought us tiles for flooring and roofing which they sold to enable them to buy new masts and purchase a return cargo.[4]

We did not have many entertainments in those days, but a very enjoyable dinner, ball and supper was held by the members of the 'Raffles Club' at the Singapore Hotel in Commercial Square on 6th July 1826 in honour of Sir Stamford Raffles' 45th birthday, the second year in which such an event had been held. Sam Bonham was in the chair, Crawfurd being overseas at the time. The gentlemen joined the ladies in the ballroom after the dinner and the evening passed off with much satisfaction. It was not until sometime later that the news reached us that Sir Stamford had in fact been

---

[4] *Oriental Herald and Journal of General Literature*, October 1826, Vol 11, p. 208.

found dead in England the previous day.[5] The following year, with Prince in the chair, only a dinner was held it being felt that a ball and supper would have been unseemly in the circumstances.[6] This Club continued for about 10 years before fading out.

For reasons best known to the directors of the Hon'ble Company, Penang, Malacca and Singapore were in August 1826 designated a separate presidency, no longer under the direct aegis of Bengal. There was to be a Governor in Penang and Resident Councillors (no longer Residents) in the three ports. Another change of title, which infuriated Flint, was that the Master Attendants at Malacca and Singapore were now to be known as Assistant Master Attendants, the post at Penang being the only one retaining the old title. The effective date of the changeover was 1st August.[7] Crawfurd officially stepped down on 14th August but had left Singapore in mid–January for Calcutta, before the treaty was signed in February after the first Anglo–Burmese War. He had been appointed Civil Commissioner for the Delta of Pegu including Bassein, Martaban and Rangoon. From March until mid–August he spent most of his time in that place and for a while Sam Bonham was left in charge.[8] Crawfurd was then appointed to head a mission in September to the Burmese court at Ava, 500 miles up the Irrawaddy River. On this journey he identified a flower new to science, subsequently named for the naturalist wife of the new Governor General (Figure 17). On the return journey due to low water in the river he was able to collect seven boxes of fossil animal bones. These were sent in due course to Sir Richard Murchison, (brother of our future Resident Councillor) in London, some of which were later identified as being from an unknown species of mastodon.

Before he first departed for Rangoon Crawfurd left considerable funds with me which he wished to invest profitably in Singapore but felt that, given he would be continuing officially as Resident for some months, it would be invidious of him to do so directly. I was therefore to buy certain

[5] *Asiatic Journal*, Feb 1827, p. 277 quoting *Singapore Chronicle* 20th July 1826.

[6] *Singapore Chronicle*, 19th July 1827.

[7] SSR A24 236 dated 24th April 1826.

[8] See Crawfurd — Account of Rangoon in the summer of 1826. *SOAS Bulletin of Burma Research*, Vol. 3, No. 2, Autumn 2005.

properties in my name and then have them transferred to his. I bought 13 for him in early June. The most desirable was a plot adjoining the market. It belonged to Che Sang who was at first reluctant to part with it and from whom I also bought three others, two in Malacca Street and one on the north side of the Square. Six others in Malacca Street, three in Market Street with two in Circular Road completed the purchases and in due course all were transferred out of my name into Crawfurd's.[9]

It was intended that Crawfurd would be replaced in Singapore by John Prince once the latter had handed over Bencoolen to the Dutch. Meanwhile Edward Presgrave, who had left Bencoolen the previous year and been employed temporarily in Penang and Malacca, was sent down in April with the official title of 1st Assistant to the Resident but actually as Acting Resident, with young Bonham serving under him as 2nd Assistant. Presgrave, a quiet religious individual who was recorded as writing to a friend that *'most Europeans live very wicked lives'*, disliked socialising and had little small talk. He was to be with us off and on until 1830. He went on furlough to China in August 1826 for four months, officially to deal with pressing private matters, leaving Sam Bonham to cope on his own which he did very competently.

Sam was a pleasant young man who usually got on well with everyone although his relations with Guthrie, over some remarks made about the latter's dogs, remained cool for a while. The dogs, as far as I remember were mongrels, not well born, whose size and ferocity deterred all but the most determined intruders and were good at catching the rats which overran the Settlement. When Sam joined the Company, his widowed mother had been living in the Lodge at Great Baddow Hall in Essex. The Hall had been bought by his uncle in 1816 from J. W. Hull, the *'Nabob'* who had lived there for some years and was a trustee of the local Free School which Sam may well have attended. His daughter, Sophia Hull now Lady Raffles, may have suggested Sam's applying to the Hon'ble Company to be posted to Bencoolen. Neither she nor Raffles himself knew anything of that place and were taken aback when they arrived, he describing the place as *'without exception, the most wretched place I ever beheld'*.

---

[9] Leong, Foke Ming. 2004. *Early Land Transactions in Singapore* JMBRAS, Vol. LXXVII, Part I, pp. 23–42.

The difference in age of 20 years between Sam and myself was not a problem and I recall one evening when he told me something of his life up to this time. His father had been a captain in the Hon'ble Company's maritime service and divorced his first wife to marry his second, Sam's mother, who gave him Sam in 1803 and a daughter five years later. He was lost when his ship, the *True Briton,* sank in a typhoon in the South China Sea some days after separating from other East India Company ships in October 1809. Sam was introduced by his shipowner uncle when he applied to the Company for employment as a writer having been '*educated in writing and accounts, humbly hoping he was qualified to serve*'. He was sent East almost immediately aboard the Company's ship *General Harris* which reached Singapore just before his 16th birthday.[10] Here Farquhar put him to work for two months while waiting for a ship to carry him on. He eventually sailed in *Enterprise* for Bencoolen via Penang.[11]

Before *Enterprise* reached Bencoolen Raffles had departed the territory for Calcutta, leaving his wife behind, and was still away. On his return in March 1820, finding that this inexperienced teenager friend of his wife had arrived, for whom there was no useful employment, he decided to second Sam provisionally, whilst remaining on the books of Fort Marlbro' (Bencoolen), to '*do duty until further orders under the Resident of Singapore.*' There was no company ship expected to call in the near future and so he had to make his own arrangements for a passage. On arrival in Singapore in June he somewhat nervously applied to Farquhar for a refund of the cost.

It was to be a comparatively short stay. He was put to work under R. P. Reed, an older man, to assist Travers in the Pay Department and help out elsewhere as required. Reed was to take over on Travers' departure but had offended Farquhar who substituted Captain Davis, his son–in–law, in November. Sam, being overlooked, felt it was an insult to his competence and despite his young age fired off a complaint to Raffles. A little over two months later, towards the end of January 1821, he received a letter from Fort Marlbro' advising him that he had been appointed Assistant to John Prince, the Resident at '*Tappanooly and Nattal*', who lived at Nattal.

---

[10] SSR L10 105 dated 2nd September 1819.
[11] SSR L10 200 dated 6th November 1819.

He immediately applied to Farquhar for permission to take passage in the *Indian Trader* to Batavia where he found a vessel to take him to Bencoolen and then onward to act *'in the room of'* Charles Halhed, the current assistant.

On arrival he spent some months learning all he could under the guidance of Prince at Nattal but in September he joined the Rev. Burton who was, with Raffles' approval, making a journey to the island of Nias and to Tappanooly to select suitable sites where Christian Missions could be started. First, they sailed west across to the island of Nias where the villages were, he said, situated on the tops of very steep hills. The street of the village of Poheelee which they visited was regularly paved, as much as the streets in London, and about 60 feet wide. He was to be based at the small island of Punchong Kechil, lying in the mouth of Tappanooly Bay about 80 miles north of Nattal. As he told me, this was something of a challenge as he was for much of the time on his own in a strange environment with people whose customs were nothing like any to which he had been used.

Sam remained at Tappanooly until called back to Fort Marlbro' to accompany Raffles to Singapore on his final visit. It was here he was put to work harder than ever before in his life. He relished the challenge and rose to the occasion. He had learned a great deal since October 1822 and these last four months had taught him more while alone at the helm of Singapore, aged just 23.

Sam as I have said got on well with all, was popular and did his best for the Settlement. He had a snub nose, a stutter and something of a lisp and although not of aristocratic mien looked the part he had to play. He did not stand on ceremony nor look down on lower mortals, had a good sense of humour which he used in the friendliest way. All servants of the Company were required to study the Chinese or Siamese languages and he chose Chinese, a most difficult language at which he laboured for many years.[12] Whether it was at this time that he took up smoking — those small Manila *'segars'* as the Americans called them — I cannot now recall but later in life he could not do without them. Lt Keppel told us that when sailing to Batavia at the end of September 1831 in *Magicienne* Sam could

---

[12] Instruction by Fullerton per letter dated 29th August 1826.

not be without his smoke. Special unofficial arrangements had to be made on that occasion as the Captain of *Magicienne* forbade any smoking on board and his word was law.

Although we had welcomed Prince's arrival from Penang by *Lalla Rookh* on 3rd January 1827, the following day was a sad one as we received the news that Raffles had died some months earlier. I asked Prince for permission, if funds were raised, to erect a monument on Government Hill. This was immediately granted following which I had a notice published in the *Chronicle* in its next issue on 18th that a subscription list for this had been opened at my house and that in due course a meeting would be held to decide the details.

In our small community deaths and departures were felt perhaps more deeply by most people than in larger cities as our lives were more closely interconnected. One such was the death in November 1826 of D. S. Napier's wife Ann whom he had married in Calcutta and who in the short five years of their marriage had given him four children.[13] There was no way these, aged four or less, could be brought up by him in Singapore and so he took them home to Scotland to be looked after by his parents and siblings, sailing for London in *Exmouth* on Christmas Eve and leaving his fine new house just built by Coleman on Beach Road.[14] Although I did not know then if he would return he did so, arriving with a new wife two years later, early in 1829.

---

[13] Married Ann Margaret Dixon in Calcutta on 15th November 1821.

[14] *Singapore Chronicle* 4th January 1827.

Chapter 8

John Prince. Court House Matters. Defence.

John Prince, under whom Sam had been serving in Sumatra five years earlier, took over as Resident Councillor on 4th January 1827 having been sworn in in Penang and Presgrave reappeared from his furlough a week later to resume his position.[1] Sam was now back to serving as Assistant to the Resident Councillor, number three in the pecking order.

Prince was described to me by a missionary as a man whose uprightness, benevolence, misfortunes and hospitality had gained him the sympathy and admiration of the East. He had been living and trading at Nattal since he was 15 and was now 45. The early misfortunes referred to were, I think, the attack in 1810 by the French who completely destroyed his property. He was away at Fort Marlbro' at the time of the attack. His assistant Hayes was however very badly treated and taken away to Mauritius as a hostage. From this interruption he had recovered, but now once again through no fault of his own he had lost, if not a fortune, at least a good competence. Prince was an efficient administrator and was thought to be the first European to walk to Bukit Timah, a 500 foot hill in the centre of the island, and back. With the road contractor it took them five hours to cover the nine miles through gambier plantations and jungle to the top of the hill where they constructed a *balei*. The contractor tendered to build the road for $440 per mile whereas the authorised budget was only $190.

---

[1] Arrived in *Milford* 16th January 1827 per *Singapore Chronicle* 18th January 1827.

Penang advised that Calcutta had forbidden more road construction, so the project lapsed but in due course a road of sorts was built. Seven years later it was upgraded for carriages by convicts, with ditches on both sides, something of a waste of money.[2] Prince also authorised the extension of the existing road from Kallang on to Qualoo Rungong. He was only to stay with us a few months, leaving us on retirement in mid–November[3] for Java where he hoped to catch *Buckinghamshire*. She was reportedly going to sail home from China a month earlier than the Captain had expected when she called in August on her outward voyage and was delayed by lightning shivering her mainmast whilst at anchor. She did not sail from China until mid–December and arrived at the Downs at the end of April 1828.

Kenneth Murchison, who had been the senior immediately available Government servant at Penang, was rushed to Singapore when Prince announced he was leaving. Whether due to instructions received or personal preference, he appeared always unwilling to take big decisions and had them lay over pending Governor Fullerton's next visit. One such was the question of how to improve the security of the jail from which six prisoners escaped one night. Construction of a new one was approved but meanwhile Fullerton decided that the old rice godown below the Resident Councillor's office was to be cleared and converted into a temporary jail for prisoners committed for trial and that within it the criminals were to be held separately from the debtors.[4]

Later the same year Maxwell encountered a problem. He had first applied for land in 1822 through a friend and reapplied later the same year on the basis that he wanted to settle permanently as a merchant in Singapore rather than being based at Batavia as heretofore. He was not successful until the Lieutenant Governor arrived. He was then granted land which included part of the old Malay burial ground but could not take possession as the Temenggong's people had not yet moved out. Crawfurd had later approved two sites for him, one in the Chinese campong and the other in town which allowed him to commission Coleman to design what was for years considered to be the grandest brick building in the Settlement. Whilst

---

[2] *Singapore Chronicle* dated 17th April 1834.
[3] *Singapore Chronicle* dated 18th November 1827 reported that he sailed in *Thalia* for Batavia.
[4] SSR N4 108 dated 1st March 1828.

approval had not been confirmed by the Supreme Government, Crawfurd had assured him that this would undoubtedly be given. Maxwell had now decided to retire to England which he did, sailing in September 1828,[5] and so came to an agreement to sell the property with a set completion date, but, as he later told me, Prince put a spanner in the works on the basis that the land on which the building stood was reserved for Government buildings. The only solution was to cancel the sales contract and rent both it and the adjoining building to them as a residence and Court House. Murchison who in the meantime had arrived from Penang to replace Prince as Resident Councillor[6] felt this would suit him well and the deal was signed. Fate then intervened. The Recorder for the Court of Judicature in the three territories, Sir John Claridge, had arrived in Penang and was due to hold a court session in Singapore. He found there were no guaranteed funds to cover his travel and expenses while on tour and that he might have to foot that bill out of his salary. He therefore refused to go and suggested in all seriousness that all prisoners for trial should be sent to Penang together with witnesses, guards, et cetera.[7] This was unacceptable for obvious reasons and Governor Fullerton resigned himself to taking the Recorder's place in the court proceedings on his regular visits to Singapore. Murchison had previously been authorised to move into the upper floor and to use the ground floor for offices. He had moved in his own furniture but was told to move this out as Fullerton, unwilling to use the house on the hill whose outhouses had been blown down in a gale and which was being renovated, would use it himself. Murchison thereafter rented from Charles Thomas his private house on the corner of Coleman Street and the Plain until his departure for Penang after Ibbetson's arrival late in 1830. It was here that he held a one–week belated dinner and ball to celebrate the King's birthday just before Fullerton's arrival. The lack of ladies restricted the amount of dancing, but the 80 guests stayed for supper and departed to their residences very happily after one o'clock in the morning.

In early January 1828 John Francis had tendered the New Tavern for use as a courthouse at Sicca Rupees 300 per month. This was accepted and

---

[5] He sailed on 28th September 1828 in *Lord Lowther* for England via China.
[6] Murchison arrived, with his wife on 27th November 1827 in *Vittoria* from Penang.
[7] SSR N4 69-73 dated 28th January 1828.

the Office of the Registrar opened there on 1st March.[8] The Singapore Hotel had been in existence for some years, not without troubles. He had been the operator of this establishment where the Raffles Club had had its dinners in previous years but had run into difficulties.[9] That building, the property of Morgans Hunter & Co was advertised for sale later the same year.[10] Francis opened a short–lived refreshment hall and billiard room in Commercial Square and then with his son started a bakery and pastry business. Shortly before I retired his firm, now based in Teluk Ayer Street, announced they had established themselves as butchers.

It was about this period that the question of the defence of Singapore was raised for the second time. Up to then although the morning and evening guns were fired at Battery Point[11] and the Military had a few more canon there, that was about it as far as fortifications went. Captain Edward Lake of the Bengal Engineers was sent down from Penang to undertake a study of our defensive needs and civil public works. Among his recommendations was the extension of the Battery Point site and erection of another at the far seaward end of Commercial Square. This caused some concern as, to have a clear field of fire between the two, various of our outhouses had to be demolished as did part of a building extension being erected by Messrs Spottiswoode & Connolly towards the sea at the back of their Commercial Square godown. We were allowed to fill up the small vacant space between us and the Battery, allowing us a building to replace the outhouses demolished.[12] The trees and jungle on the Point were cut down to make way for an extra battery to be erected there and it was hoped, fruitlessly as it later turned out, that the famous large boulder with the mysterious inscription on it could be left untouched. Sadly, this was not to be.[13] It was expected that this new work would not interfere with the facilities put up a little earlier by the sea–bathing club. These consisted of a square pagar of about 70 yards enclosed on three sides by neebungs, the

---

[8] SSR N4 88 dated 28th February 1828.
[9] SSR L13 147 dated March 1828. A "note from the members of the Committee for managing the affairs of the Singapore hotel".
[10] *Singapore Chronicle* dated 17th July 1828.
[11] SSR N4 494 dated October 1828.
[12] SSR N4 537 dated 10th December 1827.
[13] *Singapore Chronicle* dated 7th June 1827.

shore forming the inward boundary. At the centre of the shoreline and projecting some yards over the sea was a bathing room divided into apartments, a rickety building of wood and kajang somewhat rude in its construction and higher than needed over the water.[14] Close acquaintance with a shark or an alligator would be prevented and all subscribers were encouraged to make full use of it.

Another battery was to be erected on Palmer's Hill overlooking the entrance to New Harbour and Lake was in favour of the purchase of Pearl's Hill, known at the time as Mount Stamford, on which a redoubt and hilltop citadel might be constructed and to which the Sepoy Lines might be transferred from the Plain. Captain Pearl had retired, and the sale was to be handled through Mackenzie & Co, his agents, on behalf of his agents Barretto & Co in Calcutta.[15] Although approved at the price of Sicca Rupees 10,000 the deal fell through when Penang required submission of the original *'cutting paper'* giving ownership. This no longer existed, and Bonham insisted on a bureaucratic procedure which would have involved a small loss in exchange. Mackenzie & Co withdrew the offer and workmen already on the estate were hastily withdrawn by Government. In due course the matter was resolved with the Government paying interest, Bonham denying any blame for the delay, and work on the new Sepoy Lines resumed.

We had a considerable quantity of gunpowder stored at Sandy Point where it was guarded by the military, but the building was, like so many, gradually deteriorating. As, apart from our own stock, the quantity stored for others was small we were required by Government to rebuild it, a not unreasonable request.[16] By this time the import of gunpowder without a certificate from Government was prohibited and the Captain of a Russian ship who arrived with 250 kegs of *"sporting powder"* persuaded the Registrar, Presgrave, that this import should be allowed. Presgrave asked for permission not realising that such a quantity was more than sufficient for the needs of Singapore's shooting community for several decades and

---

[14] *Singapore Chronicle* dated 24th May 1827.
[15] SSR N3 63 dated 10th October 1827.
[16] SSR N4 265 dated 30th June 1828.

was roundly castigated for stupidity in not rejecting the request immediately.[17]

Partnerships and relationships change as time goes by and Hay left us in 1829 to setup on his own.[18] He was not the easiest of partners and initially at least had resented the fact that Read had a greater share in the firm than himself although he had been with me since we first set up. His strengths were his attention to detail and bookkeeping but he liked to keep himself to himself and as soon as he could afford it moved to his own small bungalow. We had many arguments over routine matters, both being somewhat hot tempered and reluctant to compromise. He was quite successful after leaving us and in 1835 took Duncan in as a partner. This only lasted until 1837 when there was an acrimonious split, possibly as the result of the arrival of Andrew Hay junior, his nephew. Queiros, who shortly afterwards left the Settlement, split up with W. R. George[19] as did George Armstrong and Thomas Crane.[20] Armstrong opened a Public Exchange, Reading Room and Circulating Library which was not a commercial success and it was later relaunched as the Singapore Reading Room with shareholders. It closed for good a year or so before I retired.[21]

As far as my own business was concerned, we continued to act as agents for a large number of square–rigged vessels many trading with London, Antwerp, Calcutta, Australia and elsewhere. We had taken on extra staff. One was young John Ellis who later left us and joined the Police. Another was Robert Jack who came to us from Batavia and joined as a clerk. He had previously been trading at Moco Moco, 100 miles or so from Bencoolen and was the brother of William Jack, the doctor and naturalist who before his death had been a good friend there of the Lieutenant Governor.[22] Although some ship names from those days such as *Nimrod*, *Lady of the Lake*, *Hero of Malown* and *Juno* remain in my memory for some reason, most I have forgotten. There was a French vessel, the

---

[17] SSR N4 392-3 dated 23rd September 1828.

[18] 26th August 1829 as reported in *Singapore Chronicle* of 27th August 1829.

[19] 30th June 1828 as reported in *Singapore Chronicle* of 3rd July.

[20] 31st July 1828.

[21] *Singapore Free Press* dated 25th November 1840.

[22] Bastin, J. 2019. *Sir Stamford Raffles and Some of His Friends and Contemporaries: A Memoir of the Founder of Singapore*. World Scientific, Singapore, p. 360.

Euphonie, which arrived in a sorry state needing to be re-coppered and refitted before sailing on to China. The Captain had no funds, so we advertised for him to raise 5,000 dollars on a bottomry bond whereby a loan is made and the security for the loan is the ship herself. I forget who came forward to invest but they lost their money. The day after her subsequent arrival at Lintin she was driven from her anchors on shore in a heavy gale and was totally wrecked with the loss of one life. Such are the risks of life at sea.[23]

---

[23] *Singapore Chronicle* dated 9th September 1830.

Chapter 9

Judicial Problems. Jail. Bridges.

I was still a magistrate and justice of the peace which at times needed a good deal of my attention and nevertheless enabled me to know something of what was going on in the various communities. One case which in the end had to go before the Governor was between George Armstrong's company and old Whampoa. They had been doing business which had ceased, and Armstrong held a promissory note from him which was long overdue for payment. Whampoa alleged that it was customary for such notes given by Chinese not to incur interest from the due date until the actual date of payment. An expert witness testified that interest was normally charged in India at 12 per cent per annum and the Governor ruled in favour of the plaintiff, which caused consternation among the Chinese community.[1]

Our system of civil and criminal justice varied over time. Initially Singapore was regarded as a military station rather than a civil settlement and Farquhar was effectively the only magistrate. This changed when the Lieutenant Governor returned in 1822 and early the following year instituted a system of magistrates and regulations for judicial matters. As I think I mentioned earlier I was appointed as one of the first magistrates and justices of the peace. Two of us were to sit with the Resident in civil and criminal cases and we were to take turns in carrying out the daily magistrates' duties. After taking over, Crawfurd swiftly changed the system and in addition to the Resident's Court set up a Court of Requests which was presided over by the Assistant Resident and could hear minor civil cases

---

[1] *Singapore Chronicle* dated 22nd May 1828.

up to an amount of 32 dollars. The bugbear was that the Resident's Court had no authority over European residents, some of whom made the most of this situation. Nor, in cases of murder, piracy or other crimes at sea, did it have jurisdiction even though the penalties for such crimes had been published by the Lieutenant Governor in 1823.[2] It was not until 1836 that a further Act of Parliament was passed which gave us Admiralty jurisdiction. When we were combined with Malacca and Penang to form the Presidency of the Straits Settlements in 1826 matters stagnated until the arrival of a new Charter of Justice from London which created a Court of Judicature consisting of the Governor, Fullerton, the Resident Councillors in the three settlements and a Recorder based in Penang who was to be a full–time qualified lawyer, the first being Sir John Claridge. The Court was to sit twice a year in each Settlement which programme was thrown into doubt by the Recorder initially refusing to travel and falling out with the Governor who had to visit us without him for the Court to be held. In June 1830, the Presidency was abolished so that all three Settlements reported to Calcutta once more and all the official titles changed. As exact titles were quoted in the charter Fullerton decided that the court could not continue, closed it and dismissed the staff. It was not until 1832 that the old titles were reintroduced, and justice recommenced until the present day. I remember well Crawfurd's problem when a confessed murderer came before him but could not legally be sentenced or set free. Similar problems arose with false cases brought before the Court by those who wished to get revenge. One such case concerned one Kim Seang, a bookkeeper at Napier & Scott. Accused of being an accessory to a plot by a Malay girl cook to poison a Chinese family, Charles Scott's evidence provided his alibi. It was proved that the poison had been provided by a former mistress of Che Sang, he having been heard threatening Kim Seang.

As in Scotland and England witnesses in court had to swear that they would speak the truth and nothing but the truth, so help them God. The Chinese consider no oath binding on them unless they cut off the head of a cock (a rather messy business), burn sacrificial paper or throw a plate on to the floor to break into pieces which shows the fate that will befall the witness should he tell a lie. These proceedings, together with

---

[2] SSR L17 683-6 dated 6th June 1823.

misunderstandings caused by the interpreters, at times stretched out the cases and strained our patience.

With serious cases only being heard twice a year numbers of prisoners put in jail by us magistrates to await trial rose and, as the native population was a shifting one, it often happened that by the time the court sat the witnesses had either left town or the plaintiff had done likewise and so the prisoner had to be declared not guilty and set free. Of course in some cases they had already been confined longer than the sentence they might have received if proved guilty. In about 1836 Sam Bonham, by then officially Governor, set up on his own initiative his own court with Wingrove, the Resident Councillor, but without the Recorder so as to shorten the waiting times and reduce the overcrowding in jail.[3] Sam, who had been at Singapore from its infancy and seen it emerge from a wilderness to a place of considerable importance was, we all agreed, deeply interested in its welfare. He had seen four recorders come and go and whilst recognising their expertise in English criminal law was of opinion that there was room for great improvement in their hearing of civil cases. The recorders had hardly time to make themselves at all acquainted with the prejudices and characters of the inhabitants frequenting the Settlements. It might indeed be said that such knowledge was not necessary for the pure administration of justice. In civil cases, if not assisted by a local jury, he would have to find justice without a knowledge of the language, character and prejudices of the parties before him. Without these the evidence had to be conveyed through interpreters who being aware that they were not likely to be detected were apt to interpret somewhat carelessly.

There had always been problems with the police jail. In the early days this was just a room in the Police post at Ferry Point. Later in 1828 or 1829 one was built on piles driven into the swamp beside the road from the bridge towards Tanjong Pagar, a most unsuitable site being in the middle of town, too small and insecure.[4] Problems abounded, and the portico collapsed shortly after construction killing a worker. For a short while my godown at the foot of the drawbridge was leased by Government as a temporary measure when the wall of the old jail needed urgent repair.

---

[3] *Singapore Chronicle* dated 4th April 1835.
[4] See the Grand Jury report in the *Singapore Chronicle* of 5th June 1828.

Within five years letters were being written to and published in the *Press* highlighting the fact that the jail compound, having subsided a foot or more was regularly flooded at high tide (being next to a creek) and that the floor of the building, being lower was on occasions flooded, the prisoners being obliged to be removed to the upper story.[5] Not only was construction flawed but the administration also. My former partner Hay after enquiry following some escapes found that prisoners were permitted to go a considerable distance outside of the white building, unattended by any guard, to fetch water for their own use and for other purposes.[6] Lights were not permitted in the jail after dark and, as a result, the body of at least one prisoner who had hanged himself was not discovered until daylight.[7] Those sentenced to death were usually hanged by the side of the street in front of the main entrance thereby encouraging passers–by to behave themselves.[8] On at least one occasion a Chinaman was hanged on the bridge itself.[9]

Convicts had their own jail and house of correction. They were transported from Bombay, Madras and Calcutta to Bencoolen but in 1825 transported to us and thereafter direct to us in Singapore. Most were male but a few were female. Some were of high caste, but the majority had been convicted of theft and murder. By way of a small return those of our non–Indian criminals guilty of serious crimes such as murder were transported to Bombay.

We magistrates came under much criticism over the state of the town, of the roads, and of the town bridges not funded by Government. The funds which were raised by a tax on property never sufficed to cope with the myriad requirements of a vocal European population. The Chinese in general had no notion of hygiene outside their own dwellings and rubbish of all sorts was thrown into the streets, the drains, the canal through town, and the river. A Government notification that such a practice was positively prohibited, and any person or persons detected infringing the order

---

[5] *Singapore Chronicle* dated 28th March 1833.
[6] *Singapore Chronicle* dated 9th May 1833.
[7] *Singapore Chronicle* dated 31st January 1835.
[8] *Singapore Chronicle* dated 23rd January 1834.
[9] *Singapore Chronicle* dated 5th June 1828.

would be subject to such fine as we, the magistrates, saw fit to impose had as much effect as water on a duck's back and the problem continued.[10] Although convicts with rubbish collection carts were sent daily round the town they could not restrain the boat population in the river throwing everything overboard causing its gradual silting up. The population was ever-changing with people arriving and leaving, not too many staying over a longer term and so lessons learned by some were not learned by the majority.

Occasionally we got some praise, and the following is from a clipping from the *Singapore Chronicle* in December 1828 which I put aside as a souvenir, reading as follows:

'It affords us much pleasure to notice the very spirited manner in which the magistrates are endeavouring to carry into effect the various suggestions contained in the presentment of the Grand Jury .... The roads and bridges which have been so long and so justly complained of as being in a very inefficient state are now undergoing a complete repair. A considerable part of the line of the road leading from New Harbour to the town is already finished; and a number of substantial puckah bridges are erected in place of the former ones which generally consisted of a few spars placed across a ditch and covered over with sand; and which were frequently in a very dangerous state especially after heavy rains.'

The satisfaction expressed did not last long as wet weather combined with non–stop usage meant that wood rotted, surface materials got worn or washed away and, in some cases, if stone was used it disappeared over-night. Government had in 1825 built a small drawbridge over the Canal, as well as a masonry bridge at the Battery. One which attracted regular comment was the insignificant but necessary little bridge which crossed the ditch dividing Circular Road, linking the big bridge with Commercial Square. Another was an old long broken–down bridge just behind the Institution which if repaired in later years would have avoided having to use a narrow rickety wooden bridge temporarily erected behind the Chinese jail. The new bridge opened in 1830 over the Sungei Rochor

---

[10] Dated 7th June 1827.

opened up for expansion the marshy area beyond and was the start of a new road out into the country.

The wooden drawbridge across the river which Government had constructed in 1823 was officially named Presentment Bridge. It was quickly nicknamed Monkey Bridge and was forever in need of some repair or other. Many of the later fortnightly issues of the Singapore Chronicle contained a complaint on this subject. *'Broken–backed'*, *'a subject of vituperation'*, *'broken railings'*, *'sunk more than a foot'*, were some of the milder descriptions used and the wife of one resident south of the river, driving to cross the bridge, insisted on getting out of the carriage and walking as *'it was so frightful'*. My own experience was no different and there were many times, not only when the road leading to the bridge was, as so often, flooded, when I preferred to cross the river by boat. By the time an official recommendation to replace it went forward in April 1829 the bridge was restricted to foot traffic. The recommendation was to no avail and the editor resignedly opined *'we must needs be content with the present rotten one until it sinks beneath its own cumbrous weight, a catastrophe which may be waited for daily.'*[11] In 1834 the members of the Grand Jury, of which I was one, seriously considered framing an indictment of the Government. On consulting the Recorder as to the proper form were advised that neither the Governor nor the Resident Councillor could be indicted under criminal information nor be obliged to attend court. An individual could however do so by civil action on the ground of expenses having been incurred such as palanquin hire &ca on the side of the river to which the complainant now had no access by a carriage of his own.[12] Government were of opinion that, while they had originally agreed to build it, they were now under no obligation to repair it and in 1835 in desperation we raised funds by subscription and repaired it at the expense of $1200 which, we were assured, would extend its life by at least three years. That same year Bengal authorised an extra bridge a little upstream and an iron suspension bridge was proposed but this could not be built until the gunpowder magazine situated on the south bank of the river was removed. The materials were delivered but Coleman then showed that a

[11] Letter from Murchison to Penang dated 3rd April 1829.
[12] *Singapore Chronicle* dated 16th January 1834.

wooden carriage bridge could be put up at half the cost. This was agreed and the materials for the iron bridge were shipped back to Calcutta at vast expense. This second bridge, *'Coleman's'*, was opened in mid–1840 and Government took the view that the old bridge was now no longer needed, their having for sale some lots of ground near the new bridge. At the time I left Singapore in December 1841 it was still standing. I am told there have since been some developments.

Chapter 10

Old Friends. Fire.
Palmer & Co., Failure. Government.

There were rare occasions when old friends came through and one such was Ralfe who appeared just before Christmas 1827 from Calcutta and left a week later for the Straits of Sunda where he hoped to find a ship to take him to England. It was a real pleasure to reminisce and get up to date. His health alas was not good, and he was going home on sick certificate. About the same time an acquaintance, G. Maclaine, arrived in *Tartar* from Batavia in connection with the formation of Maclaine Fraser & Co was to be run by James Fraser who had arrived from Forres in Scotland in 1823, had been working for Maxwell and took over his business. A few months later Napier arrived back having acquired a new wife and a daughter, the latter being followed at intervals by more daughters — poor man, think of the dowries which would be needed when they found husbands. Before long, his partnership with Scott split up and his elder brother William became his partner, with another brother Robert as clerk. He finally left the Settlement early in 1830 and died in Scotland six years later. Deaths were regrettably common. Scott's brother Harry died in 1830 at their then house on Mount Erskine. Among others I had had to help Temperton's widow. Her husband had founded a shipbuilding yard on the river next to Maxwell's ground. When he died, he was just completing a 200–ton vessel named *Elizabeth* which I subsequently advertised for sale.[1] The next to go was Flint who had been in a bad way for some time and had applied for ten months absence on sick certificate.[2] He died off the China coast on 3rd October 1828 aboard HCS *William Fairlie* in which his wife and daughter were travelling to London, he himself intending to take passage only to Cape Town where he would recuperate. He had made no will, and everything was in his own name. We were his creditors as were many others and were granted letters of administration which we later transferred to his widow. All the household effects were auctioned off some months later. Although they had the Mount Sophia and other property which could be rented out there was very little surplus cash on which she could survive. The list lengthened with the death of Graham Mackenzie who had left for China at the end of September and passed on in Macao at the end of October. To offset the bad news other people arrived, one in March the same year being Edward Boustead who fairly quickly made a name for himself, first in the new firm of Robert Wise & Co. After two or three years he left them and set up in a very successful business partnership with a young German, G. C. Schwabe who knew the arts of bookkeeping and administration while Boustead did the deals.

Presgrave had had to take over temporarily as Resident Councillor Malacca from Garling who went on sick leave at the end of November 1829. He was himself not well. Garling considered all slaves in Malacca should be freed immediately and was no longer on speaking terms with his police magistrate who considered it impossible not to let the current situation continue and only gradually sort itself out. Both had referred the difference of opinion to the Governor in Penang where a decision was awaited from Calcutta. Presgrave who suffered a bad attack of illness while he was there, handed the post back to Garling and returned to Singapore in early March where he died of paralysis the following day, aged 35. We buried him in the cemetery on Government Hill with all Europeans and many natives present. He had been a very committed Christian and, despite his disapproval of the lifestyle of many of us, was well respected and liked as was his great friend our Chaplain the

---

[1] *Singapore Chronicle* dated 13rd August 1829.
[2] SSR N4 288 dated 16th July 1828.

Rev. Robert Burn[3] who boarded with him. His wife Anne, also a convinced Christian, who had come out to Bencoolen in 1819 to marry him,
had been in 1826 in bad health and, on doctor's advice, had returned home
taking their four young children. She was finally allowed by the doctors
to return East in mid–1829 leaving the children in England with her sister.
Arriving in Penang en route for Singapore, she was handed a letter, just
received, with the news of his death. Poor woman. With the help of the
Rev. Burn and his wife she packed up, arranged for the bungalow on Bukit
Cawah to be let, went to Calcutta to see his agents, and returned to
Malacca where she had friends. It was not considered advisable to arrive
in England in winter and so it was not until just after Christmas 1830 that
she and her fellow passengers Captain Edward Lake, his wife and four
children, sailed from Singapore in *Guildford* for London. The ship was
lost in the Indian Ocean and much later another vessel, *Margaret,* sighted
the wreck. A raft constructed from the ship's rigging was also sighted, but
nobody was on it. That situation, not so uncommon, alas, of not knowing
the fate of a ship, of waiting month by month in case some news should
come, and the final acceptance that she was gone, befell the four now
orphaned Presgrave children.[4]

Fire is one of the dangers of which I am the most fearful, perhaps due
to a fortunate escape early in my life when the *Earl Fitzwilliam* came to
grief in the Hugli River. Given the huddled mass of wooden and attap
housing in the early days of our Settlement in Singapore fire was an ever–
present risk. It did break out on several occasions but by luck, great effort
or change of wind was controlled and caused but small overall damage.
I shall, however, always remember Chinese New Year 1830, the lunar year
of the Tiger, the first day of which was 25th January. Chinese business shut
down as normal allowing the traditional celebrations, gambling, eating,

---

[3] Burn had come to Bencoolen in 1824 and was evacuated to Penang in 1825 whence he
moved to Singapore and was appointed the first official Chaplain. He also covered Malacca
and in 1828 he applied to be based there but later changed his mind. As this was where he
met his future wife and married her late in 1830, she may have had some influence on this.
There was one son of the marriage who died in infancy. Burn died on 17th January 1833
aged 35.

[4] Presgrave, A. 1837. Correspondence & Brief Memorial Sketches — Mrs Presgrave,
P. Palliser, Harrogate.

and visiting friends and family to continue until 10th February during which, being the Lantern Festival and the end of festivities, crowds visited temples to pray for good fortune in the coming months.

Three days earlier on the evening of Sunday, 7th February, at about half past eight fire broke out in a blacksmith's premises at the corner of Philip Street and Circular Road. The alarm was sounded. All the nearby buildings were of wood and the fire spread with such rapidity that within the hour not less than 30 houses were burned to the ground. We, together with our neighbours from Fort Fullerton, rushed over from Tanjong Tangkap to be joined shortly afterwards by NCOs from the Artillery and Ordnance. At first sight the situation was chaotic, with nobody in charge and panic breaking out as the flames flared up. We managed at first to prevent the fire spreading across Circular Road by constantly throwing water on the exposed planks of the houses on the far side for two hours or more and thus saved from destruction all the premises on the river side from Armstrong's to the godowns of Guthrie & Clark. The intense heat, dirt, noise of the flames and the obstruction by many of the residents and onlookers made our task difficult and exhausting. As time went on more helpers arrived on the scene and had it been possible to put out the flames now reaching the opposite side of Philip Street the fire would have been confined to a very small district. The inhabitants made no such effort and, seizing what little property they could conveniently carry, left their dwellings to the mercy of the flames. When the troops and convicts arrived the town's four fire engines were found to be unworkable and their water hoses full of holes. The flames were already halfway between Philip and Market Streets. Kling Street next caught fire and shortly afterwards the whole of the eastern side of Market Street was in flames, thus threatening Commercial Square, Malacca Street and possibly even Teluk Ayer. Occupants of these premises now started to remove what they could of their property to the middle of the Square where a crowd of natives, many intent on appropriating whatever they could, had gathered. The fire was finally impeded by brick walls and, after some eight hours, by the morning was under control. The following days were equally exhausting. Making sure the fires did not break out again, we also had to search for stolen property almost every house standing as well as junks and small vessels in the harbour and retrieved substantial quantities. In the course of this, it transpired that James Fraser had between 20 and 30 barrels of gunpowder stored in his godown in Commercial Square, which had been landed without a permit. It was removed as soon as possible to the Government magazine and official enquiries were launched. One unfortunate native who had gunpowder in his godown threw the kegs down his well thinking that the water would prevent an explosion. Sadly, the remedy failed, the fire evaporated the water and a large explosion resulted.

James Fraser's gunpowder had been consigned for sale by a firm in London which was proven to have followed all the necessary procedures there. Large quantities were generally imported for sale to Malays and natives of the adjacent countries and a certain amount manufactured locally. In due course Government authorised its export but within a month orders were issued at Fullerton's insistence that local manufacture could only take place with a licence from the Police.

The disastrous failure of Palmer & Co in Calcutta on 1st January 1830, although rumoured locally there for some months beforehand came as a major shock to the Singapore business community. Palmer had last come through Singapore in mid–1828 and agreed to retain that part of his hill which Lake did not require for construction of a battery, although he could have returned the land to Government and been recompensed. We later learned he had been aware of problems as early as 1823 as mentioned in one of his letters but had kept them under control. This failure led over the next four years to the collapse of almost every one of the major old Calcutta agency houses. Alexander & Co failed on 12th December 1832 swiftly followed on 5th January by McIntosh & Co and panic ensued. I forgot to mention earlier that Macquoid Davidson & Co in Java had failed in 1825 or 1826, taking with them some £16,000 of Raffles' savings. Although this caused us some challenges, we came through with no great difficulty.

Rumours had come to our ears late in 1829 that some political changes were under consideration in London and Calcutta and, as I have just mentioned, an era ended on 1st July 1830 with our once more coming under the direct authority of Bengal. The Supreme Government, themselves under pressure from London and concerned at the implications of the failure of Palmer & Co in December 1829 which was to leave none of the agency houses there unscathed, lost no time in dictating extreme austerity. A number of officials were put out to grass, clerks dismissed, rented houses became vacant, salaries were cut, and belts had to be tightened. Property prices plunged. One who suffered in losing his position was John Leyden Siami [Siamee], Read's neighbour, who had first been employed by Raffles in Penang in 1805 and been part of his household in Java and England. A native of Siam, he spoke both Siamese and Malay as well as English and had served in Singapore in various capacities since 1819.[5] The existing Charter of Justice referred specifically to the Governor and Resident Councillors as judges but given that these titles were now abolished the courts could not sit. The whole edifice of civil and criminal justice had to be closed down with disastrous results.

Fullerton (Figure 18), who had recommended the changes but not the extreme austerity, which was imposed, decided on 29th June to retire in November and hand over to Ibbetson. Sadly, Harriet Fullerton, his wife, died the following day and the strain began to show. He had not been popular and was now blamed for the misfortunes of many.

Since early July acting as Chief Commissioner for the Affairs of Singapore, Prince of Wales Island and Malacca rather than Governor, he came down with his children via Malacca arriving at Singapore on 1st November together with Ibbetson, a widower, and handed over to him on the 12th. Murchison had left us a month earlier for Penang where he was to be Deputy Resident, Bonham holding the fort for the interim period.

It was perhaps unfortunate for Ibbetson that he was chosen just at that time to succeed Fullerton although thanks to profits from his investment in nutmeg plantations and other assets in Penang he personally felt the financial effect of the reduction in his salary and allowances less than most. He had more work to do and less help to do it. He had to maintain establishments, servants and carriages in each of the three settlements, renting a house on the Plain, and spend time in each. All in all he felt entitled to complain and did so. Murchison had had eight writers in his office and the Treasury, and these were now cut to one. The house on the hill was left to deteriorate.

Fullerton departed the same day for Europe, and it was not until about a year later that we heard he had died in London soon after his arrival. As

---

[5] SSR N1 172 and Bastin in JMBRAS, Vol 81, Part 1 (2008) pp. 1–6.

I have said, he had not been a popular man, given the various taxes he introduced in Penang to try to cover increasing costs and his insistence on carrying out the instructions from Calcutta which threw many loyal people out of work and into poverty.

I had only met Ibbetson once before and that briefly when, aboard the company ship *Hastings,* he passed through in November two years earlier en route to Batavia and Bencoolen. His task was to negotiate the release by the Dutch of those emancipated convicts and *caffrees* who had been recipients of a British government pension before 1825 and now wished to leave that place. He was successful only to a certain extent as the Dutch regulations, which they would not waive, meant families being split up but was nonetheless able to take 97 men, women and children with him back to Penang.[6]

As I think I may have explained, the island of Singapore is generally low–lying with tree covered small hills rising between widespread mangrove and other swamps. As the town spread out, jungle was cleared and swamps drained, paths were made, followed in some cases by bullock tracks. Main roads were constructed by Government in accordance with the ideas laid down by the Lieutenant Governor. The first was High Street, then River Street and once the bridge was approved Bridge Street and the road to New Harbour. Beach Road lay between the sea and the first housing lots on the East beach. Circular Road and Kling Street were thoroughfares leading from the bridge to Commercial Square and Market Street. Teluk Ayer Street, along the shore, was connected to them. River Valley Road, roads to Bukit Timah and the Ranggong River were not yet complete in Ibbetson's time and being outside the town limits were not the concern of the Magistrates. We were concerned however with those in the town and the fact that they had sunk since being laid out leading in many cases to flooding whenever there was a high tide or an extra heavy rainstorm. There was also the never–ending problem of the innumerable ditches, nullahs and creeks which needed to be bridged. We had increased

[6] *Caffrees* were the descendants of slaves imported from Madagascar by the Company between 1695 and the mid-18th century. They had all been emancipated by Raffles in 1818 but continued as labourers much as before.

the amounts payable into the Assessment Fund by an additional tax on houses, and a new one on conveyances, horses &ca. and whilst that part of the public who paid naturally expected to see improvements, the fund was never quite enough to cover what was needed.

It was about this time that Boustead, by now one of our most active merchants, commissioned Coleman to build him a large godown with living quarters on a site on the south bank of the river just upstream of the bridge and overlooking it. When completed in about 1832 it quickly became known as the House of Twenty–Seven Pillars and was an adornment to the scene, towering over the nearby godowns.

Merchant tokens were copper coins very similar in design to existing coins circulating in South East Asia. Originally issued as trade grew, they responded to a genuine demand for coin which the Company did not wish to issue. Initially resembling a 1 keping coin and later similar to the Dutch quarter Stiver, they became firmly established and were in constant demand. Protests by the Dutch led to the British Government suppressing their minting in Calcutta. Singapore merchants then produced tokens not resembling any current coin and the standard design became a cockerel, produced by the Soho Mint in Birmingham. This became a profitable line for our merchants as the value normally substantially exceeded the cost. Read, having connections in the islands, was one of the first to enter this business but I am told that, now that the Company has introduced copper coins for the Straits Settlements, demand is falling (Figure 19).

Read, my partner, had in the early days wanted to base himself at Penang as we were not happy with our agents there, but this situation was rectified and he remained in Singapore. He did travel rather more than I, visiting Calcutta in 1827 with his family, in 1834 and London in 1830. He sailed for China in 1836 and remained there and in Manila for a year or so.

Ibbetson stayed with us for three years during which time Bonham persuaded Calcutta to abolish censorship and that the Government did not need to approve each issue of a newspaper. The *Chronicle* was bought by a merchant from Penang in 1835 whereupon Boustead, Lorrain and Coleman set up the *Singapore Free Press* which only needed a year or so to drive the *Chronicle* out of business. The latter's

issue of 16th July 1836 included an unusual advertisement from a number of leading firms including ourselves. Mackertich Moses, an
Armenian, had come down from Penang some years earlier and now
fallen on hard times. All his property had been made over to his fellow
Armenians prior to his declaring himself insolvent thereby apparently
giving to his particular friends and countrymen an undue preference
over his general creditors. Instead of issuing a statement of his affairs
as was customary he made no offer of compromise or settlement but
shut himself up in his house in defiance. His creditors then had him put
in jail for debt. His wife insisted on remaining there with him despite
the Sheriff's order to her to leave. Despite Moses' actions we, his creditors, were prepared to let him out under a general release, provided he
first produced a full and satisfactory statement of his affairs with a fair
offer of composition and good security that he would not quit the
Settlement until his affairs were finally arranged. He was let out and
continued in business until his death three years ago although I understand he got into trouble after I left and was fined 50 dollars or, failing
payment, one month's imprisonment for having barrels of gunpowder in
his shop in Commercial Square.

Ibbetson, a man of simplicity of manner, readiness of access and
openness of heart, retired on December 1833 and Murchison took over in
Singapore as Governor of the three settlements. No sooner was this done
than Murchison and family, together with Ibbetson departed in *Zephyr* to
Muntok (Minto) in Banca where they would await the arrival of the
Company's ship *Marquis of Huntly* to take Ibbetson to London and
Murchison and family to the Cape of Good Hope. Murchison expected to
be away for 18 months.[7] Garling, the senior Resident Councillor, serving
at Malacca would stand in while he was away. Within days a rumour circulated that Bonham would be appointed instead leading to a letter to the
press against the appointment of such a young man. It was followed the
next day by an official announcement that Bonham was now Resident of
Singapore and thereby Acting Governor. Wingrove was Acting Resident

---

[7] *Singapore Chronicle* dated 12th December 1833.

Councillor. No sooner did *Zephyr* return than Bonham departed for Malacca and Penang but returned on 30th March 1834. The spirit and opium farms for 1834–1835 had been auctioned at a considerably higher price than before and it was hoped that the Government would now start to repair the bridge and several smaller ones near town which had fallen down.

Thomas Church, a long–term employee of the Company in Bencoolen & Penang, had previously resigned and gone back to Britain. After a few months he began to regret his decision and appealed to the directors to be allowed to re–join. Surprisingly, his wish was granted on condition that his seniority would date from the date of his reinstatement. Travelling back to the Straits via Calcutta he persuaded the Governor General that he was nevertheless senior to Bonham and therefore should replace him as Acting Governor. On 17th April he arrived with his family and, the following day, he took over as Resident of Singapore and there-fore as Acting Governor. In early September to everyone's surprise Mrs Church held a ball. She was fond of dancing and gaiety though Church considered this *'prophane'.* He was a man of narrow views and was President of the Singapore Temperance Society, but on this occasion acted as a *'very polite and attentive host'* while the supper *'was handsome and plentiful'.*[8] His appointment caused much adverse comment and corre-spondence with Calcutta leading to Bonham taking over again as Resident and Acting Governor on 2nd October until 16th June 1835, the following year, when Murchison arrived back from leave. He took over once more when Murchison left in January 1836 for a short visit to China and from 14th November 1836 when he sailed for Bengal. Bonham learned in March 1837 that he had been appointed Governor with effect from 25th December 1836, the date on which Murchison had departed from India. Thus, in the course of just under 18 years, he had risen from teenage new arrival to the highest in the land.

It was about this time that the Sultan, who had removed to Malacca the previous year, died aged 59, a man by all accounts now so fat and

---

[8] Letter from Maria Balestier to her sister dated 27th September 1841.

indolent that he could not move without help. He had divorced his first wife by whom he had a son, the Tunku Besar, since deceased, and thro' him a granddaughter and two grandsons. His second wife produced two daughters and two sons, the elder of whom, Ali, was now 11 and designated his heir. Ali has, I believe, remained in Malacca to this day. There was also an illegitimate son aged 18 in 1835.

Chapter 11

Piracy

I realise that I have not up to now mentioned the very real problem of piracy. The professional pirates with large prahus based in the Sulu Sea and known as Illanuns, terrorised vast swathes of coastline all over South East Asia. They took slaves where they could find them and used prahus up to more than 100 feet long and 15 broad, with sails, guns and carrying a hundred or more rowers and well–armed fighters. These were not alone in their profession and ranged far and wide at favourable times of the year, sweeping down on unprotected villages or vessels at sea.

Much as these were feared they were not as immediately troublesome to us as were local pirates who infested the whole archipelago, clustered off Selangor, the Sembilan Islands, Siak and the Sumatra coastline, Ramunia Point at the eastern tip of Johor and in the maze of islands under Dutch control to our southward. They were often indistinguishable from peaceful fishermen until they came up to their prey with an opening request for tobacco. To let them come alongside one's vessel was a mistake fatal to many over the years. For centuries the Malays had considered trade to be a low–class activity, especially when carried out by Chinese, but to exact tolls on such trade or to turn pirate and attack the vessels, capturing or killing the crews, and taking the ships and their cargo, was felt to be an entirely honorable profession, undertaken full time or only occasionally as opportunity offered. Many local chiefs actively encouraged such activity to support themselves. We were fully aware that the followers of the Temenggong and Sultan had been, and still were, involved in such marauding and pursuing this barbarous practice. Farquhar himself,

139

very early in 1819, had had to organise the collection of human remains, skulls and bones from the beach and then have them disposed of out at sea. Prisoners were sold as slaves in the Temenggong's campong before we put a stop to it. Reports of ships captured, cargo stolen, men killed, and other atrocities committed were common and in the 1830s were ever increasing. In 1828 it was believed that from one centre to the south of us piratical prahus with 90–100 men in each at certain seasons of the year proceeded to make regular sweeps in fleets of 10–20, each accompanied by some small rowing boats. The large prahus would take shelter in creeks or rivers or behind islands little frequented and from thence send forth their smaller boats in all directions to plunder and bring in the proceeds.

The innumerable small islands, creeks and rivers where pirates could shelter and hide, combined with shallow tidal waters were not open to our larger draught gunboats. As was stated in the mid–30s the three allocated to Penang, Malacca and ourselves had not succeeded in eradicating any pirates. Piracy was not indictable in our Courts as they had no Admiralty jurisdiction, and this gave rise to a notorious case in which four prisoners together with their accusers and witnesses were sent at a considerable expense to Calcutta to be tried. They were tried for piracy and sentenced to be executed, being reprieved until the King's pleasure (to whom a reference was made but on what grounds I am unaware) should be known. The result was that three of them were released (one having died in jail) after about a year or 18 months imprisonment and returned to Singapore having naturally become convinced that they might, whenever they saw fit, proceed to similar acts of violence with impunity and tell their fellows not to have any fear of British justice.[1]

I remember reading of the attack on the opium ship *Lady Grant*, 239 tons, on 2nd February 1836 by no less than five Malay prahus off Pulau Jarra in the Malacca Straits. They were observed standing out from the Sembilans and, as the wind fell light, they lowered their sails and pulled towards the *Lady Grant*. On observing their approach Captain Jeffrey fired at them whereupon they hoisted the black flag and redoubled their exertions to get at the schooner. She, however, taking advantage of a light breeze that then sprang up, did not await their onset, but glided away and

---

[1] SSR R3 159 dated 23rd April 1835.

left them, in the darkness of the evening, out of sight. The moon soon rose; the wind dying away left the clipper again at the mercy of the pirates, or rather to the defensive resources of her crew. Happily for the underwriters, these were not found wanting and her Commander had most judiciously determined on coming to an anchor with a spring on his cable. About 10 o'clock the prahus were observed right ahead pulling quietly and eagerly for the schooner. A small piece on the forecastle was immediately fired at them at which they yelled, beat their tom–toms, and continued pulling towards the schooner. Captain Jeffrey in the meantime, by the assistance of the spring on his cable, had brought the *Lady Grant*'s broadside to bear on them and kept up a constant, and from the result, evidently well–directed fire, the guns being ably served by the officers and six or seven British seamen shipped as seacunnies. The largest prahu came on in advance: this vessel was nearly as large as the *Lady Grant,* and so full of men that it is supposed it was the intention of the pirates to carry the clipper by a *coup de main* on boarding her. They had in this instance miscalculated, for being now within pistol shot, the rounds of grape and cannister from the *Lady Grant* drove them from their sweeps to take shelter below, and their vessel drifted away with the tide. Before daylight, the *Lady Grant* had weighed and made sail to an increasing breeze, and nothing more was seen of the pirates.[2]

In March, the editor of the *Singapore Chronicle* wrote that a newspaper devoted entirely to accounts of piracy would have no trouble in finding enough to fill its pages. The leading article listed a junk from Hainan attacked by ten prahus which opened fire killing five members of the crew and wounding others. It was then boarded and plundered, the rest of the crew being made captive apart from two who threw themselves overboard and escaped. A trading boat on her way from Pahang was attacked near the same place by eight prahus but managed to escape due to a strong and favourable breeze. A day or two later a fishing boat with seven men was attacked by 10 prahus which fired on her and wounded three men. They all saved themselves by swimming to the shore, having lost their boat and fish. The same night a boat with 12 men was going from Tanah Merah to

---

[2] Monthly Journal and General Register of Occurrences Throughout The British Dominions in the East Forming an Epitome of the Indian Press for the Year 1836, p.15.

Johor to collect rattans when they were suddenly fired on which caused them to take to the water and escape to the shore with loss of boat and all it contained. The last example was a small fishing boat attacked beyond Tanah Merah by a sampan, the crew of which stole all their fish.

Although in April the boats of HMS *Wolf* and Government Cruizer *Zephyr* and the local gunboat came up with a fleet of 18 prahus off Point Ramunia they were unable to catch or sink them.

I remember well an earlier occasion when I was sitting magistrate. A Chinese man who had come the previous day from the Carimons by *sampan pucat* came to me at the Police Office and deposed, under oath, that while he had been staying at the Carimons with the Capitan China, one Rajah Jaffir came from the other side of the island in his prahu, bringing with him for sale a large quantity of wines, gin &ca which he sold to the Capitan China. On the following day he reappeared with a similar cargo and freely admitted that he had taken it from an English vessel, the crew of which he had murdered.[3]

Government in the persons of Fullerton, Murchison, Bonham and Wingrove were all concerned to stop piracy but in agreement that with the resources available to them they did not see how this could be achieved. Various ideas which were floated invariably came up against the cost and who was to pay. This gave rise to an official proposal to tax square–rigged shipping, the proceeds of which would be used to finance anti–piracy operations. The whole idea of a tax, contrary to the ideas with which Singapore had been founded, was anathema to the European merchant community. Public meetings were held, and a petition signed by Read and Boustead with three others and supported by all was sent to London to protest at the idea and to try with the help of others there to ensure that Parliament would put paid to it. They did so but that did not solve the finance problem and piracy continued to flourish. Two American missionaries singing hymns in a sampan on their way to Bulang Bay were attacked and one severely injured. Case after case was reported.

Over 300 native prahus left Singapore every year to gather trepang and bird's nests from Burma and Mergui. Who was to know, when they returned, if their cargo was collected, bought, or stolen? *Wolf* on one

---

[3] SSR L17 473.

occasion fell in with five prahus near Cucob and as they had no port clearance or cargo brought them to Singapore where they were set free as there was no evidence to prove them pirates.

In June 1836, Bonham sailed to Rhio in *Andromache* with Capt. Chads to call on the Dutch Resident, discuss measures to stop piracy and ask for help in suppressing the pirates' nest at Gallang in Linggi. The Dutch declined to help, so *Andromache* sailed on alone and destroyed three or four villages, 14 large prows, and 30–40 small prows. She arrived back towards the end of July. She sailed on to Trengganu and Pahang, where she rescued 17 Cochin Chinese and Javanese including one woman and a child, and retrieved a junk, and Endau. He was back in mid–September in time to officiate at a marriage in his capacity as Justice of the Peace, having had the opportunity to see the problem at first hand.

Chapter 12

Americans. Tan Che Sang's Funeral.

I wrote earlier about American ships not being able to trade at Singapore. They were however able to lie at anchor in the Singapore Roads while they arranged their sales or purchases. Once all the arrangements were made by the respective parties the ship departed to nearby Dutch waters followed by a fleet of small vessels not infrequently flying the flags of other nations. This problem persisted for years and most agreed it must be solved sooner rather than later. *Sachem* made several voyages to Bangkok. Her captain believing she would be arrested if she landed cargo in Singapore, and despite offering a security bond was unable to get any guarantee that she would not be arrested. So, all her cargo, both in and out, had to be ferried by *sampan pukat, twacow* and cargo boat to and from Bulang Bay where she anchored. *Francis 1st*, *Georgian* and a few others had the same problem. News in 1834 that we would shortly have an American Consul among us proved inaccurate. Mr. Balestier did arrive with his wife and 14–year–old son, but due to bureaucratic problems his appointment did not take effect until three years later and, in the meantime, he set himself up first as merchant and then as the developer of a sugar plantation on West Indian lines. It took me some time to get to know such a very pleasant family. The custom at the time was for the newly arrived husband to call upon such persons as he desired to become acquainted with, and the visit would be returned by the lady and gentleman on whom he had called. If the commencement of the acquaintance proved agreeable the new arrivals would then be invited to dine but if not, the matter stopped there. Due largely to their lack of funds Balestier was reluctant to follow this custom, feeling he could not afford to return the hospitality offered. They were the only Americans residing in Singapore until the arrival two months later of the Rev. Ira Tracy, a Baptist missionary who had first been sent to Canton to learn Chinese which was officially forbidden there. So, he had to leave and pursue such studies in Singapore. He was joined by Dr. Parker, a medical missionary also from Canton and it was through the two of them that I first had the good fortune to meet Maria Balestier, a very worthy woman who went out of her way to help others. The Mission House had been occupied for some years by a Miss Wallace, without any companion. She had been sponsored to come from England some years earlier to superintend native schools for girls and stayed on when the contract lapsed working diligently on her own to convert Chinese to Christian beliefs. She was eccentric to say the least but good hearted and spoke their language.

One evening I was contacted by Balestier and the two missionaries. Miss Wallace had gone into China Town and put on native dress which was only a petticoat without a binding, fastened with a belt and a kind of short loose gown. She had cut off her long hair and was without shoes or stockings, had taken up her abode in a most unsuitable house and refused to leave. This was a most unfortunate turn of events as Europeans were not expected to act in such a way. In the end, she was persuaded to stay for a while with the Balestiers who felt she was harmless albeit somewhat odd.

In mid–January 1835, Tracy's fiancée arrived with two American missionary couples, all of whom were to move into the Mission House. Although Miss Wallace did not now complain she proposed to leave for Calcutta. Having been used to living very quietly and having nothing of a worldly nature to interrupt the regular habits of her life, the prospect of living at close quarters with two pregnant American wives was too much. She attended the wedding and the wedding breakfast at the Balestiers' residence as the rain poured down all day. I was present as an official witness and was able to have some conversation with her. She sailed a few days later. As we subsequently heard she disembarked at Penang and in July was officially certified insane, a sad fate which caused problems for Murchison who had no funds available to support her.

When the Company had a monopoly of the China trade, we in Singapore benefitted substantially from the fact that goods purchased in

China for export to Britain or India had to be transshipped to avoid taxes and other levies. The most important item was raw silk, followed by nankeens, coffee, spices, camphor, and Japan copper valued at nearly three million dollars. During the first 12 months, 1834–35, following the ending of the monopoly this figure dropped to only half a million.[167]

It was on 2nd April 1835 that Tan Che Sang died aged 73, and we all received printed invitations to attend his funeral. This, the most opulent that had been seen in Singapore, was watched with amazement by many Europeans and with excitement by much of the population. The walls of the room in which he died, according to Dr Peter Parker, the American medical missionary who was shown it, were lined with iron coffers containing silver and most valuable goods with a tiger's skin in the centre on which he slept. By his account there were ceremonies previous to the body being brought to its former home. A few days later the coffin of more than the usual enormous size, covered with flowers and a bag of rice on a black satin canopy embroidered with gold, was moved to a bare ground floor room where it lay in state for five or six days. At the head of the coffin on a common table stood a large silver vessel containing burning sandalwood, a small silver tea pot with a teacup and saucer and a cup of sugar. On each side on pedestals stood an image of a mandarin with a tea pot, and the everlasting cup and saucer in their hands. Before them, a table was spread with fruit and other things that the deceased was fond of; among other things he remarked a pack of Chinese cards all of which would be put into the grave with him. Two similar figures guarded the outside of the table. Large lanthorns suspended from the roof with coverings of silk richly embroidered gave a dull light, and added to the melancholy impression of the barn–like looking apartment. In the adjoining room people were eating, drinking, smoking, and coming and going all the time he stayed, while on each side of the apartment were several women and children, preparing for passing the night on mats spread for that purpose.

At an early hour on the 12th, the gongs began to make their melancholy sound as the funeral was to take place on that day. Crowds of Chinese and Malays began to assemble in the street outside the house and see the huge giant that had been constructed to precede the coffin (which had now been moved out into the street under a huge awning). It was a reddish figure made of paper at least 14 feet high, with a long flowing beard, and in addition to the two eyes that such figures are usually made with, he had a large one in the middle of his forehead. Black feathers constituted the fierce eyebrows. You would not have supposed it was made of such flimsy materials, the richness of the colours, and the manner in which the folds of the robe were arranged, gave it an imposing appearance. It was placed upon four wheels so as to be easily moved by men and beside it stood two *'devils'* in masks, armed with spears and dressed in sackcloth with long dishevelled hair over their shoulders. A large table, placed under the awning I mentioned, was opened across the street, covered with a goat roasted whole, vast quantities of pork, fruit and other things for the sacrifice and with attendants and a musical band standing by. Entering by the gate through the wall 15 feet high one could see the females of the household sitting on the ground waiting for the procession to begin.

We watched from the upper floor of a nearby house. It seemed everyone was abroad.

A number of Chinese led the procession loaded with pieces of cotton of about three yards each, which they gave to those who chose to attend it. They tied it round the head or arm, as it suited them. The Giant and his attendants came next being what is known as the *'open the way'* men to drive away any devils of men harmed by Che Sang, murdered, husbands whose wives had been seduced or victims of his other crimes. These were followed by standard–bearers of his *hoey*, of the Malacca and Hokkien *hoeys*, of the Canton, Ho Chue, all other Chinese and officers from his junks. To my surprise a band of Klings had joined in with their version of music and dancing and very soon after they passed by came the two devils, the male children and grandchildren, the coffin and pall bearers with the silver vase with burning sandalwood. The principal wife and other females of the family brought up the rear followed by a motley crowd of all and sundry.

The procession wound through Chinatown and slowly made its way to the burying ground where an attap shelter had been constructed. We rode directly about a mile and so arrived ahead of the coffin which was deposited into the prepared grave with much time spent in lining it up exactly with the head to the east. Later each of the grandchildren received 20 silver Spanish Dollars and the giant was burnt, but ceremonies continued for some days and it was said that 3,000 dollars had been expended in telling Singapore that its richest and oldest merchant had gone to his rest.

Our weather in Singapore could be summed up succinctly in the words hot and wet. The temperature varied little during the year and according to measurements made for Captain Davis between 1820 and 1826 the lowest recorded was 71°F [21.6°C] and the highest 89°F [31.6°C], the average being in the low 80s. Early morning was the coolest time and thus the favourite for walking or taking exercise. The humidity was almost always high, the exception perhaps having been during the three–month drought from January 1836. This was the worst I experienced, a tragedy for those like Mrs Balestier or Captain Scott who were keen gardeners, the rainfall being less than a fifth of normal. We relied on our own wells for the supply of water and had to be economical in its use. The heaviest rains were normally brought by the arrival of the Northeast monsoon in late November or December to early January. Heavy afternoon downpours were common at all times of the year and average humidity was 80 per cent. We were fortunate indeed not to be affected by typhoons or earthquakes and in general our climate was felt to be healthy.

Towards the end of 1837 after Read's return I took ship to Macao and Canton for various reasons which I may tell you about another time. It was a few months before this that we magistrates received a petition signed by almost all the European merchants who were not magistrates and a number of Chinese including Tan Tock Seng. This concerned the wedding of merchant Bung Wan's daughter to Beng Choon, another prominent merchant. Permission had been granted for a wedding procession from a house on the riverside to Commercial Square and back via Market Street but only on condition that gongs were not beaten nor fireworks let off. A second petition was signed by another 24 resident Chinese merchants and stated that they had hitherto been permitted the full exercise of their religious faith and all the rites and ceremonies connected therewith. According to custom in China, marriage is a religious rite, and on the day of the ceremony a procession is made through the public streets being accompanied with gongs and music and with the discharge of crackers, without which the ceremony cannot be properly performed. It was submitted that on the previous festival of the Muharam, as well as all previous ones, large bodies of men paraded the town and suburbs by night and by day bearing drawn swords, spears, banners and torches and that so great was the noise and tumult that it was impossible for those in the neighbour-hood they passed to sleep or rest at night.   Sepoys and Convicts were allowed their processions, both Hindu and Moslem. I cannot remember just what arrangement was reached but, if my memory serves me correctly, think it was acceptable to all.

Chapter 13

China. Tigers. Flooding Problems. China Expedition Forces Arrival.

I returned to Singapore at the end of July 1839 concerned with developments in China and their likely effect on our business. Annual exports of opium to that country had grown to over 40,000 chests with an estimated value of over $16 million and led to an ever–increasing drain of its silver. The previous year the Emperor appointed Lin Tse–hsu to stop the trade but as the proceeds of the sales were the mainstay of the Honorable Company's finances any interference threatened the whole government of India. By the middle of May however Lin's attitude and military preparations became so threatening Captain Elliot advised the British merchants to leave at once. Over 20,000 chests had been handed over, valued at more than £2.5 million, and were destroyed by the end of June as confirmed by an American merchant who witnessed it. Britain could not sit idly by in this situation and action against the Chinese Government was expected although this might take time.

There had been changes too in Singapore one of which was an increased number of tigers which were attacking and killing coolies in the countryside. Although it was known that some existed on the island and attention had been drawn to this in the *Chronicle* eight years earlier when a woodcutter was killed to the rear of the Chinese temple on the road to New Harbour and close to the Sepoy Lines. Some months later Mr and

Mrs Armstrong driving along the same road one evening saw a tiger cross the road ahead of them. The only European I knew who had had a contact too close for comfort was Coleman. His theodolite was attacked in 1835 whilst he and a party of convicts was surveying for a new road some four and a half miles out of town on what would become known as Tiger Hill off the Sa Rangong Road (Figure 20). The convicts ran and so did the tiger. No one was hurt. The theodolite had to be retrieved some days later. If one was not in the habit of straying far from town there was little cause for concern, but Government did introduce a bounty of 20 dollars for the carcase of any tiger. Over the intervening years, more jungle had been cleared for gambier plantations, and the deer and pig which had been the animals' preferred meal became fewer. Once a tiger has tasted human flesh it seems he or she prefers it. In the month of my return the bounty was increased to 50 dollars as a result of four men being carried off on the Sa Rangong Road. No sooner was this done than two more killings occurred, one a woman at Sandy Point and the other a man in his gambier plantation. Despite the increased offer not one animal had been killed, and more and more reports of men becoming prey to tigers continued. The situation worsened as months went by and more casualties reported until finally in May 1841 at a Chinese-owned estate close to that of Mr Balestier, the first of the destructive animals was caught in a specially dug pit and stoned to death. The captors claimed and were paid the 100–dollar reward now on offer and made another 70 by selling off the flesh at six fanams a catty and other more valuable parts at higher prices. Before I departed for Scotland another three tigers had been disposed of and I am told the problem continues to this day.

Letters on the condition of roads continued to appear in the press. One, written by *'Civis'* whose identity I believe I knew, appeared in the *Free Press* in January 1840:

> 'Your late correspondents who have been declaiming on the bad state of the thoroughfare that leads from the bridge to the Lines seem to have been mounted on a parcel of *Pegasuses* when they traversed the road in question, for notwithstanding all the fuss they have made about it, it is not so *very bad* as they represent. Most true is it that in rainy weather the

said road and the streets that lead into it are *rather* sloppy and dirty — not worse however that some streets are in many English towns at such times. It should be remembered that almost the whole of the location in question was, not many years ago, a deep swamp, similar to that now existing on the right–hand side of the road; — and in fact the road was constructed over this swamp with vast expense of labour by throwing on great quantities of clay, but which, from the soft nature of the substratum, has gradually sunk into it. It is a fact also that most of the town from the river side to near Teluk Ayer has been built on similar ground, the swampy parts having been filled up by completely levelling a hill which once stood on the very site of Commercial Square.

The jail was built on piles driven into the swamp but even thus, it has sunk 4 feet perhaps so that the ground floor was lately obliged to be raised as it used to be flooded every high tide. ....

But the Bridge Road and all the streets leading into it are still *too low*. This however may be owing to the difficulty of procuring a sufficient quantity of *proper* materials to throw on them without incurring considerable expense in cartage &ca. To preserve the streets and roads in that locality in decent condition they must still be raised 2 or 3 feet higher than they are at present — and to prevent their being flooded by high tides the old drains must be raised also as the water apparently forces its way into the streets though those channels. In truth many of the streets want new drains altogether. .... It may be asked what are the numerous convicts, which are now on the island, actually doing? That they have not been idle of late will appear very evident to anyone who will traverse the eight–mile roads that lead to Bukit Tima and the Rangong River which have been lately finished.'

This year matters in China went from bad to worse and we expected the arrival of British invasion forces. HM Ships *Wellesley* & *Cruizer* had been in port since early April and by dusk on 14th May a further 12 vessels had arrived from Penang, Calcutta, Madras and Bombay. The Balestiers had intended to celebrate their son Revere's 21st birthday with a ball at their impressive two storey rented stuccoed brick house with verandahs running round the house on both floors and a terraced roof. All was set in eight acres of ground some of which was taken up with stockades for chickens, geese, ducks and other fowls as well as a kitchen garden. His birthday fell on 15th May but with so many arrivals the guest list had to be extended at short notice to include the Acting Commander–in–Chief Sir Gordon Bremer, who had now hoisted his broad pennant aboard *Wellesley,* and many of his officers. I was invited as chaperone to Mrs Elliot, the wife of the Captain Elliot who was in charge of British affairs in China. She was staying with me. Many of the 100 or so male guests were splendidly attired in uniform and the 20 ladies did their best to rival them in colourful dresses.

More vessels arrived and by 29th May six warships, three steamers and 15 transports were present. The troops which had disembarked and camped in tents on the Plain were now re–embarked and the Balestiers held a dinner party to bid farewell to Sir Gordon. The food was good, the guests agreeable and the excitement high. The Governor Sam Bonham concluded that he had better shave before going to bed so that he *'might be up at the monstrously early hour of seven next morning'* to see the ships off. Next day, Saturday 30th May we witnessed a magnificent sight as the bulk of the fleet set off eastwards in the forenoon in three divisions under full sail. Four warships, two steamers and 15 transports, undoubtedly the largest fleet ever seen here unless by chance some native had seen the British fleet passing Singapore en route to the invasion of Java in 1811. Over the next week six more vessels departed and on 13th June HMS *Larne* which had awaited the arrival of the latest overland mail from London set sail followed by a schooner and three troop transports. Three days later Rear Admiral George Elliot arrived from the Cape of Good Hope aboard HMS *Melville* accompanied by *Pylades, Blonde* and two transports. The commander of *Blonde,* believing he was to arrest any Chinese junks he came across, sent a boarding party to one which had just sailed and took possession of her, quickly following up by arresting three more. Ashore, consternation reigned as the owners had received assurances from Government that they would not be molested. The matter was quickly put to rights and the four released while the Admiral hurried on to China after one day in port. The last steamer left on the 19th and the last transport on the 24th leaving the Plain to recover from its trampling by military boots and our society to return to its normal tenor.

It was about this time that the question arose whether tea from China could be imported into England in ships other than British or Chinese. Opinion on the subject was divided and we had several American ships unload their cargoes of tea at Bulang Bay for transhipment into English vessels so as not to run the risk of tax or confiscation.

We Europeans in Singapore were a small community, generally young in age and growing from about 20 when I first arrived in 1820 to a total of 320 in December 1840 which was less than one per cent of the whole population. Initially no distinction was made between Europeans and the few Indo–Britons who were the offspring of European males and their local mistresses. For some reason, which now escapes me, the categories were separated for the 1830 census and those thereafter. In the 1832 census while Europeans had risen to 105 Indo–Britons had done so by over 200 per cent from 29 to 94 and both categories thereafter showed steady increases, standing at 167 and 153 when I left. Human nature and its urges do not change and given the almost entire want of young European female company it was inevitable that liaisons were formed with attractive Malay girls by the younger generation. Chinese girls were not allowed to leave China and although some females were shown in the figures these were in fact almost entirely not ethnic Chinese but local wives of Chinese. As these notes are for family consumption only, I can safely give a few names as examples. Boustead for instance had at first a reputation among us for being uninterested in the opposite sex until, after three years or so, his manservant's sister named Janedah arrived from Bencoolen aged 14 and before long she produced the first of three children. One of these died very young. Jane and Eduardo were sent off initially to England and later to Germany to be educated. A native woman living with a European would be known as Nona, and so Janedah was referred to as Nona Boustead, but was not seen abroad with him or mixing in European society. James Fraser of Maclaine Fraser & Co had three by different mothers before he came back to Scotland to marry, taking with him two of the children who now remain here. Guthrie had one at least, Montgomerie had some as did Farquhar and many others.

I now realise just how little we understood the Chinese even though we worked alongside them and depended on them to bring in the produce which we exported to the West. They were forbidden by the Imperial Government to teach foreigners their language, be it the language of the literati or the common everyday dialects. The main dialects, Hokkien, Teochew, Cantonese, Hakka and Hailam [Hainanese], all spoken in

Singapore, are so different from each other as to be mutually incomprehensible although the written characters are, I am told, the same. This in Singapore was of no great help as the vast majority of the *sinkehs* were illiterate and had to patronise street letter–writers to communicate with home. On the coast of China around Canton a strange form of English called *pidgin* had developed to form a language bridge between business people who had no common language, as I found when I went there. It was not used much in Singapore where simple Malay was the lingua franca which any European merchant had quickly to master. Nonetheless some common phrases are creeping into our own language, at least in the East. In Singapore we had the *Baba* Chinese merchants who had moved down from Malacca where their families had lived, sometimes for generations, and intermarried with local Malays. Some spoke a certain amount of English or Dutch and all a version of the Hokkien dialect mixed with Malay. One such was Seet (or See) Boon Tiong with whom we did much business. His firm Boon Tiong & Co was set up with a partner See Ho Keh in 1831 the same year as he joined 35 other Hokkien merchants from Malacca to form the mutual aid association Keng Teck Whay. Each paid $100 into a joint fund and a guild house was built in Teluk Ayer Street (Figure 21). The association was exclusively for the founders and their male descendants.

Tan Che Sang, old reprobate, had himself originally been a *sinkeh* from Guanzhou (not to be confused with Guangzhou or Canton) and relied on Malay to communicate with us; yet we had no clear understanding of how his influence was maintained. We had some idea that it was not entirely *pukka* and felt it wiser not to ask, knowing we would never get a full answer.

The Chinese lived in a largely self–contained community in theory under the benevolent government provided by the authorities but in fact regulated far more severely by their own clans, societies and *kongsis*.

My health was giving me problems and retirement beckoned. I had taken on a new business partner named Drysdale at the commencement of 1841 and Read's son, W. H. as he was later known, joined us in September. He is an able young man and has already proved his worth, so I felt sufficiently confident of being able to leave before the end of the year to return to Scotland in semi–retirement. My will was drafted, signed and witnessed and my passage to Bombay booked, from which port I would proceed home by the *'overland'* route via Suez and Alexandria. It now remained to start calling on friends to say my goodbyes. The Balestiers had been living in something of a palace which was owned by a Parsee family in Bombay and by now needed considerable repairs. As the agent refused to attend to these, they had just moved into their own much smaller house at their sugar plantation, some two miles out of town off the Serangoon Road. I went out one morning to pay a farewell breakfast call on Mrs Balestier who has done so much good in this Settlement. The house which they are extending looked better than I had expected and I congratulated her on the interior which was painted white with Bengal mats on the floor and pictures on the walls. Like all of us they had their fair share of insects and lizards in the house. When I leave Singapore I shall not miss the mosquitoes, at night the loud, rasping, sudden call of the gecko up in the rafters, the scorpions which hide in one's shoes and the two sorts of centipede which can cause painful bites. I shall though miss the chikchaks, small lizards which run up and down the walls, over the ceiling searching for the flying ants which can invade the house after dark before shedding their wings. Their *'clicking'* is a friendly sound and they are quite harmless.

Guthrie and Spottiswoode were travelling in the same ship as myself, *Charles Grant,* and a farewell dinner was held for us two days before our departure. Sandy, as he was always known, had come out in 1821 and Spottiswoode in 1824 although he had spent many subsequent years at sea in his vessel *Mary Ann*. Sam Bonham was now one of the very few still remaining in Singapore who preceded us. I am not an emotional man, but it is hard to say goodbye after 22 years and although I retained my share of the business until last year those hours spent on deck on 20th December watching Singapore gradually disappear over the horizon were not the happiest of my life.

So that is that. Perhaps someday somebody will find these rambling reminiscences of passing interest and I hope my memory has not played me false in any significant way.

Part 2

Edward Boustead

DRAMATIS PERSONAE

BAIN, Robert	Former partner in A. L. Johnston & Co. From 1853 partner in Boustead & Co.
BALESTIER, Joseph	Merchant. American Consul from 1836.
BEHN, August	German merchant, Behn Meyer & Co.
BENNETT, George	Surgeon & naturalist.
BOUSTEAD, Eduardo	Illegitimate son of E. Boustead.
BOUSTEAD, Jane	Illegitimate daughter of E. Boustead.
BOUSTEAD, Helen "Nellie"	Daughter of E. Boustead.
CHIA Ann Siang	Boustead employee & later merchant.
CHURCH, Thomas	The East India Company.
CLARK, James	Merchant
COLEMAN, George D.	Irish Architect. Later Surveyor.
DUNMAN, Thomas	Commissioner of Police, Singapore
DUTRONGQUOY, Gaston	Hotel-keeper & photographer.
Janedah	Sarel's sister and later Boustead's mistress.
JOHNSTON, Alexander Laurie,	Merchant.
JOHNSTON, John	Illegitimate son of E. Boustead
LOGAN, Abraham	Lawyer.
LORRAIN, Walter Scott	Merchant.
MONTGOMERIE, Dr. William	Surgeon.
MOSES, Catchick	Armenian employee, later merchant.
MURCHISON, Kenneth	Resident Councillor, Singapore, later Governor.

NAPIER, William	Lawyer.
NIVEN, William	Husband of Helen Boustead.
PALMER, John.	Merchant & Financier in Calcutta.
PRINCE, John	Resident Councillor, Singapore 1827
QUEIROS, Claude	Merchant, agent for John Palmer.
READ, W. H.	Merchant
Sarel	Boustead's No. 1 servant.
SCHWABE, Gustav Christian	Business partner & merchant.
SHAW, William Wardrop	Boustead's later business partner.
STEBBING, Charlotte	English governess, later Mrs Boustead.
SYKES, Adam	Merchant.
TAN Kim Seng	Chinese merchant.
TAN Beng Swee	Son of Tan Kim Seng & merchant.
WINGROVE, R. F.	The East India Company.
WISE, Joseph	Merchant.
YOUNG, Jasper	Later partner in Boustead & Co.

Chapter 14

Early Days

Boustead & Co. Founded in Singapore in 1830
(As noted in all the local directories in the period 1845 to 1870)

The *Singapore Chronicle* of 27th March 1828 records the arrival on 13th March of Edward Boustead (Figure 23), a passenger aboard the ship *Hindustan*. A small vessel, she had sailed from Liverpool four and a half months earlier on 28th October 1827 and after selling her part cargo and finding another she departed for London on 26th June. Boustead had been tasked with setting up and managing the Singapore business of a new trading firm Robert Wise & Co., a partnership formed in London between Robert Wise (formerly a merchant seaman) and William Anderson (Cape Town) in August 1827 and stated in the agreement to run for seven years. He was a young bachelor, 28 years old, and was stated by C. B. Buckley[1] many years later to have previously been in China and Singapore. No record or confirmation of this is now traceable. Official permission to settle in Singapore had to be obtained from the company either in Calcutta or in London and he brought with him a licence dated 6th October 1827 from the Court of Directors of the East India Company in London allowing him to reside in Singapore.

The surname Boustead or Bowstead, which comes from the Old English 'Bula Stede' (the Bull Farm), was found in the 18th Century

---

[1] Buckley, C.B. (1902). *An Anecdotal History of Old Times in Singapore: From Foundation of the Settlement Under the Honourable East India Company...1819–1867*. Fraser & Neave, p.207.

mainly in the county of Cumberland, in North–West England on the bor-
der with Scotland. Irthington, then a small village of about 900 inhabitants, lying some nine miles to the east of Carlisle on the old Roman road
to Newcastle, just to the south of Hadrian's Wall and today just beyond the
end of the runway of Carlisle Airport, was Edward's birthplace in the last
few days of December 1800.

His father is believed to have been Ambrose Boustead, who farmed at
Irthington and married Jane, a local girl from the well–known Wannop
family, in about 1780. Jane gave birth to nine children between 1782 and
1807 of whom Edward was the seventh, and the fifth son. We do not know
the exact date of this, but according to the records he was christened at
St Kentigern Church on 19th January 1801.

Britain had been at war with France more or less uninterruptedly from
1793 until Napoleon was finally defeated in 1815. The cost to the country,
of over a billion and a half pounds sterling, had been catastrophic and as
William Hazlitt wrote in the *Examiner* in 1816:

> 'The gaols are filled with insolvent debtors and criminals driven to theft by
> urgent want, the Gazette filled with bankruptcies, agriculture declining,
> commerce and manufactories nearly at a stand, while thousands are
> emigrating to foreign countries, whole parishes deserted, the burthen of
> the poor rates intolerable, and yet insufficient to maintain the increasing
> number of the poor, and hundreds of once-respectable house-holders
> reduced to the sad necessity of soliciting admission into the receptacles
> for paupers and vagabonds, and thousands wandering about in search for
> that employment which it is no longer in the power of the gentleman or
> farmer to bestow.'

Around 350,000 men were demobilised in 1815, roughly one in six of
the male population aged between 15 and 40. The following year had no
summer, the massive eruption of the Tambora Volcano on the island of
Sumbawa in the East Indies in April 1815 having caused clouds of ash to
circle the globe. Fog, rain and floods resulted, the harvest failed, and tenant
farmers gave up their farms. How Ambrose Boustead fared we do not know.

As the fifth son it is likely that, had Edward stayed at home, he would
have ended up as a simple labourer helping on the family farm but, perhaps with the help of other relatives, he was sent away to be educated,

Where and how and for how long we do not know, although he was probably employed by the age of 15, moving from Cumberland to the growing textile centres of the Midlands and to Liverpool, cotton and mechanical spinning starting to replace the home spinning of wool.

It is possible he had previously been sent out via India to Macao and Canton to investigate conditions and possibilities there. In 1813 trade with India had been opened to all, the Honorable East India Company monopoly being ended, although that of British trade with China remained solely with it for the time being. According to the records it was only from 1827 onwards that British calicoes were able to be sold there at a profit by the Company. Singapore, founded in 1819 as a free port (Penang and Malacca becoming free ports seven years later), became a place of transhipment of goods from China and of British and Indian textiles destined for that country.

The new business would have been primarily to sell on a commission basis goods shipped from England and with the proceeds or the firm's capital to buy goods and products to be sent back for sale. Boustead must have had some previous relevant business experience. Yet it was said by his partner Schwabe[2] in later years that while he had not had overmuch business education yet he did the buying, selling and negotiating, leaving the routine, the cash and the accounts to others.

On the ship's arrival in the Singapore roads he hired a sampan and was rowed ashore, clutching a letter of introduction to one of the existing merchants. Landing at Ferry Point at the mouth of the Singapore River he made his way along a muddy lane glorified with the name of High Street hoping to find his putative host in residence. It was only just over 10 years earlier that Raffles had signed the first treaty to obtain sovereignty, covering land stretching a couple of miles along the shoreline and reaching inland as far as a cannon shot could carry. Now however the whole island, albeit unexplored, belonged to the Company and the population was surging with Chinese, Malays and folk from all over the region. The recent

---

[2] Gustav Christian Schwabe (10th May 1813–10th January 1897) was born in Hamburg, Germany. He joined Robert Wise & Co in Singapore in 1831 and became Boustead's partner in Boustead Schwabe & Co in 1834. After visits to China and the Philippines he moved to Liverpool in 1838, but remained in partnership with Boustead until 1848. They remained friends until Boustead's death in 1888.

census showed the Chinese as the most numerous at 7,575 out of 18,189. The Europeans comprised a mere 122, of whom 25 were female, and it was essential to follow the conventions. An early call on the Resident Councillor, Mr. Kenneth Murchison, was essential and it led to an invitation to a dinner and ball a month later, giving him a chance to meet almost the whole of *'society'*. He would also have attended the fourth annual meeting of the Raffles Club in July.

In 1828 for the first time a Grand Jury was called in Singapore. The purpose was to examine the evidence of criminal cases brought before it and, if the prosecution's case was considered adequate, to forward them to the court for trial. It became customary for the members also to make *'presentments'* to Government on matters they felt needed review such as the state of the bridge (frequent) and the roads. The minimum number of persons making up the Jury was 13. They were chosen by ballot but only Europeans of a certain standing were selected to stand. Unfortunately, these were small in number and Boustead was chosen for the second Jury in December that year. Although as European numbers increased the chance of being balloted diminished, Boustead served on a total of 19 occasions during his time in Singapore and possibly more as we do not have the lists of names in 12 others.

As soon as he could arrange it, he moved into a rented house and godown on the south bank of the river, upstream of that then occupied by A. L. Johnston of the eponymous firm. Boustead was driven by his determination to make money honestly and become rich. Although it was here that he held the meeting on 1st October 1829 proposing the formation of what turned out to be the short–lived Billiards Club,[3] business came before socialising or anything else. He employed for about five years a young Armenian, Catchick Moses. Catchick had arrived from Basra on 1st August 1828 just before his 16th birthday and was introduced by his uncle Aristarkies Moses who had pioneered the import of gold dust from Pahang and its export to India. He later became one of the most respected Armenians in the area. At some time Adam Sykes also joined the firm as senior clerk and took over when Boustead left it on 10th December 1831 as advertised in the *Singapore Chronicle* (Figure 24).

---

[3] Buckley, op.cit., p.206.

Adam Sykes, born in 1807, may have been related to the owners of Sykes Bleaching Company in Edgeley, near Stockport but this cannot be confirmed. His family in England had come to know members of a German family named Schwabe who, although Jewish by race, had been baptised Christians and emigrated from Hamburg to Britain in about 1817. Adam's sister Eliza (b. 1817) was to marry Stephan Schwabe in February 1833 and it may have been through her early contacts that Stephan's young cousin Gustav Christian Schwabe was sent out in the second half of 1831, aged 18, to join the firm as junior clerk. As was usual in such cases he stayed with Boustead who had now moved temporarily to Campong Glam.[4] It was the beginning of a long–lasting business relationship and friendship, the latter continuing until Boustead's death in 1888.

Late in 1830 George Bennett, a young English surgeon who later became famous as a naturalist, stayed with Boustead on his way back to England from Australia and New Zealand. While Bennett was there Boustead bought a wild Siamang (ape) from a Sumatra Malay and gave it to him to take back to England when he sailed in *Sophia* five days later. His book[5] gives an entertaining account of the ape's behaviour on board where he ate with the passengers and crew but sadly died when almost within sight of the coast of England (Figure 25).

When Boustead arrived in Singapore both it and Malacca were governed from Penang as a presidency of the East India Company. This was too expensive to run and as mandated from London, the three settlements officially reverted to direct control from Bengal on 31st May 1830 but in fact only reverted on 30th July. One of the unintended consequences was that due to the terms of the earlier charter of justice the court system had to be abolished apart from courts of requests which covered minor civil cases involving $32 or less. On 5th October 1831, following considerable unhappiness among the merchant community that no court of justice had been held in any of the three settlements for 15 months, Boustead was one of five calling on the Acting Resident Councillor, R. F. Wingrove to hold a public meeting to deplore the suspension of the Court of Judicature and

---

[4] Schwabe deposition dated 22nd December 1893.
[5] Bennett, G. (1834) *Wanderings in New South Wales, Batavia, Pedir Coast, Singapore, And China: Being The Journal Of A Naturalist In Those Countries During 1832, 1833, And 1834, Vol 2.* Richard Bentley, New Burlington Street, London, pp. 142–173.

request its reinstatement. This took place three days later. A petition to Parliament dated 4th November was signed by almost all the community including Sykes and Schwabe. It was not until the following year that the Charter was amended, and a system of justice renewed.

Although today Boustead Singapore Limited states that 1828 was its founding date it is instructive that the Straits Directory for 1846 and later editions give the date as 1830. Boustead, at the start of that year, appears to have been running two businesses in Singapore. A letter dated 2nd May 1831 from Anderson, Wise & Co., Liverpool refers to him as *'our managing partner there'*[6] of Robert Wise & Co.

This letter was produced as evidence in an 1841 court case in London. It concerned 657 bags of coffee the firm had shipped from Singapore in November 1831 in the *Lady Gordon* (Figure 26). These were consigned to importers in England effectively as payment in settlement of previous outstandings and the bills of lading signed by Captain Harmer were, unknown to him, endorsed to those importers. Boustead, as Managing Partner in Singapore, wrote to Anderson, the Partner in Cape Town, authorising him on *Lady Gordon*'s arrival to land there all or any part of the coffee shipped to one of the consignees:

> 'provided you can obtain a price which will enable you to remit in specie or good bills, or something that you are certain will pay as well, an exchange of at least 3s. 6d., per *Lady Gordon* or a very early opportunity. If you cannot do this, you will have the goodness to allow it to go on. The amount stated in the manifest includes all charges here, to which you will have to add freight and charges with you. The freight is £7 per 18 cwt. We do not think it is likely Captain Harmer will be able to get at any of the coffee of this mark; but, if you can, you will be so good as to indorse on his bill of lading what you may land, and advise Messrs John Dugdale & Brothers what you have done.'

His idea was that if a larger profit could be made by landing and selling the coffee at Cape Town than by shipping it to Britain then it made sense to do so, paying cash to Dugdales for the agreed value of the coffee

---

[6] Manning, J. (1844). *Cases Argued and Determined in the Court of Common Pleas — Brockbank v Anderson & Wise,* Great Britain Court of Common Please, pp. 295–315.

to them and retaining any extra for the partnership. This of course assumed that Dugdales themselves had not contracted to sell the coffee on. Unfortunately, Anderson, who may have been in financial difficulty, unloaded all the coffee on board on the spurious grounds that it was going bad, sold it and retained the proceeds. This hastened the break–up of his partnership with Robert Wise.

The Irish architect Coleman who had moved permanently to Singapore in 1825 was contracted by Boustead in about 1831 to build a substantial godown and living quarters on the right bank of the Singapore River just adjacent to the only bridge (Figure 29). It was completed in 1832 and, although officially *'Bridge Buildings'*, quickly became known as the *'House of Twenty–Seven Pillars'* (Figures 27 and 28). An imposing structure it lasted, with some alterations and repairs, until the Elgin Bridge was rebuilt and widened in the late 1920s.

Boustead had hoped to rent out a good part of it, but this proved difficult and so with Schwabe he had moved in by 1833. In that year Bennett stayed with him again on his way to Australia and wrote that:

'near the splendid and extensive pile of buildings, the residence of E. Boustead, Esq., is a wooden bridge at present in a very dilapidated state and impassable for carriages which is a great source of inconvenience to ladies and others who wish to visit across the water. They are obliged to stop the carriage on one side of the bridge and walk across, at the risk of deranging their curls by the breezes, or injuring the fairness of their complexions by the fervent rays of a tropical sun. And besides, they must have a conveyance in waiting on the opposite side to take them to the place they may be desirous of visiting.'[7]

Boustead employed a Malay *'No 1 Boy'* or butler named Sarel who had come from Bencoolen, the former British possession on the south west coast of Sumatra. Early in 1832 Sarel's mother and young sister managed to come over to Singapore where the mother was employed as caretaker at the new building while it was being completed. Part was designed as living quarters and Schwabe described these years later as having offices and servants' quarters on the ground floor, a dining room,

---

[7] Bennett, op. cit., p. 177.

a sitting room and another small room on the first floor and with bedrooms and dressing rooms above.[8] The staff employed were Sarel, a cook and two houseboys. Boustead had been living a celibate life and was well–known for this, unlike most of the European bachelors who had acquired local mistresses, almost always Malay given the scarcity of Chinese women in the territory. Sarel's 14–year–old sister, Janedah, was a nice girl and before long she, with her brother's blessing and as he may well have planned, became Boustead's mistress. Such mistresses were known of locally but never appeared socially or were involved in running the domestic establishment. As Schwabe stated many years later, *'Boustead was known as a very severe man and he was much chaffed the day after the 'connection' began.'*

Business may not have been good, or it may have been because of the split between Anderson and Wise that by the end of 1831 Boustead had resigned, leaving Sykes and a Joseph Wise[9] in charge of Robert Wise & Co. In the *London Gazette* it was officially announced on 30th July 1834 that due to the actions of Anderson the partnership was dissolved. The Robert Wise business in Singapore would be wound up with effect from 19th July 1834 by Sykes, who had advertised his house to let in December 1833. What appears to have been a closing sale had been advertised in the press a month earlier, the stock consisting, inter alia, of Abbott's Patent Hair Felt, anchors, Swedish tar, pale ale and whisky, blank bills of lading and a *'patent copying press'*. In September prime Irish mess pork ex *Brian Boru* and 1052–1054 gallon hogsheads of prime sherry ex *Madeline* were on offer. An advertisement dated 25th December 1834 in the Singapore Chronicle advertised that Robert Wise & Co.'s godown was *'To Let'*.

Winding up was a slow process and was never completed. On 5th August two years later an advertisement appeared stating that the name of Mr. John Holliday, who *'had been for some time a partner in the Houses of Robert Wise & Co. Singapore, Batavia and Manila'* was added to this firm and that their business would, in future, be conducted at each of the above places under the style of Robt. Wise, Holliday & Co. The Singapore operation was closed shortly afterwards and an office in China

---

[8] Schwabe deposition dated 19th February 1895.
[9] Joseph Wise (9th May 1815–24th June 1852). Possibly related to Robert Wise, John Wise and James Wise.

opened, trade with that market having been allowed to Country Traders from 1833 when the East India Company's monopoly of the trade ended. Robert Wise's interest in the firm ceased on 1st July 1839 and on the same date a John Wise (not to be confused with Joseph) and Robert James Farbridge were admitted as partners as announced from Toongkoo Bay, China in the Singapore press on 28th November the same year.

On 1st January 1834 Gustav Christian Schwabe, now 20, officially joined Boustead *'in his establishment'* and the business was to be known as Boustead, Schwabe & Co. The announcement appeared in the *Singapore Chronicle* on 9th January. According to Schwabe in 1895[10] he and Boustead were the only partners, and each put in $8,000 as capital. As Boustead was not well off most of his share was in the form of the godown, his major asset. Boustead did the buying, selling and correspondence and Schwabe handled everything else including looking after the cash.[11] There was no bank in town at the time and no banknotes were in circulation. He had had a better mercantile education than Boustead and understood office work better but was less experienced. Sykes was at this stage not a partner in Singapore, presumably to avoid any conflict of interest.

There was however another partnership agreement, between Boustead, Sykes, Schwabe, Benjamin Butler (in Manila) and Edward Little (in London) as Commission Agents. Little withdrew from this on 30th June 1838 as recorded by an announcement in the *Gazette* in London.

The arrival from America of Joseph Balestier with his wife and son in May 1834 and his rental of a godown and rooms in the Bridge Buildings for $30 per month was undoubtedly welcome. As Maria Balestier described these in a letter to her sister,[12] the rooms were *'at least twenty feet high'*, of solid masonry with the walls plastered and *'white as snow'*. There was no glass in the windows, Venetian blinds being used instead. She also wrote that:

'Mr. Boosted [sic], another of our visitors, is a young man, but he seems to have forsworn the society of ladies entirely, and when he comes to see Mr. Balestier I rarely talk to him, but as he is a very sensible intelligent

---

[10] Schwabe deposition, op. cit.

[11] Ibid., p.3.

[12] Letter dated 1st June 1834 from Maria Balestier to her sister Harriett in Boston.

man, I admire to listen to him when he is conversing. He has a fine gentlemanly appearance, and is considered the most active merchant here.'

She was probably entirely ignorant of Janedah's existence and of the birth of the first child, Jane, in 1835; her misspelling of Boustead may have reflected his Cumbrian accent.

There were three large lots of ground across the Plain on which houses facing East had been built. These were owned, running from North to South, by Charles Thomas, William Montgomerie and Claude Queiros who was agent for John Palmer of Calcutta. It had earlier been clearly made known to them that the Plain would not be further built up. Naturally, they were more than a little annoyed when on 8th October 1827 the Government announced that three lots in front of them, should be put up for tender blocking their view of the sea.

PUBLIC NOTICE IS HERE-
BY Given that Sealed Ten-
ders will be received on the 31st
Instant for the purchase of 3 Lots
of Ground on reserved Plain, each
Lot measuring on an average 254
by 240 feet, situated in front of the
Premises belonging to Messrs. Thomas, Montgomerie and Queiros,
and separated from them by a road
of 45 feet in breadth.
    These Tenders will be opened at
12 o'Clock on the day abovementioned, and forwarded to the Honorable the Governor in Council for approval. All other particulars may
be obtained by application at the
Resident's Office.
            JOHN PRINCE,
        RESIDENT COUNCILLOR.
Singapore 8th October 1827.

Public Notice for Purchase of 3 Lots of Ground on Reserved Plain

Source: Singapore Chronicle

They tackled John Prince, the Resident Councillor on this. With little to lose as he was about to depart on retirement, he took up the cudgels on their behalf and persuaded the Governor in Penang to cancel the instructions given to him on condition that the three undertook in writing *'In consideration of Government permitting the space between the sea and the piece of ground conveyed to me in Lease ( ) to remain unoccupied I hereby engage to build a substantial house of an architectural appearance on the said lot.'*

John Palmer arrived from Calcutta in November en route to Batavia. He may by now have been feeling financially less secure than in previous years and, not wanting the extra expense, instructed Queiros to sell his plot, Grant No. 554. This was bought by James Clark in two tranches, the transfers being registered on 7th and 10th August 1831. Clark had already purchased two lots facing High Street which adjoined Grant 554, Grant 205 at auction after the departure on sick leave of its owner Lieutenant Philip Jackson and Grant 555 separately.

Plan (not to scale) of Lots at the corner of High Street and The Plain.

Clark now contracted G. D. Coleman to design and build a fine mansion on land comprising Grants 554.1, 555 and 205 which on completion was most probably leased out until he went on leave in 1836. To support this it should be noted that on 29th June an advertisement regarding his current abode appeared in the press *'To let for two months or probably more the commodious dwelling house in Campong Glam belonging to, and lately occupied by J. S. Clark Esq.'* At this time he sold the land comprising Grant 554.2 to his neighbour William Montgomerie.

A commodious dwelling house situated at the corner of High Street, opposite the Court House was advertised for rent by Boustead Schwabe & Co. in January 1836 as *'now undergoing a thorough repair which will be completed in all next month'*. In July it was still available and was now described as *'That commodious dwelling house situated at the corner of High–street, opposite to the Court House — the Hall, on the ground–floor and all the upper–rooms being matted.'* It is not clear who, if anyone, rented the house and it appears it was not until 1841 that Boustead decided to lease it and move in himself.

W. W. Shaw in a deposition sworn in 1893 stated that when he spent two weeks in Singapore en route to China in 1839 he stayed with Boustead *'not exactly in a house'* but, in 1842, his three weeks in Singapore staying with Boustead were at his house. W.H. Read in a deposition sworn on 13th December 1893 stated that Boustead had been living at that time *'on the Esplanade'*. It seems that he was still at the House of Twenty–Seven Pillars when Janedah, living in the back quarters, gave birth on either 27th April or 18th May 1837 to her second child Edward (referred to henceforth in this text, except when in quotation marks, as Eduardo to avoid confusion with his father).

Some years ago a prominent Singaporean historian alleged in an article that Boustead had been given this ground in 1823 and that the Bousteads had built their family home there. From whence he acquired this incorrect information remains a mystery.[13]

The merchants of Singapore were alarmed to learn that the current Governor, Murchison, was proposing to levy port duties and, following a meeting amongst themselves, wrote to him in January 1836 asking for details of the proposals. Boustead and Joseph Wise both signed the letter which drew an almost immediate response. The Supreme Government in Calcutta wished to impose a duty on the sea exports and imports of the three Straits Settlements (Singapore, Penang and Malacca). The rate of duty was to be designed to cover the cost of a customs house and a flotilla (to suppress piracy), and although Murchison could not be specific, he estimated a probable duty of 2.5 per cent with foreign registered

---

[13] Lai, C. K. (2016). The Padang, *BiblioAsia* Vol 12, Issue 3 Oct–Dec 2016, National Library, Singapore.

square-rigged vessels paying double. This raised howls of protest and a public meeting on 4th February was held at which a number of resolutions were passed, Boustead seconding one. At the same time, he and four other prominent merchants were elected to refine the petition and forward it to Calcutta. Prior to this it was to be copied to Murchison with the request that he add his support. The success of Singapore was based on its free port status and it would be madness to change this. In the end, common sense prevailed and the proposals were cancelled. Piracy continued.

In May 1836, the formation of the Singapore Agricultural and Horticultural Society was suggested and Boustead was an early member. A petition to Government was proposed in October by Mr. Balestier and seconded by Boustead calling for a more liberal policy regarding the sale or leasing of lands to encourage agriculture. He also had a ketch named *Waterwitch*. This vessel took part in the 1837 New Year regatta and the following year took Munshi Abdullah and a Mr. Grandpre on a mission up the East Coast of Malaya as far as Kelantan with letters from Bonham who was now Governor.[14]

Schwabe sailed for China on 4th October 1836 in *Viscount Melbourne* to investigate business possibilities and stayed in Canton until October 1837 when he departed for Manila. How long he stayed in the Philippines is not known but on 22nd January 1838 he left Singapore for London in *Jessie Logan* taking with him Boustead's first child Jane, now about three years old. Due almost certainly to his introduction, Boustead gave office space to August Behn on his arrival from Hamburg in 1840 for a few months before he rented his own godown. His firm went on to become the first of many well-reputed and successful German firms, Behn Meyer & Co.

Boustead had been helping edit the *Singapore Chronicle*. In 1835 the restrictions on publications being lifted, he founded the *Singapore Free Press* in October together with his friends Lorrain, a merchant and Coleman, the architect. This interest he probably retained until 1846 when

---

[14] Trans, A. E. with notes & appendices. Coope (1949). *The Story of the Voyage of Abdullah Bin Abdul Kadir, Munshi. (undertaken in 1838 from Singapore to Kelantan).* The Malaya Publishing House, Singapore.

Abraham Logan bought the paper.[15] He was also one of the leading busi-
nessmen who in February 1837 met to form The Singapore Chamber of
Commerce for the purpose of watching over the commercial interests of
the Settlement. No member of the firm became Chairman until 1879
although Boustead himself was a member of the Committee at least for
the first two years of the Chamber's existence. He resigned as a member
in 1849 after returning from China. Later on there was a definite policy
that the company's senior staff should take no part in public life and
should concentrate their full energies on the business in hand. When the
company's prosperity might be affected there was however no hesitation
in taking up the cudgels. He was one of those much involved with the
question of steamships being used to connect London with India and on
to China, initially at the end of 1838.

Just when Sykes and Joseph Wise came to work with Boustead after
leaving Robert Wise & Co is unclear. Sykes, while at home on leave, on
20th September 1838 married Ann Burton at Tyldesley, nine miles west–
north–west of Manchester. She was the daughter of a mill owner already
wealthy and successful but destined to own one of the most extensive of
such operations of his day. One may assume the couple got back to
Singapore early in 1839.

Business continued successfully and on 23rd September 1840 Boustead
purchased a house in Campong Buyong on Victoria Road[16] and a month
later, in October, bought a plantation in Tanah Merah Road, Geylang.[17]
He arranged for Captain Arnold of *The Friends* to take Eduardo, now aged
three, to England. She sailed on 13th January 1840 and the boy was delivered in due course to Schwabe in Liverpool by *'a Chinaman'*. Schwabe
was almost certainly involved with the *'fine new ship'* Edward Boustead,
a barque built in 1842 in Liverpool and owned by Dugdales. She was
advertised in the *Free Press* as sailing from Singapore under her master,

---

[15] Makepeace, W. (1921). *One Hundred Years of Singapore, Vol. 1: Being Some Account of
the Capital of the Straits Settlements from Its Foundation by Sir Stamford Raffles on the 6th
February 1819 to the 6th February 1919. (Classic Reprint)*, Oxford University Press Pte
Ltd, Singapore 1991, p. 195.
[16] Gov. Lease No. 6000 for 999 years.
[17] Gov. Lease No. 5000.

Arnold, in January 1843. She served them for 10 years before being sold to Harrisons in 1852.

The idea of setting up a company in China may well have been under consideration after Schwabe's stay in Canton, but the political situation there deteriorated in 1838 and it was not until 1841, with the Treaty of Nanking and the cession to Britain of the island of Hong Kong, that profitable opportunities could be seen. Early in 1843 Boustead was making his preparations to go there and Janedah moved out to the house on Victoria Road. William Napier, the lawyer, drew up for Boustead a document giving her a life interest in it for 100 years or until her death provided she paid, if demanded, one cent per annum. It was dated 2nd June 1843 and witnessed by J. Wise and A. Sykes. On 9th June, a week later, Boustead sailed for Macao aboard *Pelorus* leaving Sykes in charge.

It was announced in the *Singapore Free Press* of 11th August 1843 that they had opened an agency in China called Boustead and Company which would join their other Group companies comprising Sykes Schwabe and Co of Liverpool, Butler Sykes and Co of Manila and Boustead Schwabe and Co of Singapore.

The Union Bank of Calcutta, the first bank to open a branch in Singapore and advertised as opening on 1st December 1840 later ran into problems in India over loans to indigo farmers and traders. H. W. Abbott, the second of its Agents in Singapore, moved out of the House of Twenty–Seven Pillars in mid–1843, possibly due to the closure of the bank's branch. The godown he had rented there was advertised from mid–July until the end of March 1844 as being '*to let*' but it seems there were no takers perhaps due in part to the March 1842 violent robbery of the store of a moneychanger who had established his headquarters in the verandah of the building.[18]

The House of Twenty–Seven Pillars was put up for auction, to take place on 15th June 1844 (Figure 30). Whether it was sold is unknown to the author. If sold, it must have later been repurchased or leased, as it is referred to in the Muncipal Engineer's report of 10th March as '*the Godowns of Messrs. Boustead & Co.*' and recorded in the *Singapore Daily Times* on 31st March 1882. Boustead, until he sailed for China, had been

---

[18] Buckley, op. cit., p. 376.

living in the house on the corner of High Street and the Esplanade, opposite the Court House.

It is not clear just when this No.1 on the Esplanade became a hotel (Figure 31). According to Buckley, Boustead was living there in 1842 as was confirmed many years later in a sworn statement by W. W. Shaw.[19] Mr. Tom Church, the Resident Councillor, was at No. 3 which he had leased on his arrival in 1837 and bought the following year for $4,600. Dr William Montgomerie had been living between them at No. 2 which he owned. His wife had gone home with the children in October 1841 and after her departure he moved out to his sugar plantation at Kalangdale.

A Mrs. Duncan had advertised on 1st June 1841 in the *Singapore Free Press* that she had opened the Singapore Hotel *'in High Street leading from the Court House'* and on 28th August a Mrs. Milne was offering to teach girls sewing and reading in a *'house opposite the Singapore Hotel'*. Early in 1842 the hotel moved to the Esplanade but did not stay long. An advertisement dated 27th December 1843 headed *'To be Let or Sold'* appeared stating *'The house No. 2 on the Esplanade at present occupied by Mr. John Duncan will be vacant on the 1st February 1844'*. A further announcement dated 17th January 1844 stated that the hotel would move on 1st February *'from the Esplanade'*. On 1st March Mr. Dutronquoy leased the site from Montgomerie and moved his London Hotel *'to the house lately occupied as the Singapore Hotel on the Esplanade.'* A year later on 2nd April 1845 he leased *'the house adjoining'* and on 20th November advertised that he had:

> 'just completed the enlargement of his Establishment, in doing which he has spared no expense or labour to make it a most comfortable and suitable house, for those who may favour him with their patronage, it being by far the most elegant, spacious and airy house of any in Singapore. It is situated on the Esplanade facing the sea commanding an extensive view both of land and sea. It is the first house that meets the eye of the Stranger on landing — it being close to the landing place.'

He bought the site of No. 2 in July 1850 (Lots 553 and 554.1)

---

[19] Deposition by W. W. Shaw dated 13th December 1893.

The *Anglo Chinese Calendar* for 1845 shows Boustead as being resident in Macao with Boustead & Co having five assistants. R. Aspinell Jr., Marten Wilhelmy, (a German) and W. C. Farquhar, (British) are not shown as based in any particular city. Two other British men were W. Hutchinson who was in Shanghai and Francis B. Birley in Canton. Butler, Sykes and Schwabe were shown as overseas partners. The Calendar for 1846 shows the partners as being the same but the locations are not given. Birley had left and set up on his own in Hong Kong and Canton. 1847 showed Boustead as now based in Canton with Aspinell and Wilhelmy plus Joseph Wise who had arrived from Singapore. A new recruit Edward Burton was in Shanghai with Hutchinson and Farquhar and early in 1848 there had been no changes.

Boustead, who apparently enjoyed country walks, signed a letter on 18th February 1848 referring to the problems for foreigners who wished to ramble outside Canton. In early June agreement was reached that Schwabe, with whom he remained friends until the end of his life, would leave the partnership. The Singapore firm would henceforth be known as Boustead & Co and the company in China would be wound up leaving that field to Schwabe and Sykes. The change of name was shown in an advertisement dated 8th June in Singapore. Boustead must have returned to Singapore fairly soon after this as he was visited there by W. W. Shaw, whom he had known for some years, returning to the United Kingdom from Shanghai where he had left the employ of Thomas Ripley & Co. Joseph Wise had also come back.

It may have been through the introduction of his good friend Tan Kim Seng that Boustead employed on his return a young 16–year–old who had arrived from Malacca. This boy, Chia Ann Siang, did well and by 1856 was the company's chief produce storekeeper. He built up a large fortune and died a wealthy man, with the hill in the centre of Chinatown still named after him today.

New business for the company was shown in an announcement dated 12th January 1849 that it had been appointed Agent for Royal Insurance of Liverpool, followed three days later by a similar announcement for Asiatic Marine Insurance Office.

Joseph Balestier who had for some years been United States Consul left Singapore, a sick man, in May 1848. The young American he had appointed to be *'locum tenens'* died some weeks later and the only other American on the island felt unable to take over. There was thus no US Consul until 12th November 1849 when Balestier, now tasked with arranging trade treaties with South East Asian countries, as an envoy of the President of the United States, arrived back in *Braganza.*[20] The same day, before sailing on to Hong Kong, he persuaded Boustead to take the position on. Boustead pointed out that he planned to retire to England early in 1851 but realising that the position could give the firm extra profitable business which they could handle, consented. It was just prior to this that Boustead had added his name to a letter dated 3rd November 1849 signed by a number of leading merchants and addressed to Sir James Brooke, Rajah of Sarawak, supporting his moves to suppress piracy. This was only published on 8th March 1850 by *The Straits Times* whose editor was vocally anti–Brooke. At the same time the paper published a list of Singapore firms with the date of establishment given. Boustead & Co is shown as starting in 1830. The company had been Brooke's agent in Singapore but, perhaps due to Boustead's absence in China, this agency had been transferred to W. R. Paterson & Co.

Boustead was able to help Balestier who came down from Hong Kong on 6th November 1850, before travelling on to Batavia on 7th December. His son had died in 1844 and his wife in 1847, both being buried in the cemetery on Government Hill. Several American vessels passed through Singapore at this time, all except one being headed for Calcutta. The exception, the *Santiago,* had arrived in Singapore consigned to Boustead & Co. on 22nd October from Boston via Batavia, with her captain, Stephenson, seriously ill with Java Fever. A week later he died and, a new captain appointed, she sailed for Boston on 14th November. Assuming the corpse was to be taken home Boustead, who had known the Balestiers since 1834, suggested that three would be as easy as one. Balestier, who by now, in contrast to when leaving Singapore in 1848, had sufficient funds to afford this, arranged the exhumation of their remains and off they were taken to Boston where they were reburied by his in–laws in the Old Granary Graveyard.

---

[20] Notice in *Singapore Free Press* dated 12th November 1849.

William Wardrop Shaw[21] arrived back in Singapore aboard the P & O *Pekin* on 3rd May 1850 and moved in with Boustead who was staying in Campong Glam. In December, the same year a letter, signed by Boustead and others, addressed to and supporting William Napier was published in the press. An old lawyer friend of Boustead, Napier had edited the *Singapore Free Press* until 1846 and from 1848 was for a short time Lieutenant Governor of Labuan before being given the sack by James Brooke, Rajah of Sarawak who was in overall charge.

There is no record of Boustead's exact date of departure to the United Kingdom, but circumstantial evidence points to very late February or March 1851 as he was balloted to be a member of the February Grand Jury. Shaw, who together with Wise was now a partner in the firm, had, in a letter dated 10th February to Balestier, confirmed his willingness to take over the Consul's role from Boustead and this was publicly announced in the press on 20th March. Shaw married Emily, the young third daughter of Thomas Crane, at St Andrew's Church on 8th October 1852. Joseph Wise, a man from Cumberland like Boustead, had died earlier on 24th June 1852, aged only 37, and a new partner, Robert Bain, was brought in on 1st January 1853 having previously been a partner in A. L. Johnston & Co. The same year a young Archibald Buchanan Brown joined as bookkeeper, and became a partner on 1st January 1856, the day after Bain, who later set up his own business as Commission Agent on 19th September, stepped down. Brown married a young Scots girl in June, and they lived with Shaw. Shaw found this difficult and referred to it in his letter of 21st September to Boustead after a brief trip up to Penang:

'I feel all the better for my trip for I was getting nervous and irritable before I left, and owing to Mrs. Brown's continued ailings and Miss Jessie's disagreeable manners my home residence was far from agreeable. What a pity for a young strong chap like Brown to buckle to with such a partner.'

---

[21] William Wardrop Shaw (1816–1895). Before joining Boustead, he had been in Burma and China. He married Emily Crane, daughter of Thomas Crane, at St Andrew's Church on 8th October 1852. Returned to England 1860. Retired 31st December 1878.

He adds later that '*For the few times I have seen her during the three months she appears a very nice person.*' He intended to sail on 23rd October but Brown, who was behind with things, he felt needed to shape up. However, '*they are going on in the office as well as they will do if I am away*' and the three young '*griffins*' Frolich, Lipscombe and Young were turning out well, supported by James Henry Leicester (1820–1891) who had been chief clerk since the early 1840s and was one of the very prolific family of that name from Bencoolen. His father Edward at this stage was a government pensioner and James had brothers in the Governor's office, the Master Attendant's office and the Export/Import office. He married twice and had a total of nine children.

Chapter 15

United Kingdom

Boustead now had the chance to get to know his two children who had been sent to Europe. Janedah had had another who died at or soon after birth. Both Jane, and later Eduardo, had been settled by Schwabe, at that time a bachelor, with a Mrs. Isabella Martin, who lived at 13 Blackburn Road, Liverpool and was the sister–in–law of Dr. Martin of Singapore. He married Helen Dugdale in 1842 and by 1851 they lived some five miles out of Liverpool at 71 Yew Tree Drive, West Derby next to the site where he had Broughton Hall (Figure 32) constructed and into which they moved in 1860. When the children were with Mrs. Martin and had holidays both would visit the Schwabes. According to a court statement made by Schwabe many years later, his wife had at first been reluctant to allow this, saying that they were evidently of Malay blood and feared that their friends would think they were her husband's bastards, *'but in the end she was persuaded to allow it.'* The Schwabes later moved south to London, first to 22 Cleveland Square where they were in 1881 and then to 19 Kensington Palace Gardens as recorded in the 1891 census.

Schwabe said later[1] that he could not remember just when the two children were sent over to Hamburg, first to his sister Frau Fanny Maria Wolff. She fairly soon moved them to live with Frau Hermann, a widowed cousin. Doubtless they went to school there and *'Jane became a fairly accomplished young lady. She spoke German fluently. Eduardo, I should say had a good education.'*

---

[1] Schwabe deposition dated 22nd December 1893.

In England Boustead registered a new company, Edward Boustead & Co., and first settled in Manchester, at 104 King Street. It was from here that he acknowledged Wise's private note of 5th April 1852 telling him that Janedah had given birth to another son in November 1851. This was most unwelcome news and initially Boustead refused to acknowledge the child as his own. He repudiated him in a letter to Wise dated 22nd June (two days before the latter's death in Singapore).

'I regret exceedingly that the existence of the youngster is known, but of course such a thing could not be kept secret. The worst of it is that Jane and Edward [Eduardo] it appears were told in their infancy that their mother was dead, and which I did not know until lately. I would not for the world that they should know, yet I fear it will reach them somehow or other. I still doubt it is mine and would rather it should never come to England, at least it must never come bearing my name. Could it not be sent to Australia or elsewhere under the name of Wilson or Smith or some such name? Call him young Smith for the future so that if your letters fall into other hands it will not be known who you mean, with a certain sum settled on it in some way.'

Both children had come back from Hamburg and Eduardo, now in his early teens, was enrolled in the Liverpool Collegiate Institution Middle School in December 1851 where he remained until early 1854. Frau Wolff's son Gustav had started there as a pupil in 1848. Jane needed a Governess and through Schwabe's introduction a Miss Charlotte Stebbing was employed in this capacity. By February 1856 Eduardo (*'He will never be clever but is a very amiable boy.'[2]*) had been dispatched back to Hamburg to work in an office and by this time Boustead and his household had moved down south, settling initially at Irwell Lodge, Thornton Road in Clapham Park (Figure 33). Clapham, originally a Saxon village in farmland some five miles south of the City of London, began to develop in the late 1700s when many large houses were built for those wealthy people who valued the relatively easy access to the City. In 1825 Thomas Cubitt, the builder later responsible for many fine buildings and residential squares in London, bought the

---

[2] Letter from Boustead to Shaw dated 10th February 1856.

225 acres of Bleak Hall Farm and began to develop it with detached houses designed to appeal to the wealthiest of society. Thornton Road was an early part of this development.

Jane was seriously ill. According to her father:

'She and Edward were much respected by all who knew them and while Jane was well [she] was received everywhere, even by Mrs. James Fraser who has driven out to Clapham Park purposely to call on her. She speaks and writes German and French same as English and before her illness sang with great taste and very well. She is still a very fair performer on the piano and, notwithstanding her illness, is still very lively and cheerful as a cricket. I spent a fortnight with her at Torquay last month most happily altho' I had to carry her upstairs to bed every night. Her illness has done us both good. I have now more consideration for others.'[3]

Miss Stebbing turned out to be an excellent choice in more ways than one; love blossomed, and Boustead married her on 22nd April, a very happy occasion. They went on a three–week cruise in August and on 23rd January 1857 she gave birth to a daughter, Helen. Meanwhile Jane's health deteriorated and sadly she finally died, aged 21, of consumption on 22nd October 1857, being buried in the family vault. Very soon after this the family moved to 1 Clarence Road. Less than four months later, on 3rd February 1858, Charlotte, his new wife, died and he was left on his own to bring up Helen, his one year old daughter.

The Thornton Road house, although very adequate for a short period, was merely a stepping stone before moving a few hundred yards up the road towards London to the new, far grander mansion just completed. During the 30 years he lived there Boustead made a number of improvements and changes but the description when the house was sold in 1888 after his death, even allowing for estate agents' superlatives, gives a good idea of the place:

'One of these well–known properties of distinctive character and possessing all the attractions of a country residence, within three quarters of an hour's drive of the City. It comprises about 9¾ acres and for about

---

[3] Ibid.

30 years past has been in the occupation of the late Edward Boustead who from time to time has made considerable outlay in additions and improvements, rendering the property perfect as an abode for banker or merchant. The Cubitt–built mansion, well situate and approached by a carriage–drive from the Clarence Road is entered by a large enclosed portico, and contains 12 bed and dressing rooms, with bath room, and boudoir on the two upper floors, reached by two staircases, spacious drawing room, dining room and library on the ground floor, and complete domestic offices and cellarage; excellent stabling for five horses, fitted in a costly manner, with apartments for coachman and groom. Adjoining the house are three large vineries, and in addition to the charmingly–timbered ornamental pleasure grounds, is an extensive and well–stocked kitchen garden, with ranges of pits, tool–house, yard and outbuildings, including cow–houses, loose boxes and poultry sheds, and an enclosure of meadow, belted by finely–grown trees and shrubbery.'

The, as yet unnamed, illegitimate male child was still with Janedah in Singapore. Boustead decided it was time for him to be sent elsewhere and letters went back and forth to and from Shaw, who by now was fully aware of the whole sorry story. The boy was put under the care of Captain Scott of *John Brightman* which sailed on 20th July 1856. As agreed beforehand Scott had him christened John Johnston at the Scots Kirk in Calcutta and placed him at the Parental Academic Institution Doveton College. The junior school accepted boys from three years old upwards and had a matron to look after them. The cost including board, textbooks and clothing was $40 per month, with some expenses extra. Boustead was paranoid that his name should not be known, and that the child's existence should not become known in Singapore or in England. Shaw pointed out that not only did he look like his father *('something of your phiz')* but had a picture of him and knew his name.[4] Two shops or other property in Singapore (up to a value of $8,000 if necessary although only a cost of $5,000 was expected) were to be purchased and put in the name of Trustees, the rent from which would be used to pay the fees and when the boy came of age would give him some assets. Tan Beng Swee, the son of Boustead's old friend Tan Kim Seng, agreed to act as Trustee. As Shaw was going on

---

[4] Letter from Shaw to Boustead dated 11th May 1856.

home leave shortly, Dunman, the Commissioner of Police, would deal with correspondence so that, as Boustead wrote *'no one at the office will have any occasion to interfere or to be troubled in any way in these disgusting private matters'*.

At this stage Boustead intended that John Johnston should remain in India where he would have a better chance of getting on than in Europe. He wrote that:

> 'it is a mistake to bring those sort to Europe both for health and the chances of getting on. Jane, poor thing, cannot possibly last long and Edward, from all appearances, will go the same way. If sent to Singapore he might have a chance but this is impossible. He is at present in Hamburg and I fear his breaking down there this winter.'[5]

Shaw, replying on 21st September 1856 to Boustead's letter of 9th August, was far from well and looking forward to his leave:

> 'I do sincerely hope that Jane and Edward may never hear of their mother or brother, which he most certainly is, and I fear his resemblance hereafter may tell tales but I think you should not hesitate to inform your wife as it may accidently come out some day and then you would never be forgiven. She must know that Jane had a native mother, and she must also know very well that such must not be known by her. But have no secrets from your wife. You will feel happier and easier and 'tho she may storm a little at first she will see that there will be ample provision for the family she is likely to have from you.'

---

[5] Letter from Boustead to Shaw dated 9th September 1856.

Chapter 16

Janedah

Before leaving Singapore for China in 1843, Boustead had made careful arrangements for Janedah, now in her early twenties, wanting her to be financially secure and to have somewhere to live. She was given a monthly allowance of $20 and had moved to a house in Victoria Street [formerly Road] in which she was given a life interest. She had also been given a life interest in a coconut plantation on Tanah Merah Road, Geylang. Although it appears she did not move back in with Boustead between his return from China in 1848 and leaving for England in early 1851, she gave birth to his son in November, as noted above. Writing to Wise, Boustead refers to her as *"the old woman"* and wishes she could be persuaded to leave Singapore by buying a house or something and settling on her for life. *"It must be our object to get her off to Java, Bencoolen or elsewhere and be done with her."*[1] It seems that in the stress of the moment he forgot that he had already given her the interest in a house and plantation.

As mentioned earlier in February 1856 Boustead had decided, although still not admitting that the now five–year–old boy was his, that the child must be sent to India to be raised and educated so as to give him a chance in life. Janedah was not prepared to let him go. Shaw threatened that she would lose her monthly allowance of $20 and he would sell the properties (he did not then know of her life interest). She came to see him (he found her '*grown enormously fat*') and showed him a document, of which he made a copy. She was reluctant in the extreme to allow the boy

---

[1] Letter from Boustead to Wise dated 22nd June 1852.

to be sent off overseas, and said it was cruel to the child and that Boustead had never told her when one had died, had never mentioned it. This must refer to her third child, Robert, who died in infancy and of whom we have no other detail.

Shaw tried to persuade her to return to Bencoolen but, understandably, she replied that she *'left young, that all her known relatives are in Singapore so she would not go there.'* She *'has only to die, as all her children are gone.'* She had one adopted child, her nephew, to whom she wanted to leave the plantation. Three or four days before the ship was to sail, she demanded an advance of $500, then came down to $200, without which she would keep the child. Shaw called her in with her brother and somebody named *'Samchi'* and announced that he would have no more to do with her and that the child would go. She rushed to Kim Seng and after further discussion he recommended a payment of $55 to cover clothes and *'susah ali.'* Shaw agreed and the boy left for Calcutta.

Shaw felt that the discarded mistresses of European bachelors of earlier years should no longer be seen or heard:

> 'She [Janedah] has been badly advised by some of the neglected ladies here and I hear chiefly by Mrs. [sic] Lewis Fraser, a very bad character indeed. The place has receded much in these matters for now the drive at the seaside round the plain and the band playing is completely surrounded by the ladies from Campong Bencoolen dressed out like Europeans, no shame in them at all.'[2]

Janedah, hearing from Shaw of Boustead's marriage, complained that he did not want her anymore and that she should get married. She decided to go on the Haj to Mecca and negotiated an advance of 18 months allowance to cover the cost. On 10th March 1859 Boustead wrote to Shaw, now back in Singapore *'perhaps the best thing would be to buy an annuity for the old lady, so that she would be no further trouble to anyone. But I must think well about it....'*

A month later he wrote, *'See that the old lady does not want but if satisfied with her monthly pay better not disturb her. The way of transgressions is hard.'*

---

[2] Letter from Shaw to Boustead dated 17th July 1856.

By July, writing by the mail, he had further ideas:

'I think it would be well to sell the house the old lady lives in, provide her another she would like as well and at less expense which she might live in free but if in her own name somebody might do her out of it. Then get a mortgage to give say $25 or $30 per month which Beng Swee would no doubt collect and pay her.'

A fortnight later he clarified his idea and said that *'a special sum should be invested in a mortgage.'* Two weeks later he wanted Shaw to confirm he had placed enough funds with Tan Kim Seng to cover her allowance for six months and asked him to place the grants of the properties with Kim Seng or Dunman *'when you leave, if they will be bothered with them.'* On 27th September he wrote again:

'Regarding the old woman I fear if she got married it would just be to get hold of the money, that her husband would soon spend it and leave her, and she would be reduced to want. I could never think of her being so circumstanced and if she could be got into a small house of her own with a monthly allowance that she could not touch, it would be best. Then she could not starve. I ought to have thought about this before but it is such a disgusting humiliating business that I cannot bear to refer to it and I only wish it could be buried in oblivion. If nothing has been done in the matter I think we shall be able to arrange it through Kim Seng, who is very kind, after your return home. I hope you destroyed all the old books and papers and took care of the lease or grant of the house the old woman occupies.'

Shaw retired to England and the matter moved no further forward despite correspondence with Tan Beng Swee, the son of Tan Kim Seng who had become his father's partner in Kim Seng & Co. in 1852. A very striking and magnificent silver epergne (Figure 34) was presented in January 1862 by Edward Boustead to the two of them *'as a mark of esteem and friendship, and in acknowledgment of the many and valuable services rendered to himself personally as well as to his firm during an uninterrupted friendly intercourse of nearly a quarter of a century'*. Undoubtedly the help with Janedah was the major factor in this presentation.

In November 1866 Boustead wrote to his lawyer in London, J. D. Marsden, instructing him to draw up a power of attorney to enable

Dunman[3] to sell on his behalf a piece of ground in Victoria Road [sic] and all buildings thereon being Lot 2 of Lease 662 covering 21,150 square feet on 999 years lease from 15th February 1829 @ $3 per annum purchased by him in 1840. Within two days he had written both to Beng Swee (whose father Kim Seng had died in Malacca on 14th March 1864)[4] and Dunman on the subject, but to the latter wrote *'Since Shaw left Singapore Beng Swee has kindly paid the old lady $20 per month which with some little rent she has got for the two properties referred to [Victoria Road and Geylang] have given her in all about $30 per month, ample for her to live on.'* This may explain Shaw's earlier statement in about 1850, that Janedah was living in a back street not far away [rather than Victoria Street]. Boustead also brought up again the idea of an annuity so that she would not be financially affected in case of his death.

He hoped Dunman would discuss the ideas with Beng Swee and advise what they felt would be the best to do:

'The old lady said some time ago that the house in Victoria Street wanted large repairs, that the Municipal Commissioners had given notice to that effect which may, or may not, be true. But I do not want to spend more money on it or wish to retain the two properties in my name. I shall therefore send Beng Swee [sic] power next mail to sell them. I do not want Lipscombe[5] or Young[6] to know anything about this unpleasant affair.'

---

[3] Thomas Dunman (1814–1887) came to Singapore in 1840 to join Martin Dyce & Co. In September 1843 he was appointed Deputy Magistrate and Superintendent of Police. A popular man, he led by example, building up the efficiency and morale of the Police which was recognised when, in 1857, he was appointed Commissioner of Police. Married to a daughter of Thomas Crane, he retired in 1871 to his coconut estate in Katong (Grove Estate) and four years later moved to England where he died on 6th October 1887 in Bournemouth.

[4] Song, O. S. (1922). *One Hundred Years' History of the Chinese in Singapore*, 1967 Reprint by University Malaya Press, p. 49.

[5] George Lipscombe joined Boustead & Co in 1855. Admitted as a partner (together with Jasper Young) 1st January 1861. Married Mary Anne Green in Devon on 1st September 1865. Retired from the partnership and returned to England 1870. No children.

[6] Jasper Young was born in 1833 in Kilmarnock, Scotland, and had twelve siblings. He went to Singapore in 1855 and joined Boustead & Co. Admitted as a partner 1st January 1861. Married Margaret Henderson in England in 1863. Left Singapore in March 1873 but remained a partner and joined Boustead in London.

Two weeks later, having omitted to send Dunman a copy of his letter to Beng Swee, Boustead continued to harp on the idea of an annuity. Failing this, *'I fancy the only thing will be to give the old lady a life interest in, say, $5,000 placed in the hands of Trustees who will be empowered to invest it for her benefit and at her death it comes back again to my estate, for I daresay she will live longer than I will.'* In December he had heard that property prices in Singapore were down and suggested buying a shop in a good situation to rent for $30 a month.

It seems that producing a power of attorney was proving difficult and he wrote to his lawyer again on 6th February 1867 giving details and adding *'do not describe Singapore as being in the 'Empire of China' as you did in the last power. It is not within a thousand miles of the nearest part of China.'* Two weeks later the document was in his hands, signed and witnessed, and sent off to Dunman with further instructions:

> 'The plantation was expressly bought for Noonah [the old lady] and would have been put in her name at the time but I was afraid it might be made away with and she would never get any good out of it. However I do not wish to keep it any longer in my name and if she objects to the sale of it with the view of providing amply for her otherwise you may transfer it to her and if she will not take care of it I cannot help it.'

He enclosed a note to Lipscombe instructing him to take the two leases out of the iron chest and pass them over to Dunman. On the same date he added to Beng Swee that he cared very little how it was all done as long as he and his executors were clear of all further interference in the matter and Noonah comfortably provided for life.

The idea of an annuity found favour and although in June this was being pursued through Maclaine Fraser & Co and the Sovereign Life Assurance Company he later heard that such an annuity could not be bought. Writing to Beng Swee on 17th October he said:

> 'Mr. Dunman suggests Tanjong Pagar Dock Debentures which I think will be best so that if you will kindly act for me in this matter please invest $4,000 in Dock Debentures in your own name, giving me a letter saying they are on my account, interest to be paid to Noonah during her lifetime after which they are to belong to my estate, attaching a copy of

this letter to the debenture bonds so that in the event of your death your executors will know to whom they belong. If you will kindly do this you will oblige me very much....... The bonds pay 9% which will give $30 per month, ample I fancy for the comfortable support of the old lady, Boustead & Co have orders to pay you $4,000 whenever you please to ask for it.'

Matters were evidently not quite as simple as expected. Beng Swee could find nobody prepared to sell the required debentures but would keep trying. On 27th August 1868, 10 months later, Boustead wrote to Dunman thanking him for his letter of 7th December: *'I have been anxiously expecting to hear that Beng Swee has got $4,000 worth of Tanjong Pagar Dock debentures or something else equally secure.'* He had heard in London that the Dock people were again in want of money and might be obliged to issue fixed dividend preference shares. If so, these might be preferable to the debentures but, if the dividend was to be lower than expected, up to $5,000 was available from Boustead & Co. Occasional correspondence with Dunman and Beng Swee continued and on 6th May 1869 as Janedah had objected to the house being sold Boustead wanted it put in good repair. No debentures or preference shares had been purchased and he now thought it best if $5,000 were placed in Beng Swee's name with the Oriental Bank on fixed deposit, even though they were only paying 5 per cent per annum. On 15th July he wrote hoping the house and plantation had not been sold. He would like both to be transferred into Janedah's name to do what she liked with. The monthly $20 should still be paid by Beng Swee pending allocation of 50 $100 Tanjong Pagar preference shares at 7 per cent per annum which he had applied for through the company's agent in London and which he expected to receive in September or October. The interest on 35 of these would be used by Beng Swee to pay the monthly $20 payment. In the meantime Beng Swee had deposited $4,800 with the Oriental Bank at 5 per cent per annum as advised in his letters of 17th and 21st June, and Boustead acknowledged this on 10th September. Dunman, who was about to depart on leave, had the titles to the house and plantation registered in Janedah's name on 7th September. At the end of 1870, 34 Tanjong Pagar Dock Co preference shares were transferred to Beng Swee and from then on he used the dividends to pay Janedah's allowance until her death in May 1884.

After getting the news of Janedah's death from a letter sent to Jasper Young, Boustead wrote to Beng Swee. He asked him to transfer into his name the 34 Tanjong Pagar shares, but also offered to accept only 21 shares, the other 13 *'to be divided as you think best among those in your establishment who have had trouble in this matter. It is only right that I should make some little recompense for such long and kind services.'* In the event this generous offer was not accepted and the full 34 shares were transferred back, added to the 379 shares already held by him. Beng Swee himself did not long survive Janedah, and after an illness of two months died on Tuesday 4th November 1884 at his house, Panglima Prang, in River Valley Road. Learning of this, Boustead wrote a letter of condolence to Beng Swee's brother on 12th December.

Records show that, on 18th February, less than a month before her death Janedah had sold the house in Victoria Street to Lee Cheng Wee for $2,900. Whether or not Boustead got to know of this is not recorded.

Chapter 17

The Company

Shaw found that his leave had improved his health, as had being with his wife and young children. He returned to Singapore on 29th October 1858 and remained until late in 1859 when Brown returned from a year's leave in England. Boustead had written in September, *'I fear Brown will break down and we will either have to close [at the] end of 1860 or find someone else. It is a pity after all we have missed Wood. He is a fool I think to stay where he is.'* Brown retired from the partnership on 1st January 1861. George Lipscombe and Jasper Young were admitted as partners on the same day, but Henry Frolich continued as an assistant until 1866 when his brother Charles took his place. This was a difficult year for those engaged in American business as, to a large extent, were Bousteads. The Civil War had broken out and it was difficult if not impossible to get insurance cover for cargoes shipped in American bottoms even if the ships were to be found.

In 1857, after the Indian Mutiny, there had been agitation locally to remove the Straits Settlements from the clutches of the East India Company or India Office and instead to become a crown colony. This was not achieved until 1st April 1867. Boustead had doubts and wrote to Dunman in November that *'I hope the change of Government will be in your favor [sic] altho' I think the thing was a mistake.'* Colonel Harry St. George Ord was appointed Governor with instructions to reorganise the administration. He considered that as the Queen's representative he should be treated like royalty and be provided with accommodation and transport of a standard he considered appropriate. He did not return the calls made on him by foreigners, which was considered locally a grave insult:

> 'Notice is given, that His Excellency the Governor purposes [sic] transacting business at his office, at the public buildings, on some mornings during each week, between the hours of twelve and two [sic], on which occasions a flag will be hoisted on the staff at the buildings, to denote that His Excellency is ready to receive Gentlemen desirous of seeing him on business.'

This announcement, as well as his order that a new Government House should be built in time for the late 1869 visit by the Duke of Edinburgh, and various measures which the merchants considered harmful, were not well received. Their concerns were relayed to those merchants who had retired from the East but retained their investments there. As a result, a decision to set up the Straits Settlements Association on 31st January 1868 was taken at a meeting in Boustead's London office. The membership consisted of a number of members of parliament as well as others who had worked in Singapore and Penang. The objective was to represent the interests of the Straits Settlements through direct contact with the Colonial Office. Boustead was a committee member and during Ord's governorship the Association was very active in its opposition to much of his policy. Thereafter, with a more accommodating Governor in place, it did little until it was resuscitated in 1888.

George Lipscombe retired from the firm in 1870, the exact date being uncertain. He was replaced possibly only as a temporary measure by John Stow Young, believed to have been a cousin of Jasper, who had joined in 1863. He was now running the Penang branch set up in 1864. He continued there until his *'interest and responsibility in the company ceased on 31st December 1872'*, as announced in the press on 25th February 1873. Jasper Young left Singapore in March aboard the P&O liner *Travancore,* remaining a partner and joined Boustead in the London company. His cousin also joined that office as Corresponding Clerk. Over the years following Boustead's move to the United Kingdom the percentage share in the Singapore firm held by each partner varied as partners came and went, and as results increased or were reduced. In 1878 the new two–year arrangement was 25 per cent for Boustead, 25 per cent for Jasper Young and the remaining 50 per cent allocated to the three partners running the business in Singapore.

Young had been a leading member of the group being formed in February 1871 to build a railway from town to the docks at Tanjong Pagar, but this did not come to fruition.

Following Young's departure three new partners were admitted. Farleigh Armstrong (joined from his own firm in 1872) who ran the Penang operation, Isaac Henderson (whose sister was Jasper Young's wife) and Thomas Cuthbertson who had both joined in 1871.

Chapter 18

United Kingdom Again

1858 had been a sad year with Boustead's wife Charlotte's death in February but life had to continue. Eduardo had been sent off to Manila from Hamburg to work in a trading company, Tillson, Herrmann & Co. Their senior partner was an Englishman Edward Parr who was known both to Schwabe and to Boustead, and Herrmann was a member of the family young Eduardo had lived with in Hamburg.

Early in 1859 Boustead decided that John Johnston should not be left in Calcutta and wrote to Shaw on 11th April *'I shall be very glad if you will get any information that can be relied on about the little fellow at Doveton College. ... If the little fellow is at all strong I must have him home as soon as I can find anyone that will take charge of him.'* By July he was writing that *'the boy must not arrive in the winter, say not before May next.'* Shaw had consulted a Captain Viall who recommended something in the Orkneys and in September Boustead decided that the child should remain in Calcutta until he could discuss matters with Shaw. In the end the boy came to Scotland and was later found a job in a shipbroker's office in Aberdeen. This was no great success and, having come of age, he attempted to ascertain his parentage and if he had property in India. He was brusquely told that *'the gentleman who sent you home died many years ago so that you have no funds in India to look to.'* He was then placed in *'an advantageous partnership'* with a mill owner in Manchester. This too did not work well and, at his own request, in 1874 he shipped off to Australia and was never heard of again.

One of Boustead's oldest friends, William Henderson of Liverpool, a draper by profession whom he had helped financially in earlier years, had a daughter Margaret. She and a young man from a good county family had fallen in love but both realised that due to their difference in class they could not marry. Boustead suggested that, to have a change of scene, she should come down to Clapham and look after Helen; her parents approved, and she accepted the idea. Jasper Young returned in 1862 on his first home leave and, having now lost both his parents who had lived in Kilmarnock, Scotland, was invited to stay with Boustead who treated him like a son. Before long, love blossomed between the two young people. They were married in September 1863 and arrived together back in Singapore in the P&O *China* on 14 December that year.

When in Singapore Boustead was said never to have attended a church service apart from one occasion when he went to listen to an American Baptist preacher. It seems therefore that his commitment to the Particular Baptist Church began after his return to England. He was a member of the congregation at the Metropolitan Tabernacle at Newington, Surrey. Here the renowned Baptist preacher C. H. Spurgeon was pastor. Spurgeon appealed for funds to organise a *'colporteur'* organisation (one which would sell or distribute free copies of the bible or religious tracts) and in the next issue of *'The Magazine'* it was reported that one gentleman had written in offering generous aid in establishing colporteur work. The gentleman was Edward Boustead and the year 1866.

In November 1866 Helen, known as Nellie, now nine years old, was *'getting tall'* and had great talent for music. Five years later when the census was taken, she was shown as being a student at Surbiton House, The Globe, Camberwell.

Eduardo had settled into his work in Manila and in 1864 his father made him an interest-free loan of £14,000 to enable him to become a partner for 10 years in Tillson, Herrmann & Co.

It is not clear how Eduardo found out that his mother was a Malay, still living, and that he was illegitimate. Find out he did and wrote a bitter accusatory letter to his father in London dated 20th September 1866. This diatribe caused Boustead genuine distress. Receiving it in early November he replied at length two days later.

'I need not tell you how deeply grieved I am to think I am the cause of occasioning you so much unhappiness. You have no reason to be ashamed of your position. I am entirely to blame and it has been the cause of shame and regret to me for many many years and must be until my dying day. It has long been a question with me whether to tell you or leave you to find it out and I decided on the latter, either that I did not wish to hurt your feelings sooner than it could be avoided or thinking as you got older and saw more of the world, you would be better able to bear it. If I have done wrong in withholding it from you, I hope you will forgive me. I acted from the kindest motives, but above all I must ask your forgiveness for having placed you by my great wickedness in the humiliating position in which you are. I hope God has forgiven me and that I shall never act towards you except as a father, so long as you act as a dutiful and prudent son. I have done all in my power to repair the injury I have done to you. I sent you home at an early age, gave you an excellent education and when you decided on being a merchant you were placed in an office in Hamburg; and as I could not send you to Singapore while your poor mother is living, you were sent to Manila where you found Mr. Herrmann who treated you as a brother and, at your own request and Mr. Herrmann's, I advanced you a large sum by way of capital to make you a partner in a respectable and old–established house.'

Having got what he wanted and made a partner in the business Eduardo changed his lifestyle and:

'began to squander away most foolishly, under the impression apparently that because you had only [then] discovered your position, you thought others would also and that you would be disgraced. It is not so. Mr. Herrmann and Mr. Parr have known all about you since you arrived in England as a child, Mr. and Mrs. Schwabe, the Dugdales, Mr. and Mrs. Wolff and all your Hamburg friends all know exactly what you are, yet as long as you conducted yourself properly you were treated by all with the utmost respect. When Mr. Herrmann arrived in England he spoke of you to me in the highest terms and said that ever since you went to Hamburg he had regarded you as his own brother and was most anxious you should join the house in Manila.'[1]

---

[1] Letter from Boustead to Eduardo dated 7th November 1866.

Herrmann had said that Mr. Parr intended to retire at the end of the current partnership agreement in 1874, and that he would then move to Europe leaving Eduardo in charge in Manila. He had changed his mind and planned to retire himself as he was not prepared to leave him uncontrolled in Manila but, perhaps at Boustead's urging, Herrmann was now prepared to continue in Manila and Eduardo was instructed in no uncertain terms to behave himself, get out of debt and realise that a partner had to work even harder than a clerk.

At this period in Europe a person with part Asian blood, or who looked as though he (or she) had, would always suffer discrimination, overtly or not. Among Europeans recently arrived in Asia to remark that someone had been *'country born'* was somewhat derogatory. Boustead undoubtedly portrayed a certain wishful thinking when he wrote: *'Dismiss from your mind that men are respect[ed] or despised according to their parentage. It is according to their own conduct and character that they are judged.'* He held out the possibility in a few years of a position in the recently opened branch of Boustead & Co in Penang *'where you would find the Browns and the Scotts, the first houses there, exactly in the same position as you are, born in Penang of native mothers yet highly respected and moving in the best society.'*

The next letter, written in March 1867 in response to his written apology in January, confirmed that Mr. Herrmann would continue but Eduardo was still overspending and was $5,000 in debt. Boustead had had second thoughts about Penang and felt the Straits might not be the right place for him despite giving further examples of Straits–born children. *'My own impression is that after what has happened, and from your still spending more money than you have any occasion to do that it would be imprudent for you ever to be left to yourself again.'*

A good deal of the overspending may have been due to Eduardo's courtship of Dolores, a young Filipina, reportedly of Spanish extraction, whom he married the following year (1868) and to whom, in due course, two daughters were born. The next year Boustead, without telling them, made a £20,000 settlement in favour of the whole family, subject to Boustead's own life interest and with power of revocation.

Eduardo continued in the firm in Manila yet did not mend his ways and when in 1874 the partnership agreement expired Herrmann was glad to be rid of him. He stayed on in Manila and tried to establish connections with the correspondents of the firm in a manner which called forth the strongest rebukes from his father.

By July 1875 he had negotiated a partnership agreement with a Mr. John Ph. Hens, the senior local partner of the large and well-known firm G. Von Polanen Petel & Co. Boustead was unwilling to continue the original £14,000 loan until full accounts of the old partnership with Herrmann were shown to him and was furious when he received a telegram from Eduardo in October 1875 asking for £8,000 to be remitted to him. After explanations he sent £10,000 direct to Hens asking that it be used to wind up Eduardo's affairs. In the end he had to pay about £30,000 to clear all the known debts, although afterwards new ones surfaced rendering his son liable to criminal prosecution.

A more pleasant event occurred in 1876 when on 3rd August Helen, now 19, married a 29–year–old architect, William Niven at the Anglican St James's Church, Clapham, and moved to live at 31 Princes Square. Her dowry was £25,000. Their son, William Edward Graham Niven, was born the following year on 24th June and Helen sadly died shortly afterwards.

The debt problems in Manila took time to sort out and it was in 1878 that Boustead offered Eduardo £500 per annum not to go into business again but to remain where they were, as his wife had connections. Notwithstanding this, the following year he agreed to pay the family's fare to Stuttgart in Germany, where he wished them to settle. This did not appeal and instead they took a house in Bayonne, south–west France. The funds settled on them earlier were invested in stock, the certificates being held by Shaw, and they were to live on the income of £900 per annum without touching the capital.

From Boustead's letters in 1882 he was under the impression that Eduardo had turned over a new leaf, become interested in Baptist missionary activities and that his wife had left Roman Catholicism behind in Manila. '*I note with pleasure,*' he writes on 15th August:

'the interest you take in good work but you must guard against your name appearing in any Missionary reports which would be sure to find there [sic] way into religious publications here and I might be asked some questions which would be rather unpleasant and inconvenient. With the exception of two or three old friends, no one in England knows of your existence and I do not want any more to know. So please, in your intercourse with Europeans, English especially, never mention my name. It would do you no good and place me in a very unpleasant position in many quarters. Those who now treat you with respect, if they knew the whole truth might look down upon you and I might also be treated here in a similar way. I never mention you to anyone and even post all my letters to you myself so that no one may suspect the connection. My old friends who do know never mention you in the presence of others. On this account I can never have you in England in my lifetime nor indeed should I ever wish you to come to England. I shall take care however that you and your family shall not suffer in consequence for I am solely to blame in the matter.'

By the end of the month he had been worrying more and on the 30th suggested that Eduardo consider changing his name and assuming French nationality, taking advice from a French lawyer. As an illegitimate son under British law he would inherit nothing.

From the correspondence available to us it is clear that Eduardo, hurt by the fact that he was illegitimate, knowing his father was rich, took a perverse delight in living beyond his means partly as a form of revenge in the knowledge that his father would always, despite complaining, cover the debts. He also realised, though this was never mentioned, that a word spread in England would destroy his father's reputation in society and in the Baptist Church where he, or perhaps his generosity, had earned a good name.

The next letter which has survived was written on 18th February 1886 and starts, *'The more I think of your present position, the more I am shocked at your utter want of principal [sic]'*. If, when Eduardo had first got into difficulties in Manila, he had owned up, he might have got out of it at a cost of £4,000 but as it was, Boustead, by his various specious representations, was swindled out of at least £30,000 to avoid further mischief and protect the family name. Later in August 1883 Boustead, thinking he could now be trusted, revoked the £20,000 settlement made at the time of Eduardo's marriage and sent him East India Railway stock for £16,600 and a government annuity for £112.10 the whole of which would yield an annual £900, double the amount he had been allowed. In 1885 he had also advanced £5,200 to finance the purchase and furnishing of a house for them in Biarritz (in south–west France) and as Eduardo had overspent by £5,000, had to realise some of the Railway stock.

'You are again in difficulties, from what cause I know not as you decline to tell me, but you must tell me in full before you get another penny from me. I fear it is extravagant living, buying carriages and horses and spending money on building operations far beyond your means.'

Eduardo replied on the 20th saying that his father's letter had quite crushed him. Boustead wrote back on the 24th that:

'I fear you have yet to learn what prudence and common honesty means…. The only way you can be helped is to stop all supplies and this I shall now do……. You will get no help from me. I regret having sent the 3,000 francs under the impression your debts and liabilities were not over 15,000 francs and that a true statement of your real position was on the way. Get out of this trouble and keep out or you are sure to bring yourself and family to ruin, soon.'

Eduardo now brought his wife into play. She wrote to Boustead on 11th March, apologising, and asking for forgiveness to which, he replied, he gave. He spelled out the problems, saying that she could not have been aware of them as he was sure she would not have allowed the situation to develop. Yet once again, he gave in. *'To prevent your furniture being seized and sold and you and your children being turned out into the street I have engaged to meet all payments due up to 15th April'* leaving Eduardo to sort out the rest of the mess. *'Make your husband promise you to run up no bills whatever, pay cash for everything and owe no man anything.'*

Some hope!

On 5th January 1888 when he was already ill Boustead had written:

'You must distinctly understand that you will get nothing more from me' and underlined this.

On the same date he wrote to Shaw:

'I wrote to Edward's wife to assist her husband in keeping down expenses or they would soon be in trouble again and not to expect further help from me.'

The last letter available to us was written by Eduardo from Clarens, in Switzerland on 15th February. A Mrs. Dunn had allegedly agreed in early October 1887 to rent the house in Biarritz for the winter at 2,000 francs per month, *'but on hearing of the illness that had been in the house she threw up the bargain as she was afraid to enter it with her young boy of about eight years of age. We are thus about 10,000 francs out of pocket.'* Boustead wrote on the letter *'Answer 20th February. I have been ill for two months and if I die you will get nothing from my estate. Your name does not appear among my papers.'*

He died nine days later. According to Jasper Young, writing on 14th April to a correspondent named Fay in the United States, *'the death of our worthy Senior will not affect the business in any way .... seeing that we are worth £300,000 or about $1,500,000 I don't think the credit of the firm is likely to be dented.'*

Boustead's story is of a young man whose main object in life, at least when he arrived in Singapore, was to get rich quickly and honestly and then get richer, to the exclusion of almost everything else. By the age of 31, and when temptation was offered in the form of a young, though sexually mature, girl, he followed for 11 years the custom of European bachelors of the period. Four children resulted, of whom one died, one later disappeared and two grew to adulthood in Europe. In all cases he ensured that they were educated and supported. He was scrupulous in taking financial care of his now discarded mistress and this continued throughout his life. Once back in England he continued to work night and day to build up his assets, in which he was very successful. At this stage, he appears to have 'found' religion and bitterly repented of his early life and its consequences. He was terrified that his carefully constructed respectability in Baptist circles would be shattered by scandal, should tales of his early life come out.

Boustead is alleged to have been a founder of The Tanjong Pagar Dock Company Ltd., the first joint stock company formed in Singapore, other limited stock companies operating there being registered elsewhere: this may well be strictly incorrect. Before the company was registered an organising committee was announced but Boustead was not among them. He was of course not in Singapore and neither of his Singapore partners were mentioned either. It was announced in *The Straits Times* of 12th September 1863 that 616 $100 shares had been taken up. At an extraordinary meeting on 18th January 1864 the authorised capital was changed to $200,000 (2,000 shares of $100) with power to increase this figure and applications were invited. At the same meeting seven directors, who each had to hold at least 20 shares, were appointed. The partners of Boustead & Co. resident in Singapore, Lipscombe and Young, were not among them and according to Bogaars' history of the company there is no record of the names of all the early holders. It was only when an issue of preference shares was made in 1869 that Boustead himself became involved and gave support to the raising of funds in London. In later years partners in Boustead who were in Singapore acted as directors.

It was agreed on 31st January 1868 at a meeting in Boustead's office in the City, attended by many merchants and others, to form the Straits Settlements Association.[2] Those who had retired from the East in particular saw the need for a lobbying body in London. It was from the start dedicated to the defence of British commercial interests in South East Asia. Although most, if not all, of those involved knew his story there was an understood code of conduct and his past would not have been mentioned. Investigative and trouble making journalists did not exist.

An indication of his attitude in business can be inferred from a case he took to court the previous year in which he sued a Mr. Auton for £500. *'I have no idea of losing £500 for want of looking after it'* he wrote to his lawyer. Business continued much as usual and Shaw continued in the partnership until he retired at the end of 1878.

In October 1881 Boustead was a witness in court at the trial of a man named Clarke who, dressed as a clergyman, called upon various people fraudulently soliciting contributions to his *'homes at Enfield for destitute children whom he had rescued from the street'*. He had been approached twice, in December 1880 and June 1881 when he gave the man £5.

On 12th December 1884 writing to Beng Swee who unbeknownst to Boustead had died five weeks earlier he referred to *'the contract for the new steamer was very carefully made by Mr. Thos Cuthbertson and a very efficient person appointed to superintend the building who reports to us the work as it progresses and you may rely on no pains being spared on our part to secure the steamer being finished to your entire satisfaction.'*

---

[2] National Archives, Kew CO/273/24, pp. 189 & 199 and CO/273/25 p. 423.

Chapter 19

Afterwards

The first requirement in his will was that his *'funeral be conducted in the most simple and inexpensive manner.'* He was buried on 3rd March 1888 in his own vault in Norwood Cemetery joining his daughters Jane, Helen and his wife Charlotte, the officiating priest being a Baptist minister. The Will, with codicil attached, was proved on 13th April by his executors W. W. Shaw, Jasper Young and Isaac Henderson, the estate totalling £223,933.1.4. £75,000 was left to his grandson, William Edward Graham Niven who was now aged 13. The balance of about £145,000 was left in trust to the Executors (who were each to be paid £2,000 for their work):

> 'to apply to such purposes as they think fit as shall most fully & effectually carry out my own views and wishes in relation to the application thereof, they being well acquainted therewith and I am fully satisfied to leave the matter in their hands without any limit.'

Specific legacies, to cover operating expenditures and not to be regarded as endowments, of £5,000 were made to the Reverend Spurgeon, Stockwell Orphanage (where Spurgeon was president), The Baptist

Missionary Society and to William Birch,[1] a merchant of Chepstow Street, Manchester. Two others of £3,000 each went to the Metropolitan Tabernacle Colportage Association and the East End Juvenile Mission (which was under the direction of Dr Barnardo).

Once probate had been obtained and as investments were liquidated the Trustees began the task of distribution. Much was given to Baptist charities, orphanages, boys' homes and hospitals. £2,000 went to the Royal National Lifeboat Association and an additional £2,000 to Dr Barnardo. In addition £5,101.5.6 was distributed to Mrs. J. L. Parr, who had married Edward Parr in 1862 and was the sister of his deceased wife. A further £3,000 was passed to Miss L. M. Parr (a niece of Mr. Boustead's deceased wife), being balance of a marriage portion. £3,000 went to the Misses Fraser but whether they were relations or Baptists who did good works we do not know. Sums of £2,500 each were paid to Charles Frolich (who had served in Singapore for about seven years from 1866) who was now a book–keeper at the London office, John Stow Young (who had also served in the Singapore and Penang offices, most probably a cousin of Jasper Young and was now Corresponding Clerk at the London office) and James Wise (Clerk in the London office and who may have been the brother of Joseph Wise referred to in Boustead's letter to him of 22nd June 1852 *'I have got your brother here and I think he will do')*. Amounts ranging from £1,000 for a Mrs. M. S. Mollen Gothenburgh, daughter of an old clerk to £10 for a Mr. Bird *'an old promise to a former clerk'* were made as was £4,390 to the Straits Benevolent Fund *'portion of £5,000 intended'*.

In all £96,531.8.6 had been distributed and then, on 1st March 1889 lawyers appointed by Boustead's son–in–law Niven, on behalf of his young son, told the Trustees that the distribution was totally void and that the son should inherit the entire estate. This caused panic. They took out

---

[1] Birch, who was born in 1837, would only have been in his teens when Boustead lived in Manchester. He later became a merchant and Baptist minister and in 1863 during the *'cotton famine'* began fostering children informally and then bought houses in Cornbrook St, in Hulme for use as an orphanage. He employed a matron, Mrs. Blinkhorn to run the place. In 1866, there were 29 children and by 1868 it had risen to 43 with around 50 in 1871. The orphanage closed in the 1890s after William had moved to Auckland, New Zealand in the second half of 1889.

a summons to have it declared in court that the trust of the residual estate was charitable and thus legal. This view was supported by Shaw's affidavit, but he rather ruined the show stating that his role *was 'to patronise the diseased's [sic] relations for whom provision ought to have been made'*. The expert lawyer consulted said they had no case and confirmed that the whole estate should go to the grandson, making the trustees personally liable for the amount already distributed. After much negotiation and discussion the case was submitted to the Attorney General who in August 1890, much to the relief of the Trustees, approved a compromise settlement and the donation of £10,000 for good works in Singapore. There a local committee was formed to decide how it should be spent. Of this £1,000 was to go to the Trustees of St. Andrew's House and it was decided (mainly at the urging of Messrs. Thompson (of Tanjong Pagar Dock Company and involved with three Masonic groups) and Thomas [or Thomsen] who, according to the *Straits Times* article of 24th June 1892, were the fathers of the scheme) that the balance should be for the construction and maintenance of a centre for visiting seamen, to be named the Boustead Institute. This three–storey building was later built near the entry to the Tanjong Pagar docks on a site donated by the Tanjong Pagar Dock Company and was formally inaugurated by the Governor in the presence of a large crowd of the great and good on 2nd July 1892 (Figure 35).

As a well–patronised recreation centre for seafarers it provided a reading room, library, billiards, a refreshment bar serving only beer, no spirits, and accommodation for a small number of seamen. Sold in 1958, the new owners allowed a Nigerian, one 'Toby', to open a *'watering hole'* on the ground floor but he was expelled from Singapore in September 1959. The bar reopened under a new owner until the building was demolished in 1976.

It seems that relations between Niven, his daughter Helen's widower, and Boustead had been frosty at best. Niven wanted to assure himself that he would get maintenance for his son. He had moved from Prince's Square in 1885 when the boy was eight to 15 Dean's Yard, part of the site of the old Westminster Monastery not occupied by the Abbey. As an architect he may have been involved in some way in the building of Church House there and his son may have been studying at Westminster School.

During all this time Eduardo had liquidated all the stocks remaining to him, and, seeking more funds, wrote to the Trustees asking for his inheritance. They replied promptly that there was none and thought no more about it.

An unexpected letter arrived in June 1892 from a Spanish lawyer acting on behalf of Mrs. Edward Boustead claiming the inheritance she alleged had been promised by her father–in–law, which claim was refuted. Eduardo then set off for Singapore to find witnesses who would back up his claim that his mother had married Boustead. Charles Carnie, C. R. Rigg, James Guthrie and W. R. Paterson, all old–time residents of Singapore, meanwhile gave sworn statements in favour of the defendants. The Trustees' lawyers demanded that Eduardo's witnesses in Singapore be examined under oath, but he took no action and a court order to that effect was obtained. When the first two witnesses were examined, their evidence was damaging and seeing this Eduardo, without advising his London lawyer, ordered that no further examinations take place. He visited Singapore a second time when he registered as Mr. Roy and rounded up two old natives as new witnesses. With some difficulty he located his mother's grave which he found overgrown and arranged for it to be cleaned before returning to England with Syed Mahmoud, another 'witness'.

A letter dated 21st December 1893 addressed to Edward Boustead was delivered to Edward Boustead & Co., 34 Leadenhall Street and was opened by them thinking it was a business–related letter. It was intended for Eduardo and seemed to point to a serious attempt to tamper with Janedah's tombstone. Later one of the two new witnesses in Singapore admitted he was employed to help the plaintiff falsify evidence.

In due course the case was won by the Trustees and final disbursements were made to charitable institutions.

The later fate of Eduardo or how he earned an income is not known apart from the fact that the 1901 census shows him living at 18 Guildford Street, Holborn, London with his wife, son and younger daughter who married a Belgian in 1917. Eduardo died on 11th December 1921 in Brussels. He had been a good friend of the young doctor José Rizal, the Filipino nationalist, who had stayed with them in Biarritz in 1891 and who had wanted to marry his daughter Nellie. To do so she insisted that he become a Protestant like herself, but he felt unable to do so and they parted good friends. He was executed in the Philippines in 1896. She went on to marry Daniel Earnshaw of Manila on 25th September 1895 at St. Andrews Cathedral, Singapore and was later to be divorced sometime before 1916 when he remarried.

Figure 23: Edward Boustead (1800 – 1888).
Public domain, via Wikimedia Commons.

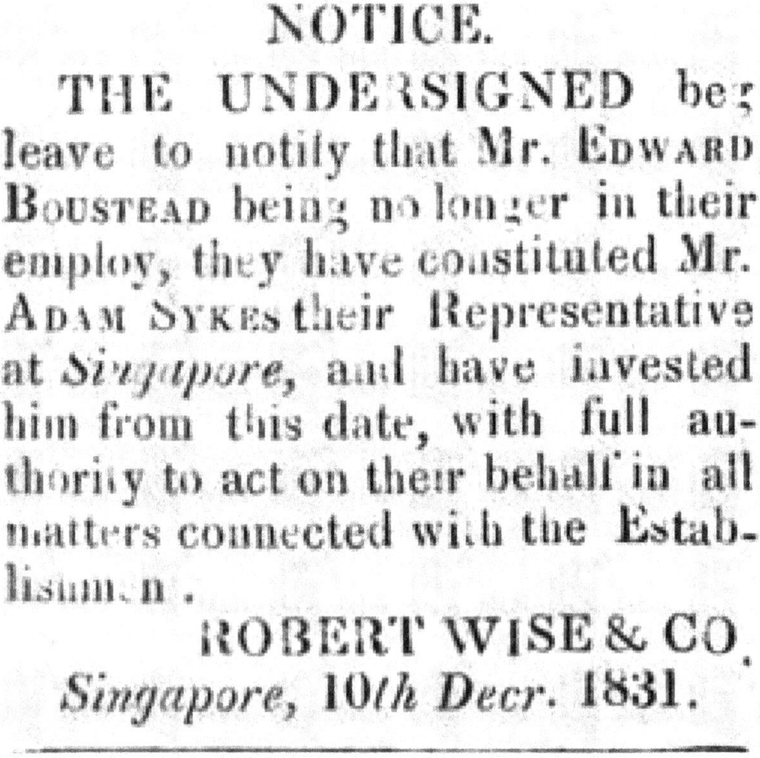

NOTICE.

THE UNDERSIGNED beg leave to notify that Mr. EDWARD BOUSTEAD being no longer in their employ, they have constituted Mr. ADAM SYKES their Representative at *Singapore*, and have invested him from this date, with full authority to act on their behalf in all matters connected with the Establishment.

ROBERT WISE & CO.

Singapore, 10th Decr. 1831.

Figure 24: Robert Wise & Co. Notice. Excerpt from the *Singapore Chronicle*.
Source: *Singapore Chronicle*, 10 December 1831.

Figure 25: George Bennett & Siamang Illustration
Source: Bennett, G. (2012) *Wanderings in New South Wales, Batavia, Pedir Coast, Singapore, And China: Being The Journal Of A Naturalist In Those Countries During 1832, 1833, And 1834, Volume 1.* Nabu Press, pp. 142–173.

Figure 26: Lady Gordon Advertisement. Excerpt from the *Singapore Chronicle*.
Source: *Singapore Chronicle*, 26 October 1831.

Figure 27: Detail from a print based on drawings made during the visit of the French naval vessels *L'Astrolabe* and *La Zélée* from 28th June to 3rd July 1839 showing the House of Twenty–Seven Pillars in the centre. Private Collection.

Figure 28: The House of Twenty–Seven Pillars taken circa 1867 after the original 'Monkey Bridge' had been replaced.

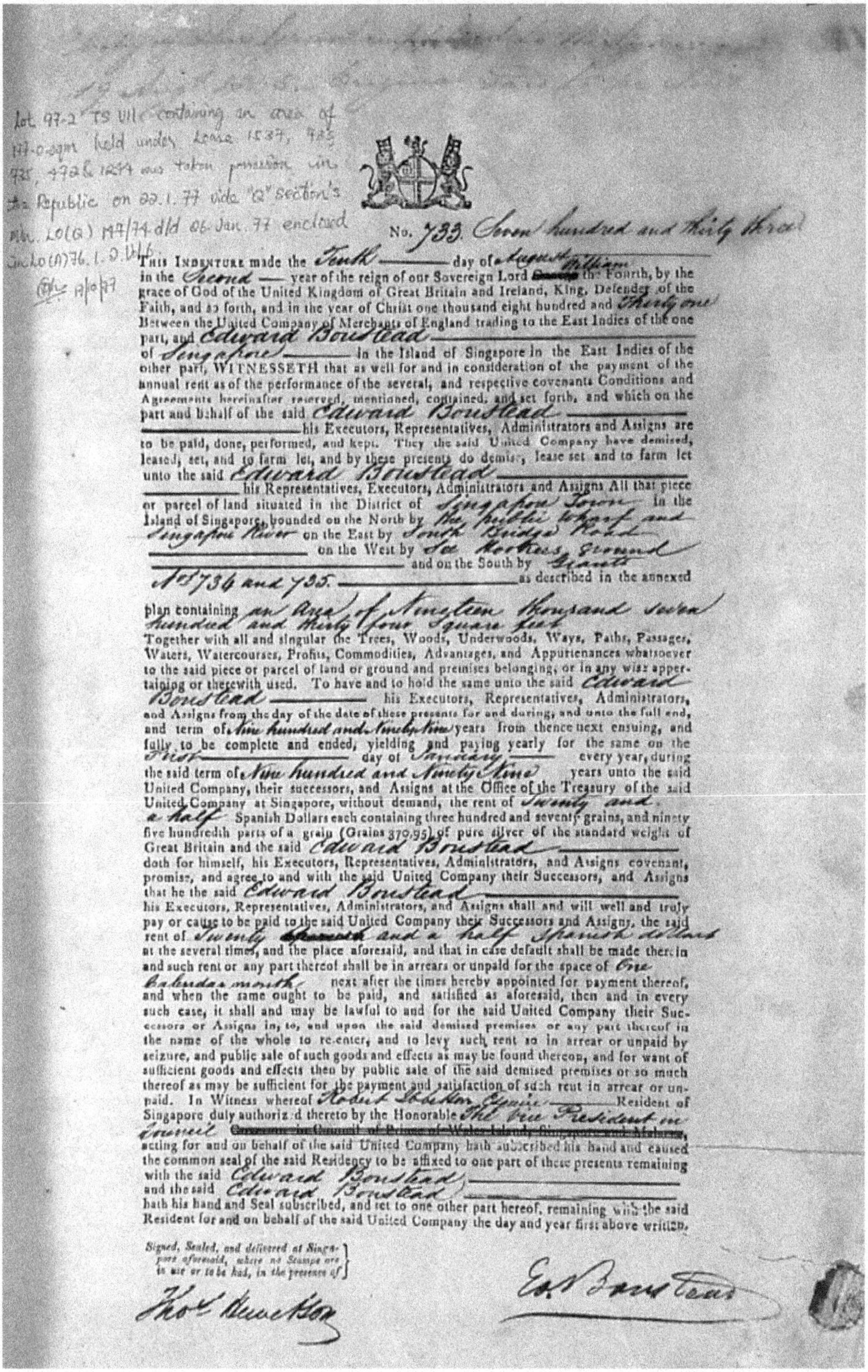

Lot 97-2 TS VII containing an area of 177-0 sqm held under Lease 1537, 733, 735, 472 & 1274 was taken possession in the Republic on 22.1.77 vide "Q" Section's Min. LO(Q) 197/74 d/d 06 Jan. 77 enclosed ... LO(A) 76.1.0 Vol 6 ... 17/10/77

No. 733. Seven hundred and thirty three

THIS INDENTURE made the Tenth day of August in the Second year of the reign of our Sovereign Lord William the Fourth, by the grace of God of the United Kingdom of Great Britain and Ireland, King, Defender of the Faith, and so forth, and in the year of Christ one thousand eight hundred and Thirty one Between the United Company of Merchants of England trading to the East Indies of the one part, and Edward Boustead of Singapore in the Island of Singapore in the East Indies of the other part, WITNESSETH that as well for and in consideration of the payment of the annual rent as of the performance of the several, and respective covenants Conditions and Agreements hereinafter reserved, mentioned, contained, and set forth, and which on the part and behalf of the said Edward Boustead his Executors, Representatives, Administrators and Assigns are to be paid, done, performed, and kept. They the said United Company have demised, leased, set, and to farm let, and by these presents do demise, lease set and to farm let unto the said Edward Boustead his Representatives, Executors, Administrators and Assigns All that piece or parcel of land situated in the District of Singapore Town in the Island of Singapore, bounded on the North by the public wharf and Singapore River on the East by South Bridge Road on the West by See Hookees ground and on the South by Grants No. 736 and 735. as described in the annexed plan containing an Area of Nineteen thousand seven hundred and thirty four Square feet Together with all and singular the Trees, Woods, Underwoods, Ways, Paths, Passages, Waters, Watercourses, Profits, Commodities, Advantages, and Appurtenances whatsoever to the said piece or parcel of land or ground and premises belonging, or in any wise appertaining or therewith used. To have and to hold the same unto the said Edward Boustead his Executors, Representatives, Administrators, and Assigns from the day of the date of these presents for and during, and unto the full end, and term of Nine hundred and Ninety Nine years from thence next ensuing, and fully to be complete and ended, yielding and paying yearly for the same on the First day of January every year, during the said term of Nine hundred and Ninety Nine years unto the said United Company, their successors, and Assigns at the Office of the Treasury of the said United Company at Singapore, without demand, the rent of Twenty and a half Spanish Dollars each containing three hundred and seventy grains, and ninety five hundredth parts of a grain (Grains 370.95) of pure silver of the standard weight of Great Britain and the said Edward Boustead doth for himself, his Executors, Representatives, Administrators, and Assigns covenant, promise, and agree to and with the said United Company their Successors, and Assigns that he the said Edward Boustead his Executors, Representatives, Administrators, and Assigns shall and will well and truly pay or cause to be paid to the said United Company their Successors and Assigns, the said rent of Twenty ~~Spanish~~ and a half Spanish dollars at the several times, and the place aforesaid, and that in case default shall be made therein and such rent or any part thereof shall be in arrears or unpaid for the space of One Calendar month next after the times hereby appointed for payment thereof, and when the same ought to be paid, and satisfied as aforesaid, then and in every such case, it shall and may be lawful to and for the said United Company their Successors or Assigns in, to, and upon the said demised premises or any part thereof in the name of the whole to re-enter, and to levy such rent so in arrear or unpaid by seizure, and public sale of such goods and effects as may be found thereon, and for want of sufficient goods and effects then by public sale of the said demised premises or so much thereof as may be sufficient for the payment and satisfaction of such rent in arrear or unpaid. In Witness whereof Robert Ibbetson Esquire Resident of Singapore duly authorized thereto by the Honorable The Vice President in Council ~~Governor in Council of Prince of Wales Island, Singapore and Malacca~~, acting for and on behalf of the said United Company hath subscribed his hand and caused the common seal of the said Residency to be affixed to one part of these presents remaining with the said Edward Boustead and the said Edward Boustead hath his hand and Seal subscribed, and set to one other part hereof, remaining with the said Resident for and on behalf of the said United Company the day and year first above written.

Signed, Sealed, and delivered at Singapore aforesaid, where no Stamps are in use or to be had, in the presence of

Thos. Hewetson

Edw. Boustead

Figure 29: Indenture dated 10th August 1831 covering the site of the House of Twenty-seven Pillars.

PUBLIC SALE OF VALUABLE LEASE-HOLD PROPERTY.

WILL BE SOLD BY PUBLIC AUCTION,

At 12 o'clock on Saturday, the 15th June next.

ON THE PREMISES,

THE whole of BRIDGE PROPERTY on the River side at the South end of the old Bridge ; consisting of two excellent Dwelling Houses with Out-offices, and extensive Godowns underneath, and five small Godowns behind, now renting at 5 dollars per month each. The whole are built on Grant No. 733 containing an area of 19,731 square feet, held on a Lease from the Honourable East India Company for 999 years. Merchandize can be landed or shipped from the wharf at all states of the *Tide.* Part of the purchase, money will be allowed to remain on mortgage if requisite. Further particulars may be known and permission obtained to view the premises by application to

BOUSTEAD, SCHWABE & Co.

Singapore, 7th May, 1844.

Figure 30: Bridge Property Public Auction Notice. Excerpt from the *Singapore Free Press*. Source: *Singapore Free Press*, 7th May 1844.

Figure 31: House No. 1 (Lots 554.2 and 555) in later years, probably about 1860.
Photograph in private collection.

Figure 32: Broughton Hall, at Yew Tree Lane West Derby, Liverpool, built in 1860
for Gustav Christian Schwabe.

Figure 33: Clapham Park — 1893 Map.

Figure 34: The Epergne Presented by Boustead.
The Peranakan Museum.

Figure 35: The Boustead Institute circa 1901 before the advent of electric trams. Photograph in private collection.

Figure 36: Brechin Castle, 1804, by James Fittler, *Scotia Depicta*.

Figure 37: An 1870s Sachtler photograph originally incorrectly labelled 'View of Mt Palmer'. It is in fact a view from Mount Palmer of Guthrie's Hill behind Guthrie's Village.

Figure 38: The Bridge over the Creek. Photo taken in 1881.

Figure 39: David Skene Napier by John Syme.
Source: Artnet.

Figure 40: Signor José d'Almeida's musical party
Source: Edward Cree 1844.

Figure 41: Jackson's drawing. 1823 National Archives, Kew, London.

Figure 42: East Indiamen in Convoy. Nicholas Pocock.
Source: Wikimedia Commons.

Figure 43: East India Company Flag 1801 – 1858.
Source: Wikipedia.

Figure 44: Balls of Opium L'Illustration 1896 Opium in Indochina.
Fernand Honore.

Part 3

Alexander Guthrie

Chapter 20

Biography

Brechin Castle in the Scottish county of Angus (Figure 36), part of the Dalhousie Estates, still stands proudly on a massive rock bluff above the River Southesk and the small town of Brechin, on the site of a much older fortress belonging to the Scottish Kings. The house was reconstructed in the 1700s and incorporates parts of the original Castle dating back to the 13th Century. At the end of the 18th Century it was the home of the Fox–Maule family who were related to one Alexander Guthrie, a farmer living three miles to the northwest at Burnside Farm which he had inherited from his father, the great grandson of the Laird of Guthrie Castle, located a few miles to the South of Brechin. They were an old and well–respected family but faced the same problem as have many others over the years when the family land was insufficient to support younger brothers and their families. Through the kindness of the Fox–Maules, Alexander's young brother Thomas had been introduced and apprenticed to the Marine Service of the East India Company and gone to sea at the age of 12 in 1790. He became a close friend of another boy who had joined at the same time, one Thomas Talbot Harrington who some years later was promoted to command the *Ganges* bound for China. Among his passengers on that voyage were Thomas Raffles, his wife Olivia, his sister Mary Anne and 16–year–old Robert Ibbetson, all destined for Penang. They disembarked at Madras in mid–August to join another ship while *Ganges* continued to Calcutta reaching Penang only in November. Ganges sank on the return voyage, all crew and passengers being saved, and Harrington was given further vessels to command. Some years later terms and conditions changed, and he decided to settle in St Helena. Having made extensive preparation he found no welcome from the newly appointed Governor and so proceeded to South Africa where he established himself and developed a business supplying St Helena where Napoleon was now in exile.

Alexander Guthrie's youngest son, also christened Alexander but always known as 'Sandy', had been born just before New Year's Eve on 30th December 1796. He idolised his uncle Thomas and, looking for a job given that the Napoleonic Wars were over, asked him for an introduction to his very successful and well–connected businessman friend now based in Cape Town.[1]

Sandy, who now being away from his father we shall call Alexander, and later Guthrie, was welcomed there in 1816. A document is still in existence signed by him on behalf of T. T. Harrington headed:

> 'The Memorial of Thomas Talbot Harrington, Merchant, requesting His Excellency the Right Honorable Lord Charles Henry Somerset, Governor and Commander in Chief at the Cape to permit the shipment by the vessel Marquis of Wellington of 2,000 pounds of flour to St Helena, to the order of Messrs Balcombe & Co, Purveyors to General Buonaparte'.

The choice of vessel seems appropriate.

Raffles, now Sir Thomas, with his second wife sailed from England in *Lady Raffles* for Bencoolen in Sumatra and, after a voyage of 14,244 miles with no calls at intermediate ports, anchored off the town on 19th March 1818, less than a year before his first arrival at Singapore. Once that Settlement had been founded in 1819 Raffles lost no time in writing to all his contacts encouraging them to set up shop there sooner rather than later. It seems probable that Harrington received such a letter and acted upon it as permission was granted by the Governor General in Calcutta on 10th April 1820 for Alexander to travel to *'any of the principal settlements belonging to the said United Company in the East Indies, there to reside*

---

[1] Cunyngham-Brown, S. (1971). *The Traders — A Story of Britain's South-East Asian Commercial Adventure, 1st Edition,* Newman Neame, London, p.17.

*for the transaction of the business of the house of Messrs Harrington &
Company.'*

Until Harrington arrived back from England whence he had departed
at the end of October 1819, expecting to be away less than 12 months and
where his wife had died in March 1820, Alexander could not sail.
Although he may have left aboard an East Indiaman it is more likely that
he took *Mary,* a brig of some 120 tons which had been chartered by
Harrington to serve St Helena but could not now be used for that purpose.
To do so would enable Alexander to take a full cargo with him for sale in
Singapore and on arrival store in the ship, until he had a godown available,
the woollen cloth, cotton twist, nails, axes, knives, clocks, stationery,
brandy and sherry he had brought with him.

He anchored in the Singapore Roads on 27th January 1821, a week or so
short of two years since Raffles had first landed. Rowed ashore past the
various local vessels, prahus and junks lying at anchor and avoiding local
boats serving them, he landed on the beach and asked in halting Malay how
to find his countryman Alex Johnston, who was already an old hand of
nearly three months residence, in the hope that he would give him some
guidance while he found his feet in this alternately dusty and muddy village.
He was not disappointed and was soon able on behalf of Harrington to rent
for a year from John Dunn a bungalow near the Reservoir[2] as well as his
under–used brick–built godown in River Street, a track leading off what was
already grandly known as High Street. Dunn, employed for many years by
the British Government both in Batavia and the island of Banka, had been
sent over in *Indiana* from Bencoolen by Raffles the previous year in charge
of a shipment of nutmeg and clove plants and seeds to be used to start a
Company spice garden.[3] These had been produced in Bencoolen from seeds
and plants collected when the British had been in charge of the Molucca
Islands during 1810 to 1817 and although cloves were by then grown in
other countries the Dutch had previously done their best to prevent nutmegs

---

[2] SSR L5 237 attachment dated 1821.7.11.
[3] *The Journal of the Indian Archipelago and Eastern Asia,* vol. II (1848). "100 Nutmeg
Plants in 3 boxes, 100 Clove Plants in 3 boxes, 1,000 Nutmeg seeds, half of them in a
double row. 350 Clove ditto. 25 large Nutmeg plants and the same number of Cloves."
J. R. Logan, Singapore., p. 558.

being so produced. Dunn was a naturalist and hoped to start his own plantation, a site for which Farquhar, the Resident in charge of Singapore, was
instructed to grant him.[4] He was initially to be employed at a monthly allowance of $100 in the Boat Department of the Master Attendant's Office.
When Farquhar discovered that he could speak fluent Malay his duty was
increased to include the oversight of day labourers carrying out public
works. Government finances were tight and on instructions from Bencoolen
his allowance was, without notice, a few months later reduced to $75 from
1st May 1820. Whether or not he learned it through private correspondence
his position was discontinued with effect from December 1821, although
the official letter advising Farquhar of this was not received by him until 25th
July 1822, indicative of the communication difficulties with Bencoolen.
Dunn had died in Batavia in May 1822 but before leaving Singapore sold
his godown to two newly arrived Armenians, Aristarkies Sarkies and
Sarkies Arratoon Sarkies who wanted it for their own use and were not
prepared to renew the one year lease to Alexander when it expired.[5]

Harrington and his 11–year–old daughter Marianne soon arrived for a
brief stay before continuing on to China to look for business opportunities.
They had spent some time in Malacca where his wife, now deceased, had
relatives living. Alexander, meanwhile, as one of the half dozen or so
European merchants, was persuaded to sign a joint letter to Farquhar concerning the arrest by the Sultan of the Nakhodah (Captain) of the first junk
arriving direct from Amoy in China.[6] This earned them all a strong rebuke
for interfering in political matters but they, in reply, pointed out that it was
the fault of Government insisting that native nakhodahs must pay a courtesy call on the Sultan.

On his arrival in early 1821 Alexander had applied for a piece of
ground and been granted Lot No. 2 on the beach towards Campong Glam.
He had taken no action to develop this as, although a prime site for a personal dwelling, it was not suitable for a godown. When advised that he
was not going to be able to extend his lease on what had been Dunn's
godown he approached Farquhar as a fellow Scot to help him out of this
crisis and in April 1822 wrote to him as follows:

---

[4] SSR L10 124 dated 1819.8.18.
[5] Wright, N. (2019). *The Armenians of Singapore*, Malaysia. Entrepot Publishing, p. 59.
[6] SSR L4 280 and 284.

'In reply to your letter of yesterday's date requesting my opinion of the suitableness of the Plain between the Cantonment and Campong Glam for mercantile purposes and also requesting my opinion of the most eligible situation here for carrying on a general and extensive commerce. I beg leave to state that the principal objections which appear to me against the Plain between the Cantonments and Campong Glam are the shallowness of the sea on the beach along the Plain and the difficulty and expence [sic] that would occur from that, and from the considerable surf which breaks on that part of the beach, in landing and shipping merchandize and which would be all avoided by having the warehouses along the banks of the Singapore River and between that and the Cantonments. My opinion therefore is that the most eligible situation here for carrying on a general extensive commerce is the banks of the Singapore River and between that and the Cantonments, particularly so here where much of the produce imported and exported is bulky and of small value.'[7]

Although not stated by him specifically it was only the north bank that was suitable, the only possible ground on the south bank having been allocated by Raffles to Captain Flint, Master Attendant and Raffles' brother–in–law. The rest of the south bank was soft mud and mangrove swamp routinely flooded at high tides and although by now numerous Chinese had built huts on stilts above the water it was not a place one could build anything more substantial. When Farquhar initially found himself unable to help, Alexander threatened to leave the Settlement. This, of course, could not be allowed as others might follow and, strange to say, a site between Ferry point and the Temenggong's compound became available for him. Although not actually on the riverbank he accepted this thankfully and proceeded to build on it. No title deeds were issued and it was clearly accepted that should the site be needed by Government in the future, however unlikely that might seem, he would give it up.

Raffles, after his arrival in October 1822, announced the revocation of all leases on the north bank of the river without compensation which caused much ill feeling. Guthrie wrote to him on 16th December:

'Agreeable to your proclamation with date 2nd instant unwinding and annulling the grants of lands made at Singapore by the Resident Lieut.

---

[7] SSR L7 183.

Col Farquhar, and requesting that the parties who thought themselves aggrieved might state the scene in writing previous to the 20th instant, I therefore beg to lay before you the condition on which I received from Lieut. Col. Farquhar the ground on which my house and godowns now stand. Arriving at Singapore in the early part of February 1821 with a considerable investment of British goods, I was so lucky as to procure for rent for a twelve month a brick built house & godowns, but at the expiry of that period the owners sold it to certain Armenian merchants who, wanting the house and godowns for their own accommodation did not chuse [sic] renting them. Having then goods on hand to a valuable amount and not being able to rent godowns where I could place them with safety, I was under the necessity of applying to the Resident for a grant of ground to build a house and godowns, and he, on consideration of the case, gave me that on which my house and godowns now stand, under the conditions that should it at any period be required by the Company, I should be obliged to give it up to them on being paid the amount I had expended on the same.

I have the honor to be, Sir, your most obedient and humble servant,
A. Guthrie'[8]

In due course, despite a letter from Farquhar to Raffles concerning *'the unfounded assertion by Guthrie that should it be required by the Company he should be obliged to give it up on being paid the same as he had expended.'* Raffles relented.[9] The house with brick foundation, formed timber superstructure, a tiled roof, and with outhouses some of timber and some of attap, was valued at $2,000 for workmanship and $1,500 for materials by F. J. Bernard and once full compensation was, in due course, paid and construction completed, Guthrie moved his godowns across the river to the new Boat Quay.[10]

There were strict rules to prevent unauthorised import of opium which did not come from the Company's own sources, but he received permission in 1822 to import 27 chests of Turkey Opium for reexport, against security.[11]

---

[8] SSR L6 151.
[9] SSR L11 149.
[10] SSR L6 190.
[11] SSR L13 24, L13 21.

Business was not easy, but on occasions commodities could be sold to Government, and shortly before Christmas 1822 Guthrie tendered 1,000 bags of Bengal Koongy rice of 2 maunds each at Spanish Dollars three and one eighth ($3.60) [sic] per bag payable by bills on Bengal at exchange 200 Sicca Rupees per $100: to be delivered at A. Guthrie's charge into the Company godown in course of the ensuing week.

It seems, although there are no details, that Guthrie applied to Raffles for a further grant of land. The result might be inferred from the tone of Farquhar's letter dated 12th February 1823 to his assistant Bonham, Registrar, which read *'Sir, You will herewith receive two letters, one from Captain Methven and the other from Mr. Guthrie applying for grants of land, with the Lieut. Governor's remarks on the back thereof, which you will be pleased to make known to the parties accordingly.'* It may have referred to the hill and land at Tanjong Pagar which Guthrie acquired at an early stage. A year later Duncan reported in his diary, having reached the spot by sampan, that Guthrie's coolies were making good progress in clearing the valley between his hill and Mount Palmer (Figure 37).

It was only just short of a month later in March that Farquhar was attacked and stabbed by an assailant and was carried into Guthrie's house, bleeding profusely from a chest wound. The assailant was killed, and Farquhar recovered but the incident emphasised the small size of the European community viz–a–viz the *'Native'*.

Harrington and his daughter had come back from China at the beginning of 1823. Guthrie and Harrington in April that year tendered to supply Spanish Dollars in cash against Bills of Exchange drawn on the Company in Calcutta. Accepted for $3,500 at an exchange rate of 207½, this was a way to transfer funds overseas. He wrote on 2nd May to Harrington, who was temporarily away in Malacca, telling him the news of Farquhar's dismissal and of his own appointment as Magistrate with effect from the 15th. The official swearing in of all twelve appointed magistrates took place on 2nd June when all swore:

'We the undersigned being appointed and commissioned to act as Magistrates of Singapore under Regulation No III of 1823 entitled *'A regulation for the establishment of a provisional magistracy and the enforcement of an efficient Police at Singapore with certain Regulations*

& Provisions for the Administration of justice in cases of emergency' and also under Regulation No II [sic] of 1823 entitled 'a regulation in furtherance of the objects of Regulation No II of 1823 and containing additional provisions for the administration of justice at Singapore' do hereby make oath and swear that we in execution of the duties thereof will do equal right to the poor and the sick, without favor or partiality to any, and to the best of our judgment and conscience and according to such rules and regulations as are now and may hereafter be laid down for the Guidance of the magistrates of Singapore, so help us God.'

Magistrates, despite their official duties, are human and Guthrie's temper was not always completely under control. A young country–born writer from Malacca, John Sergi, was up before him on a charge of drunken affray. Receiving a dressing down from a foreigner as young as himself wounded Sergi's pride and he complained to the Resident, Dr. John Crawfurd that Guthrie had intentionally set his dogs on him as he passed his house. An official letter dated 14th October 1823 was sent:

'To A. Guthrie Esquire, Singapore. Sir, I beg herewith to enclose copies of affidavits sworn to, touching a complaint made by a country-born Portuguese inhabitant of this place, named John Sergi, against you for an assault, and request you will be pleased to favour me with your reply for the information of the Rt. Hon'ble the Governor General in Council. I have &ca. Signed J. Crawfurd, Resident.'

This was a serious matter and could, though unlikely, lead to his expulsion from Singapore. He had dogs which were boisterous and inclined to bark at passers–by. He responded at once and the following day received a further letter from the Resident:

'I beg leave to acknowledge the receipt of your letter of yesterday's date stating that you had been informed that my assistant Mr. Bonham had, while sitting with me in public court, made an attack upon your character by openly asserting that it was a common practice with you to set your dog on persons passing by your house, & requesting me to call upon Mr. Bonham to substantiate his assertion by evidence. It gives me great pleasure to inform you in reply to this statement that the charge alleged against Mr. Bonham is incorrect. Mr. Bonham made no assertion whatever derogatory to your character in open court. What he stated in regard to you was incidental, and arose out of a conversation purposely made a private and confidential one by removing it out of the public court into an adjoining chamber. The assertion made by him to the best of my recollection amounted to this, that you made it a frequent practice to set your dogs on other dogs passing by, but not on passengers or travelers. This amounted at best to no more than charging you with practice somewhat inconvenient to the public but as everything stated by Mr. Bonham to me in reference to this subject tended to extenuate, rather than to aggravate, the share you had in this transaction. I feel assured that there could have been no intention whatever on the present occasion to create a bias against you. Whether there was or was not, however, I can with great sincerity assure you that such an effect has not been produced. I trust after this explanation and the pains I have already take personally to assure you on the subject that any further discussion of it will not be considered necessary.'

Johnston and Maxwell poured oil on troubled waters and in due course bad blood thinned. However relations between Guthrie and Bonham remained cool for some time to come.

The partnership with Harrington had been amicably dissolved on 8th November 1823 but he and his daughter remained until 8th March 1824 when they sailed for Malacca early in the morning, having boarded the vessel the previous evening after an enjoyable dinner at Alex Johnston's house enlivened, according to W. S. Duncan in his diary, by Harrington's *'jokes and pregnant bursts of laughter'*.

His new partnership with one James Scott Clark, a quiet, unobtrusive and efficient man, had been signed by Guthrie on 1st Feb 1824. Two days later Guthrie and nine others were appointed to form a Coroner's Inquest into the death of Captain John Hale and James Young of *Philotax* who had been killed when their ship, which was beached, rolled over on to them. Death by misadventure was the verdict.[12]

It was early in 1825 that rumours reached Singapore of a paddle steamer being built at Sourabaya for service in the Dutch East Indies.

---

[12] *Singapore Medical Journal* 2005.

Subsequently a certain Mr. Morris contacted the Master Attendant, Captain Flint with a prospectus for obtaining a steam vessel from the United Kingdom to run a regular service between Calcutta and Batavia, calling at Penang, Malacca, Singapore, Rhio and Minto en route. Flint called a meeting of subscribers at the Court House on 3ʳᵈ October 1825 and a committee consisting of Guthrie, Maxwell, Paton, Read, Syme and Spottiswoode was elected to take the matter forward. No further record is available, and it seems the project withered on the vine.[13]

The next few years passed with a lot of hard work, buying local produce such as rattans, tin, pepper, sugar, gambier etc. from native merchants, shipping it to Europe, and receiving for sale consignments of various goods from Britain and opium from India. Following the receipt in February 1827 of news of Raffles' death, he was on a committee to decide on a memorial to perpetuate the name and to raise funds therefor. He gave $25, rather less than other merchants.[14]

In 1828 the Government was looking for a new Cantonment site for the troops and he tendered what he thought was a suitable plot of land. It turned out it was not considered by the Board at Penang as required for public purposes, but they directed that the Superintendent of Lands would report if it were suitable for a cantonment. There is no record of the final outcome, if any.

Along Boat Quay near Guthrie's godowns lay a small public bridge over the creek which, along with many others in the low-lying swampy island, was forever in need of repair (Figure 38). In April 1829 repairs were officially authorised and by October the same year completed.

Starting in 1828 Grand Juries were called to decide on which criminal cases were to be brought to Court and to bring attention to matters concerning the state of the Settlement. Names of those regarded as being suitable were drawn up and 13 names balloted for attendance on each occasion. Guthrie was first balloted in February 1829 to scrutinise seven murder cases and eight others. At the end of three days, the Foreman (Edward Presgrave, who was himself a civil servant) in the presentment of the Jury drew Government's attention to the need for Night Watchmen, a

---

[13] *The Oriental Herald and Colonial Review*, Vol 10., p. 369.
[14] *Singapore Chronicle* 1827.2.1.

'*pukka*' bridge over the freshwater stream, a long–standing complaint, the state of the bridge across the Singapore River and finally the urgent need for a Pauper Hospital and how to fund it.[15]

Raffles himself had ordered the establishment of a Pork Farm in November 1823. This, of course, was not an instruction to Major Farquhar to start breeding pigs. It was a way of raising funds for Government by annually auctioning the monopoly right for an individual to slaughter hogs and sell the pork on a retail basis, against a monthly advance payment. It had been done in Penang, not as a revenue raiser but rather to fund a poor house for indigent and sick local people.

Dr. Crawfurd, the second Resident, discontinued the farm on the basis that it was effectively a tax paid by only one part of the population, the Chinese. For religious reasons the Malays, Jews and some others did not eat pork.

By the end of the 1820s, the ever–increasing numbers of Chinese public beggars, who since their emigration to the Settlement had fallen victim to disease such as to prevent them from earning an honest livelihood, was causing rising concern to the European community. The wheels of Government moved surprisingly quickly and only just over a year later it was reported by the *Singapore Chronicle* on 22nd April 1830 that the Pork Farm had been awarded for a year at a monthly fee of $820. Special regulations for this were promulgated.

'It consists in the exclusive privilege of killing hogs and selling pork within the Settlement. No person can kill a hog for an entertainment or for family use without a licence from the farmer who shall have authority to demand one Spanish Dollar for every hog killed. The renter or farmer, however, shall not exercise any control or interference with hogs killed by European butchers for sale to Europeans, or by Europeans for their own use, they being exempt from the operation of the regulation. The farmer, further, is not to demand a higher price for fresh pork that 22 cents per catty nor is he allowed to sell unhealthy hogs or weighing less than 60 catties or blow water into the meat, under a penalty of paying 50 Sicca rupees. Importers of salt pork from any of the adjacent states shall

---

[15] *Singapore Chronicle* 1829.2.26.

furnish the renter with an account of the whole previous to landing. In default to pay 50 Sicca rupees. All the revenue that may result from the vesting of this farm shall be appropriated to the purposes of supporting a Native Poor House and Infirmary for the benefit of such fixed residents of the Settlements as may from time to time require such privilege.'

Temporary accommodation was put up and in March 1831 some sixty lepers and other diseased persons were being supported.

Following the formation of the Straits Settlements as a Presidency in 1826 official costs had soared to an unacceptable level and only four years later in 1830 the territory was downgraded to a Residency under Bengal. With this change came drastic austerity. No longer was there a Governor in Penang, nor Resident Councillors in Singapore and Malacca. In their place, at vastly reduced salaries and allowances were a Resident and two Assistant Residents, none of whose titles gave them authority to administer justice. The Court system closed down.

It has been written that as Guthrie had now been away from Scotland for 13 years and felt that, with Clark running the office well, the time had come to go back on furlough. Apart from reasons of health this would give him an opportunity to see Lady Raffles whose interests in Singapore he had been looking after. In addition he might find a suitable younger member of the family at home to come out to learn the business and eventually become a partner. This suggestion, though logical, seems unlikely. He sailed on 14th November 1829 in *Agnes* for Calcutta and if he from there travelled on to Britain, he could hardly have arrived before mid–May. As it was, his nephew James, aged 17, sailed from the Clyde in *Alexander* on 16th June via Madeira, St Helena and Batavia, arriving in Singapore on 1st January 1830 with two fellow European passengers as well as *'two Chinese ladies and a Chinaman'* about whom Mrs. Balestier wrote in 1834:

'There are but two Chinese women in the Settlement. It is death for women to leave the [Chinese] Empire. These two women have been in England and are sisters, and have little feet. They were smuggled out of China and kept for a show while in England. They speak English and have a good many visitors, I have not yet seen them, although they live but a short distance from us. They are wives to one man who is a house carpenter.'

Guthrie himself was *'out-station'*, arriving in *Penang Merchant* from Calcutta or Penang three weeks later just in time to witness the big fire on 7th February. The Guthrie & Clark godowns were spared through herculean efforts and the magistrates gave a dinner four days later to thank the European officers of the 25th Madras Native Infantry, the Commander of *Madeline*, a free country trader, and his crew for their efforts in extinguishing the blaze.[16]

In February 1830 as Chairman of a group of leading merchants he published three agreed resolutions. First, that on account of the losses sustained in the late fire, the sufferers should not be harassed for immediate payment for their present debts, provided they showed a disposition to act fairly and honestly towards their creditors. Secondly, that in consequence of much inconvenience having been experienced from the system which has hitherto prevailed here, of the native dealers not liquidating their debts as they become due (nor of paying interest on the account), upon all sales which take place after the 1st March next, interest shall be regularly charged in account, at the current rate, after the expiration of the stipulated credit. Thirdly, that the rates of commission and godown charges agreed to at a meeting of the merchants held on the 16th October 1824 be rescinded, and the annexed rates be substituted from and after 30th April next.[17]

He was appointed Justice of the Peace with effect from 1st June. In August in a court case Syme v Ong he gave evidence which may or may not have helped Robert Diggles, the plaintiff, recently arrived head of Syme & Co., to the effect that a few days after the 5th February he had heard one Kong Tuan state that he was not a partner of the defendant.[18] In November the firm Hunter Watt & Co., successors to Morgans Hunter & Co. assigned to him as joint trustee all their assets for the benefit of their creditors and in December advertised their property for sale.

On the night of Sunday 23rd January 1831 a daring burglary took place at his godown. It appeared that entry had been gained through the

---

[16] *Singapore Chronicle* 1830.2.11.

[17] *Singapore Chronicle* 1830.2.25.

[18] *Singapore Chronicle* 1830.8.12.

next–door former premises of Armstrong & Co. which were under repair. The burglars then opened a part of the roof, let themselves down and succeeded in carrying off a quantity of blue English *moorees* [cloth] to the value of nearly 600 Spanish Dollars. Four carpenters who were sleeping in the adjoining house were arrested on suspicion but subsequently let out on bail.[19]

The company was, around this time, acting as property agent for the owners of a number of houses, godowns and other premises. These included Napier & Co's godowns in River Street, Napier's house in Campong Glam, the house and hill called Raeburn *'lately occupied by Charles Scott',* the house at the corner of High Street, another house at Campong Glam and the house and godowns formerly occupied by Holdsworth Smithson & Co.

A public meeting called by the Sheriff, following correspondence in the press, was held on 8th October 1831 to protest at the continued absence of a court of justice in the Settlement and to adopt such measures as might be considered best calculated to obtain the re-establishment of a court of justice in Singapore. The copies of the petition, later signed by almost all English–speaking gentlemen in the Settlement, to both Houses of Parliament were signed by Guthrie, Boustead, Diggles, Shaw and Fraser and dispatched in *Fanny* on 16th November. The duplicates went off in *Colonel Young* which sailed on 24th November. To send duplicates by a later vessel was normal practice at this time to insure against one or the other set being lost in transit. The practice continued in commercial firms for many years, and in the case of banks well into the twentieth century. A satisfactory answer addressed to Guthrie was written by Charles Grant of the India Board on 15th June 1832 and received by him in early December.

Before this the titles Governor and Resident Councillor had been reinstated, without much of their former power, allowing the Charter of Justice terms to be fulfilled. Ibbetson, now Governor, and Bonham called the strangely named Oyer & Terminor and Gaol Delivery court, the first for two years. The Grand Jury included Guthrie who was particularly vocal on the subject of beggars. The foreman of the Grand Jury, A. L. Johnston, in his presentment found that the Poor House and Infirmary did

---

[19] *Singapore Chronicle* 1831.1.27.

not by any means answer the wise and humane purposes for which it was established. The building was *'a miserable attap bungalow, much too small and confined, which, together with the exceedingly injudicious plan upon which it was constructed, rendered it altogether unfit either for an hospital for the sick or an asylum for the poor.'* He recommended that, as it was totally unsuitable, the surplus funds of over 17,000 Spanish Dollars should now be used to construct forthwith a substantial and commodious Poor House and Infirmary in every respect adapted to the exigencies of the Settlement. The funds available were amply sufficient to authorise the immediate commencement of the building and the surplus revenues of the farm which would accumulate before the whole of the present funds were expended, would be found more than sufficient for the completion of such an edifice as was required. The number of beggars, chiefly Chinese, who were continually to be seen in all parts of the town, many of whom were affected with the most loathsome diseases should be conveyed by the Police to the Infirmary.[20]

No progress had been made in the next year and the Presentment of May 1833 reiterated what had been said about the Poor House.

At the end of January 1833 Guthrie's partnership with Clark came to an end and each continued business in his own name. He was appointed joint trustee for the creditors of Lou Ah Sing and Cho Ah Ham in the firm of Yam Hap in October the same year and again as trustee in March 1835 for the creditors of Chin Chune & Co.

The need for a proper Anglican church to replace the Missionary Chapel had been felt for some years and following a meeting in October 1834 organised by the visiting Bishop of Calcutta he subscribed individually $50 towards the construction of what would be the first St. Andrew's Church. Other individuals gave between $15 and $50 whereas most firms gave $100.

Duty on the Grand Jury could be quite time consuming. He had had to sit again as Foreman on 6th January 1834 and on eight subsequent days while the fates of 41 accused were decided. 16 were discharged and 11 were sentenced to be transported to Bombay, seven for seven years, one for 14 and three for life. Three were sentenced to death, one for wounding

---

[20] *Singapore Chronicle* 1832.5.10.

and two for murder, this being carried out by public hanging in front of the jail. The remainder were sentenced to hard labour.[21]

Guthrie's next turn came on and after 22nd December when 25 prisoners were convicted but 33 let off, mostly because the accusers or witnesses had moved away.[22] Almost immediately and before the departure of the Recorder for Malacca a Special court was convened on 19th January 1835 with the same jury members to try a convict, a sand carrier, for the murder of Lalloo Singh, his overseer. Named Nasing Rao, he was thought to be of higher caste and had been sentenced to transportation from India for treason and rebellion, being a son of a minor Rajah. His victim, an overseer of convicts, was said to have made improper solicitations of him. He showed no remorse, was found guilty of murder and hanged.[23]

The next Court was held on 30th March 1835 before the Acting Governor Bonham and Resident Councillor Wingrove. Among the 40 criminal cases involving about 70 prisoners were four cases of murder. Guthrie was once more balloted to serve on the jury and elected Foreman. In one murder case they could not agree on a verdict, so the Court discharged them from giving one. The five prisoners concerned had to be discharged but warned they were still liable to be charged again. 21 cases of larceny were convicted and all except two sentenced to two years' imprisonment and hard labour. One remaining got only three months hard labour and the other transportation to Bombay for seven years. For burglary, assault, riot and tumult, the twelve cases all received the standard two years with hard labour. Highway robbery, four cases, earned them transportation to Bombay for five or seven years and two cases of cutting and wounding with intent to do bodily harm got transportation for 14. One murderer was to be executed the following morning. 24 prisoners were acquitted.

Not long after this in early 1835, it transpired that the certificate from the Registrar of Imports and Exports, covering certain goods exported to Calcutta, had not been accepted by the Collector of Government Customs there, leading to the imposition of additional duty. The Collector had

---

[21] *Singapore Chronicle* 1834.1.23.

[22] *Singapore Chronicle* 1835.1.10.

[23] *Singapore Chronicle* 1835.1.17.

found the wording of the certificate to be irregular but as the goods, when imported into Singapore, were taken direct from the ship to the importer's godowns against a previously obtained landing permit, without the Registrar or his clerk sighting the goods, the official wording could not be used. Guthrie claimed a refund of the additional amount paid and eventually, after official correspondence between the Acting Governor and the Supreme Government, he received it.[24]

Robberies were regrettably frequent and on 14th May 1836 the dwelling houses of both Messrs. Fraser and Guthrie, immediately adjoining each other, were entered by thieves. From Mr. Fraser's, all the hanging lamps in the upper verandah were taken away, as were the lamplighter's steps, which they took across to Mr. Guthrie's. From the latter only one lamp hanging at the bottom of the staircase was taken as the thieves could not ascend it, the door having been locked.[25]

His nephew James Guthrie had proved satisfactory and was made a partner with effect from 2nd January 1837. Shortly after this there had been discussions of possible formation of a Chamber of Commerce which led to a meeting at the Reading Room on Wednesday, 8th February, appointing a five–man committee to make proposals. Guthrie, Boustead, George and two others were elected and by the time of a formal public meeting 12 days later they had circulated the proposed rules in English, Chinese and Malay. 26 Chinese firms subscribed and the 11–man committee elected for the first year included six British (including Guthrie), two Chinese, and one each American, Armenian and Arab.

As did many others, Guthrie subscribed to and took an interest in the Singapore schools, attending the subscribers' annual general meeting in June at which the move from then various quarters they occupied to the Institution Buildings was approved.

He was back in Court again as a member of the jury on Tuesday 4th April 1837 with 70 prisoners to deal with, four of whom were on murder charges. On Monday 28th August 1837 another session was held, but without the Recorder present, to opine on the 38 prisoners already in gaol for

---

[24] SSR R3 101.
[25] *Singapore Chronicle* 1836.5.14.

minor offences. Guthrie was the Foreman of the jury and all cases were concluded the first day. He did however bring up, as had been done many times before, the ongoing and increasing problem of diseased vagrants begging on the bridges.

A year earlier in the issue dated 2nd July the editor of the *Singapore Chronicle* was of the opinion that the Government was entirely entitled to take over the Infirmary (now known as the Chinese Hospital) and use it as a convict gaol as it had already done, but this view was robustly attacked five days later by the editor of the *Free Press*. The paupers had been removed to an attap bungalow far too small for the number of applicants, which resulted in many being refused entry and returning to the streets. A year later in September the *Free Press* revealed that the Supreme Government in Bengal whilst insisting on austerity were about to abolish the Pork Farm and the revenue it produced as it pressed in an undue degree upon the Chinese part of the population. The Chinese had not requested the abolition, but the Poor House was to be done away with and the hospital was only thereafter to treat acute cases. A presentment in February the following year called for the reintroduction of the farm, the arrest and confinement of beggars, new build-ings and a wing of the hospital for the use of European seamen.[26]

He was requested in 1838 by its owners to advertise for sale the site on which the Court House stood, with its current lease to the East India Company. Details of a sale of Landed Property to be sold at his godowns by public auction at *'12 o'clock on Wednesday the 1st September next'* appeared in the press on the 12th August 1841.

> 'The ground contained in Grant No. 243 extending from High Street to the Singapore River, containing as area of 82,080 square feet with the Court House and various other buildings thereon erected. The ground is held on grant for 999 years on payment of an annual quit–rent of 85 Spanish Dollars and is at present let to the East India Company on a lease which expires on the 30th April 1844. The Court House was erected during the years 1826 & 27 under the superintendence of Mr. Coleman, architect, and is built of the best materials. The property has a frontage along the river side of 240 feet which at the expiry of the present lease will afford a very superior situation for the erection of godowns or shops

---

[26] *Singapore Free Press* 1838.2.22.

as there is sufficient vacant ground without in any way encroaching in the Court House or out offices attached to the same. To parties who may wish to invest capital in landed property this affords a most favorable opportunity for doing so.'

The Government were under the impression that the lease expired on 30th April 1839 as shown in Bonham's letter to Bengal dated 17th September, so possibly there was a five–year lease extension being discussed at the time.

Both Guthrie and Coleman offered a lease at $100 per month, but on 26th October 1841 the ground was sold for $15,600 and transferred to Thomas Church who, just under a year later, transferred it to Governor Bonham for account of the East India Company.

In September 1840, together with James Clark, his former business partner, he was joint attorney for the executors of William Farquhar, the first Resident of Singapore, who had died in Scotland on 11th May 1839.[27]

Guthrie was yet again foreman of the Grand Jury in June 1841; proceedings being spread over nine days to deal with the 51 prisoners.

His brother Thomas, unsure if he was still in Singapore, had written to him from Burnside on 11th May that *'the interest of the mortgages on Burnside bear rather hard on me and in the event of either of the present securities being called up, which is not improbable, I may require your assistance.'* This was received on 31st July and may indicate that he had good reason to go back to Scotland.

On 20th December 1841 he sailed in *Charles Grant* for Bombay, his fellow passengers being Alex Johnston who was going home on retirement and William Spottiswoode. All three continued on to England by *Berenice* from Bombay to Suez and *Oriental* from Alexandria to Southampton, a journey of three months. How long he remained away is not known although he was back by 1844 and acting as Business Assessor for the Chamber of Commerce.

Sir William Norris, the fourth Recorder opened the Court on Saturday 4th October 1845 and it was immediately adjourned to Monday 13th as it was feared *'that the time of the jurors would be engrossed during the following*

---

[27] *Singapore Free Press* 1840.9.10.

week by the receipt and dispatch of the Overland and other mails'.[28] On its resumption the Recorder made a strong statement recommending the re–introduction of the Port Farm and suggesting that a memorial on the subject be submitted to the Supreme Government. The European community and a few Chinese were at present supporting 150 paupers but 50 to 60 were still begging and 70 had died from starvation or disease in the previous year. Guthrie in his position as Foreman of the jury forthrightly supported this view. He was, he said, backed up by the richer Chinese merchants, and raised again the question of the $17,000 from the earlier farm which still remained unaccounted for. An impressive new hospital building was under construction thanks to the generosity of [Mr Tan] Tock Seng and this sum should be disbursed to help with the running costs, overseen by a joint com-mittee of merchants and civil servants. The Grand Jury *'cannot for a moment suppose that an enlightened and liberal government like the Supreme Government of British India would appropriate for the use of the state the revenue arising from a tax levied for a specific purpose'.*[29]

On the Grand Jury again in October 1845, now as Foreman, Guthrie made a strong statement. He was on 1st December 1845 a steward at the St. Andrew's Day Ball and Supper. The Chamber of Commerce elected him its Chairman for the year 1846 and, according to their records, also for the following year, 1847.

His nephew James, who had increasingly taken over much of the busi-ness, on 14th August 1845 sailed in *Anna Maria* for the Cape and London. Almost a year later James married Miss Suzanna Scott in Scotland. Together they returned to Singapore, travelling through France and Italy to Brindisi, to Alexandria, up the Nile, across the desert to Suez and on to Ceylon. Here, after a month's unexpected delay, they caught *Braganza*, a new paddle steamer, at Point de Galle and finally reached Singapore on 11th January 1847.

The happy couple had only a few weeks to settle in before Guthrie, having sat on the Grand Jury yet again in January, departed aboard *Braganza* on Monday 1st March 1847. *'Mr. Guthrie',* reported the *Singapore Free Press* a week later:

---

[28] *Singapore Free Press* 1845.10.6.
[29] *Singapore Free Press* 1845.10.23.

'was one of the earliest of the European merchants who settled in Singapore. He was distinguished for sound judgment and sterling integrity. And during the long course of his residence he has always occupied a high standing in the estimation of the community, whether as a member of society, a merchant, or a magistrate. He carries with him the best wishes of the community of Singapore that he may long enjoy health and happiness in his native country to which he now finally returns'.

1846, wrote the editor of the *Free Press* in January, had not been a good year for business. The market was overstocked, and demand diminished, many houses stood empty and rents were down. The *Lady Mary Wood* had on one occasion arrived from Galle without the European mail and while some 2,000 indigent and secret society related Chinese had arrived from Rhio, other Chinese were flocking to Johore where the Temenggong had opened up rivers to settlement and agriculture. At Easter, some 500 Chinese Roman Catholics had attended services at the Church of the Good Shepherd and 300 the funeral of one of their number at which Father Maudit officiated. Although relations with the local officials were good, those with the Supreme Government were the opposite, and although a new gleaming hospital had been built by the generosity of Mr. Tan Tock Seng it remained unopened through lack of operating funds.

During his sojourn in Singapore Guthrie had acquired much land at Tanjong Pagar as already mentioned and by the time of his departure he also had *'Everton'*, a 45–acre estate with 2,250 nutmeg trees bearing fruit, and *'Claymore'* on Orchard Road. The nutmeg trees originally grew in Ternate in the Moluccas but the Dutch, in order to control production, removed them all to the Banda Islands. These were occupied in the early 1800s by the British who, to break the Dutch monopoly, sent seeds to Bencoolen and elsewhere. The trees normally grew to a height of 20–30 feet and took several years to bear the fruit of which one tree could produce a thousand per year. When ripe the husk would be broken off, the mace removed, and the nut used to spice meat, etc. In Singapore, growing nutmegs became something of a craze until, in the 1850s, a disease spread through the plantations. 10 years later production had ceased, and the land had been at least partially built over.

He arrived in London, basing himself at the well–established Oriental Club, at that time situated in Hanover Square, a home from home for those who had held senior positions in the East, before moving into his new home at 3 Tenterden Street just off the Square. He had plenty to keep him busy and in 1853 the Indian Government announced its intention to make their own copper coins, fractions of a rupee, legal tender in Singapore. Although the silver rupee itself was legal in the Straits it was not used in business, the normal currency being the Spanish silver dollar as it had been from the start. The double pice, half pice and pie were to equal the cent, half cent and quarter cent at a ratio of 100 to 220. In Singapore meetings were held, petitions drawn up and sent to India. James wrote to his uncle who, gathered a number of old Singapore hands and called to protest to the President of the Board of Control, the organisation which oversaw the Indian Government. To cut a long story short this, together with actions by others, put paid to the proposal.

The news of the 1854 serious rioting in Singapore in early May was received with dismay. Guthrie could do nothing about it, but he was able to help recruit, at the request of the Municipal Council, a new man, Graham Wahab of the London Police, early in 1855. He was to take over as Deputy Superintendent of the Singapore Police and arrived there to do so in August.

In the 1860s he made several calls, individually or with others, on the Duke of Newcastle to further the proposal that the Straits Settlements should be removed from the aegis of the Indian Government and become a Crown Colony.

According to Cunningham Brown in The Traders, to the surprise of all in 1864 he sent out to Singapore his *'son, John Guthrie'* to join the company. Details of the young man's age or the identity of his mother are not known. He seemingly did not *'fit in'* as he went to sea in the autumn of 1866 and was not heard of again. There are many errors in that book and, as there are no cross references, we should perhaps charitably assume John was merely a young member of the Guthrie clan who needed help.

Guthrie died at 8 Upper Wimpole Street, London on 12th March 1865.

Part 4

Other Merchants

Chapter 21

Other Merchants — 1819–1829

Guthrie and Boustead are still well–known names in Singapore. Johnston is not, even though he was until recently the only former long–term resident of Singapore commemorated by a named sculpture. This is located on Boat Quay next to Cavanagh Bridge. Raffles was, of course, not a long–term resident.

Besides the well–known names are many merchants who arrived in Singapore between 1819 and 1829, did business, left or died. About these detailed information is sparse but listed below are such details of some of these as the author has been able to uncover in his research. The list is of course far from complete.

21.1 Choa Chong Long

Born about 1788 in Malacca where his father was Capitan China, Chong Long migrated to Singapore soon after the new settlement was established. He had been well educated, spoke English and had plenty of money. Already known to Farquhar he was, as far as we know, perhaps the only Chinese at the time that British merchants regarded as a friend. He lived and worked in Commercial Square and is known for a large dinner party he held on 8th September 1831, his 44th birthday by Chinese reckoning, which was reported at length in the *Singapore Chronicle* the next day.

He built a house in Campong Glam but never lived there, and it was used for some time as a theatre before being sold to Mr. Carnie, who rebuilt it and sold it to James Fraser.

The *Singapore Chronicle* of 25th April 1833 announced that Chong Long had won the Opium Farm for 1833–4, bidding $4,000 per month. He had also been successful when he bid $3,440 the previous year.

Chong Long gave notice on 19th March 1836 that he intended to leave for China in about two months. As it was probable that he would remain there for several years anyone with any claim or demand on him should send it in for settlement. His will was drafted and signed, covering his houses and extensive property in Malacca and houses, shops, bazars and plots of land in Singapore. Here on a plot below Government Hill he had erected a building *'for charitable purposes for the performance of religious ceremonies according to the custom of his ancestors.'* After bequeathing sums to each of his children the remaining property was bequeathed to William Spottiswoode and two other British persons in a trust to repair the building and carry out ancestor worship. Chong Long left for Macao and on 11th October a horse, a mare, a palanquin, two buggies and a coach were auctioned for cash at his house in Commercial Square by John Gemmill.

He was killed in 1838 in Macao when his house was burgled. The Trust with his property led to lengthy legal cases over the years.

21.2 James Scott Clark

Details of his origins are lost as is the date of his arrival in Singapore but on 1st February 1824 he formed a partnership with Alexander Guthrie under the name Guthrie & Clark which lasted until the end of January 1833. On 12th May 1828 a piece of ground close to that owned by Colonel Farquhar was transferred to him, a condition being that *'in consideration of the Government permitting the space between the sea and the piece of ground conveyed to me ....to remain unoccupied'*, he would build *'a substantial house of an architectural appearance'*. George Coleman designed this, the closest to High Street of the three houses facing the Plain and after its completion Clark married on 20th October 1831 Elizabeth, the widow of Andrew Farquhar for whom he was executor. Their son was born on 22nd August 1832. Three months after the dissolution of Guthrie & Clark, he formed Clark Davidson & Co. with G. F. Davidson, but this was short–lived, being dissolved just over a year later on 9th October 1834. His next venture, with James Stephen was equally brief, being wound up by Stephen on 7th November 1835 almost a year to the day from the date on which it was formed.

Meanwhile his wife gave birth to a second son who only survived three months. The house facing the Plain having been put on the market for lease, they were now living in a house in Campong Glam, but this too was advertised to be *'let partly furnished for two months or probably more'.*[1] They sailed in *Thetis* on 19th May 1836 for Calcutta. Her captain was named Clark and his wife was aboard, so one wonders if there was not some family connection.[2] When *Thetis* returned to Singapore on 3rd September after a 16–day passage with Clark on board, but not his wife and family, the vessel was consigned to his company.

At this period, a number of smaller vessels are recorded as being con-signed to him including *Rembang* commanded by Clunies Ross of the Cocos Island family.

On 8th September 1840, he and Guthrie as agents for the Executors of William Farquhar, former Resident and former father–in–law of his wife, announced the auction on 22nd September of the house and ground situ-ated between High Street and the river, which was then rented by the shipwright Joseph Melany. Also included were four lots of ground with the buildings thereon at Campong Glam, adjoining Dr d'Almeida's.

On 11th October 1848, Clark was dismissed as Coroner by the Governor, Colonel Butterworth, regarding the very irregular performance of his duties and replaced by Dr Little. This may have been due to the fact that he was, without leave, absent in Labuan in Borneo whence he had gone to review prospects in the new British colony and only returned on 26th November aboard *William Shand.*[3]

Thereafter in 1851 he appears to have been living in a house on North Bridge Road.[4] He evidently continued his Labuan connections as a report in the *Singapore Free Press* of 20th September 1866 stated that he had

---

[1] *Singapore Free Press* 1836.6.30.
[2] *Singapore Free Press* 1836.5.26.
[3] *The Straits Times* 1848.11.29.
[4] *Singapore Free Press* 1851.7.11 See sale of property opposite Mr J. S. Clark's.

been sent over from Labuan by H. M. Government to recruit for the police and had succeeded in obtaining the number of men required. They were to be accoutred and dressed in the same manner as the Singapore Police Force.

It is possible he was the Clark mentioned as travelling from Labuan to Singapore in *Cleator* early in 1873.[5]

21.3 John Connolly

Born about 1796 at Tullamore in the centre of Ireland, west of Dublin, nothing is known of his early life until he landed with his wife and William Spottiswoode in Singapore on 23rd February 1824 aboard the brig *Guide.* After leaving Madras in July 1823, they had been trying to sell their cargo of piece goods along the west coast of Sumatra. Having had little success they arrived with over 300 packages unsold and lodged with C. R. Read and his family while waiting for the completion of their own house. They settled down as planned, founding the partnership of Spottiswoode & Connolly and acquiring business premises in Commercial Square, backing on to the sea.[6] In April 1826, due to the very confined nature of their out–offices, they decided, with a view to enlarging them, to take in a small piece of ground in addition to what had already been reclaimed from the sea. This reclamation was covered by a Government grant. It was left to settle and become stable, as well as to see what effect another monsoon might have on the sea–face. In March 1827 they con-structed a foundation for the new buildings, a seawall and a jetty. Some months later the Inspector General was checking on the new military defences and found that their new walls, which were now 14 feet high, partly blocked the line of sight from the new Prince's Battery to Fort Fullerton and must therefore be demolished. Compensation of $560 for the demolition was requested and granted and they were allowed to retain the land and the jetty.[7] On 15th April 1828, the couple sailed for London aboard the British barque *Mary Ann,* of which Wm. Spottiswoode was the

---

[5] Hale, R. E., Ross — A Lifeline for Labuan, unpublished manuscript, p. 67.
[6] *The Straits Times* 1883.1.25 Duncan's Diary 1824.
[7] Straits Settlement Records N3 4.

master. With them must have been their daughter who was left at home for her education.[8] In October 1829 the firm requested permission to take over a passage to the north of their property lying between it and that of Choa Chong Long. This was granted.[9]

John Connolly was evidently back in Singapore by July 1830 as he was a co–trustee of the Estate of Meera Hussein on behalf of whom four brick–built houses in Cross Street, opposite Mr. Scott's gate were auctioned on 30. On 10th September Mrs Connolly returned in *Castle Huntly* *'from Madras, Penang and Malacca.'* She returned from a brief trip to Malacca in May 1833 perhaps for her health. A year later Mrs Balestier described their house:

'The house is very large and has a very grand scale. You enter by a covered way up stairs, to a large–scale gallery paved with black and white marble, then raised two steps and separated by pillars is another gallery, ornamented with cushions, sofa, pictures, and old china arranged on glossy stands. Some of it is beautiful, but to the fanciers of this sort of thing beautiful, for the venerators of dragon–like forms, with the rich colours, of which the principal is green. Then you enter a drawing room very handsomely furnished. Behind that is the dining room, and on each side are the sleeping apartments and sleeping rooms.'[10]

The Connollys held a ball in honour of the Recorder Sir Benjamin Malkin and Lady Malkin in the middle of June 1834, but a month later, after a short illness, Mrs Connolly died unexpectedly, aged 33.[11]

Connolly, a committed Roman Catholic, supported and raised substantial funds for educational purposes. He was a member of the Schools Committee *'a gentleman unremittingly zealous in aiding and assisting the Schools.'* He acted again as co–trustee when Merryweather & Co failed in November 1834 before he left for London in *North Briton* on 31st January 1835.

---

[8] Hale, R. E. (2017)., *The Balestiers: The First American Residents of Singapore*, Marshall Cavendish, Singapore, pp. 35–6.

[9] SSR A62 105.

[10] Hale, op. cit., pp. 35–6.

[11] *Singapore Chronicle* 1834.7.17, p.3.

He returned and on 18th June 1843 laid the cornerstone for the building situated at the corner of Bras Basah and Queen Streets which would become the Church of the Good Shepherd (later cathedral).

The company handled a large number of vessels in the 1830s, mainly trading directly with London and became agents for the P&O S N Co from 1845 when the paddle wheel steamers *Lady Mary Wood* and *Braganza* started their regular service between Point de Galle in Ceylon and Hong Kong. Connolly himself made a short visit to Hong Kong taking one of the two ships and returned to Singapore on 8th November 1845 in *Lady Mary Wood.*

Between 1830 and 1847, Connolly was 12 times one of those balloted to be on the Grand Jury, meeting to review those arrested on suspicion of crime and make recommendations to Government. He was Foreman in May 1839 when he brought to the attention of Government the sad state of affairs where minor criminals were confined for months without trial, due to the absence of judges. The same year he wrote to the editor of the *Singapore Free Press* complaining that according to that paper the Hodgson & Abbott's beer which Connolly imported was not as much in demand as that of Bass and Allsop.[12]

Charles Spottiswoode was brought in as partner on 1st January 1841 and on 18th October 1842 Connolly was for a third time appointed a co-trustee, this time of the Seth Brothers who had become insolvent.

The *Free Press* 'noticed' the arrival at Calcutta on of John Connolly and his daughter on 20th January 1845.

He was appointed Sheriff for Penang, Malacca and Singapore in 1848 and by virtue of a writ of Fieri Facias auctioned off on 24th June a 200–ton Chinese junk '*in the cause of Lim Tong Yan v Toah Tee*'. This was preceded on 15th March by another '*in the cause of John Connolly and others, Plaintiff v Joseph Balestier, Defendant*' in which case he, among others, must have lost a good deal of money financing Balestier's sugar plantation. On 8th October 1848 he departed for Bombay in the P&O steamer *Achilles* and returned in the same vessel on 10th December. Three months later he died on 24th March.[13] A plaque hangs in his memory to this day in

---

[12] *Singapore Free Press* 1839.5.30, p.3.
[13] *Singapore Free Press* 1849.3.29, p.2.

the Cathedral of the Good Shepherd, given by his nephews John and Andrew.

21.4 José d'Almeida

José d'Almeida Carvalho e Silva, to give his full name, was born in Portugal on 27th November 1784. He qualified as a doctor and enlisted in the Portuguese navy as a ship's surgeon. In 1808 he was appointed senior surgeon of the line–of–battleship *Vasco da Gama* then stationed at Lisbon to avert a French invasion. He soon volunteered to move out East as the director of St. Raphael's Hospital in Macao where he married his first wife in 1810. Early in 1820 on a passing visit he was attracted to Singapore. Before leaving he decided to buy land and, leaving funds with Bernard, Farquhar's son–in–law, contracted with him to do so and build a house. This was done and the house built at Campong Glam facing the sea (Lot 207 or originally Lot 10) two doors down from Middle Road on the town side. In 1820 a liberal revolution occurred in Portugal but news of this took time to reach Macao and, when it did, ties with Goa were broken. The Governor of Portuguese India in Goa sent a military force to retake Macao, d'Almeida was arrested and in late 1823 sent to Goa for trial where he was imprisoned. The King promised an amnesty but, tired of waiting for this to occur, d'Almeida escaped to Bombay with Father Francisco da Silva Pinto y Maia and came to Singapore in 1825. Bernard who with his family had been living in the house until then, moved out. d'Almeida moved in and after a short stay sailed for Macao. Families were forbidden to leave but they managed to do so and arrived back on 23rd December 1825 to settle down and then set up a dispensary in Commercial Square. By chance, a Portuguese and a Spanish trading ship each with perishable cargoes were held back in port due to bad weather and had to sell much of these. Being of the same nationality with one and speaking the same language he became their agent and, adding to his medical work, set up José d'Almeida & Co. to become a merchant.[14]

---

[14] Scott, M. *Sir Jose d'Almeida – A Catholic Pioneer in every sense,* The History of the Catholic Church in Singapore, https://history.catholic.sg/sir-jose-dalmeida/.

His house was built on ground leased for 15 years and he started to fill up the swampy ground included in it. To ensure he could continue to live there on expiry of the lease he requested in 1828 a long–term grant on terms less than those normally charged. This request was denied but it was recognised that in recognition of the money expended he should have the right, on the expiry of the lease, to receive a formal grant of the ground.[15]

About this time Father Francisco da Silva Pinto y Maia arrived and, there being no Catholic church in Singapore at the time, celebrated Holy Mass for many years in the d'Almeida house on Beach Street. Murchison, the Resident Councillor who had taken over in November 1827, spoke no French, Spanish or Portuguese. This was a great embarrassment on occasion, and he arranged with d'Almeida to take on the job of interpreter and translator for $100 per month. Requesting approval from Fullerton, he was turned down flat. *'The necessity of appointing d'Almeida as interpreter and translator is not apparent.'*[16]

In his book *The Eastern Seas*, George Windsor Earl paid tribute to d'Almeida for his assistance in gathering information about neighbouring lands.[17]

Business went well until mercantile misfortune overtook him in the mid–thirties. His medical skills then stood him in good stead and by economy, perseverance and good management he staved off the calamities, helped considerably by the end of the war in China in 1841.

A keen agriculturalist, d'Almeida tried growing, at Tanjong Katong, various strains of cotton, vanilla, cloves, coffee and cochineal, but was not successful. He then tried coconuts which did well, and he was a founding member of the Agricultural and Horticultural Society in 1836. With Dr Montgomerie he was convinced of the usefulness of Gutta Percha, using it for dental mouldings. He opened up the Bandula Estate (about five

---

[15] SSR N4 297.

[16] SSR N4 254.

[17] Earl, G. W. (1837). *The Eastern seas, or, Voyages and adventures in the Indian Archipelago, in 1832-33-34 : comprising a tour of the Island of Java-visits to Borneo, the Malay Peninsula, Siam, etc; also an account of the present state of Singapore with observations on the commercial resources of the archipelago*, W.H. Allen, London, p.344.

miles out along the Serangoon Road) and acquired Raeburn from Charles Scott in the 1830s and subsequently Spottiswoode Park.

He had a large family, both before and after his second marriage in 1838 to Maria Isabel Nunes. 19 children are known of, but many died young. All were musical and concerts were a regular and popular feature at Lot 207. Burglaries did happen and he advertised a reward of 20 dollars for the return of a very flat gold hunting watch which had been stolen on the night of 21st September 1833. This was described as made by McCabe, with a coat of arms consisting of three boars' heads with the motto *Libertas* engraved on the outside of the case.[18]

He went back to Portugal for the benefit of his health on a visit by the *'overland'* route in 1842 and was knighted by the Queen of Portugal and later by the King of Spain, also being appointed Portuguese Consul in Singapore, all in respect to the services he had given to their shipping over the years.

A note in the *Singapore Free Press* of the 5th September 1845 mentioned the favourable response by the Bengal Government to his request for land at Malacca on behalf of several persons wishing to grow sugar there.

Edward Cree, a surgeon in the Royal Navy and accomplished amateur water colour artist visited the d'Almeidas while his ship was docked for repairs in September 1844. As he noted in his diary on the 26th:

'Went to a musical party at Dr José d'Almeida's (Figure 40), a Portuguese merchant who lives on the Campong Glam and has a large family of daughters — and sons too I believe, but they are kept in the background. They are all very musical and get up delightful concerts in their house, twice a week, to which some of us have a general invitation. The ladies are not good looking .... but they sing and play various instruments divinely. There are ten daughters and four sons. We were received by an old priest, the father confessor of the family. Old José introduced us separately and individually to each member of the family, a formidable affair, and lastly to the Madam, a leaden coloured, fat old Malay woman who informed us *'Me no speakee de Engleezee'*. Some of her relations, Malay rajahs, were there and treated us to a hornpipe — one played on

---

[18] *Singapore Chronicle* 1833.9.26.

a fiddle some native airs, monotonous enough. It was a lovely moonlight night and the large room open to the verandah all round made it cool, so we were able to enjoy the quadrilles and waltzes — with a little flirtation.'[19]

D'Almeida's death on 17th October 1850 gave rise to a special obituary in *The Straits Times* in which he was described as an old and worthy settler whose moral worth and social qualities, his benevolence, hospitality and enduring friendships were proper tributes of respect — were the best criteria of the manner and extent in which he was esteemed. He was truly mourned from the top to the bottom of society.

21.5 Walter Scott Duncan

This young man, born about 1807, was from Lerwick, Shetland Islands as was Andrew Hay who encouraged him to travel to Singapore. He arrived on 14th November 1823, lodged with Hay and was given a position with A. L. Johnston & Co., unpaid until he was sent by them to act as their agent at Rhio six months later. His main claim to fame comes from the publication years later after his death of his diary containing refreshingly blunt comments on the local scene for the months of February to early June 1824.[20] We do not know when he returned to Singapore from Rhio or when he left A. L. Johnston & Co. to set up on his own.

Apart from his sailing across to Rhio in the Dutch barque *Sarah* on 21st March 1832 we have no details of his business dealings until October 1835 when the British brig *Mavis* having come from China was consigned to him.[21] By this time he had been five times balloted to sit on the Grand Jury, called to consider criminal cases before they were tried, indicating that he had some position locally. He had contributed $50 to the building fund for St Andrew's Church.

---

[19] Cree, E.H. (1981). *The Cree journals: the voyages of Edward H. Cree, Surgeon R.N., as related in his private journals, 1837–56,* — Webb & Bower, UK, p. 131.
[20] *The Straits Times* 1883.1.30, *"Sixty Years Ago"*.
[21] *Singapore Free Press* 1835.12.10.

In November 1833 the *New Jersey,* an American vessel en route to Canton from Gibraltar carrying a cargo of quicksilver and lead, was wrecked on the Louisa Shoal in the South China Sea. Early in 1834 on the captain reaching Singapore Duncan and certain others chartered *Madeline* with divers under the charge of Joseph Melany to salvage as much of the cargo as possible. She set off in late January and successfully recovered 25,000 Spanish Dollars' worth, whereupon in April she was followed by *Lucile*, which in turn recovered a further 7,200 dollars' worth. Duncan's share was one tenth in the first and two tenths in the second. All concerned received their rewards but at the end, after all outgoings were considered an amount of $2,771.46 remained. Duncan was offered 65 per cent of this by the owners of *New Jersey,* which he felt was insufficient. Agreement could not be reached and so the case Brown & Others v Duncan came to court. The verdict awarded him in early 1836 only $1124.92 out of which he had to bear the court costs. The verdict led to considerable correspondence in the *Singapore Chronicle* and later an appeal which was refused.[22]

It was on 25th November 1835 that he and Hay announced the formation of Hay & Duncan. His yacht *Radical* took part in the 1837 New Year races, and in April they advertised having Japanese goods and Birds of Paradise for sale. Two months later an extended stock list appeared, including anchors, salt beef and pork, brandy, sherry, claret, madeira, arrack and vinegar, gin and Champagne, rope, coir cables, copper sheathing, patent felt, paint as well as silk cloaks, ladies' worktables and boxes, metallic mirrors, jewel boxes, and birds of paradise of the finest plumage.[23]

The partnership did not last and there was an acrimonious split, with dissolution on 30th November 1837 and Duncan responsible for winding it up.

By July 1838, his list of goods for sale had expanded and now included Manila Cigars and Hats, as well as candles, various navigational books, and charts. In October 1839, he was involved with the new Singapore Coffee Company set up to manage and develop a 5,000–acre plantation under the supervision of a Monsieur Le Dieu. After the death

---

[22] *Singapore Free Press* 1836.5.12.

[23] *Singapore Free Press* 1837.4.6.

of Mr. Moor, he became the secretary of the company and presided over its sale and liquidation two years later. Only 100 acres had been cleared and planted.[24]

The 1840s saw occasional Dutch and other small vessels consigned to him and he donated to funds for a spire for St. Andrew's and generously for the new Seamen's Hospital. New items for sale included Allsop's beer and beaver hats.

On 1st June 1843, a large fire broke out in a small street running from Commercial Road to the Canal and his large range of godowns, in which were stored quantities of tar, coals, wood and spirits, backed on to the burning buildings. They only escaped destruction by constant streams of water being directed over them although the metal window frames were red hot.[25]

The sale of a yacht was advertised under his name on 19th February 1845, which may have been his *Radical*.

News of the unfortunate loss of his cutter *Dolphin* reached Singapore in October 1846. Due to wind and currents, she had drifted far from the wreck which was her destination and run out of water when she was spotted by another vessel which came to her rescue, towing her astern. A sharp squall blew up, the tow parted, and *Dolphin* was swamped, sinking at once. The crew were all rescued and brought safely back to Singapore.[26] At the beginning of the previous year, her then crew had murdered the Captain and Supercargo and taken the vessel to Lingin, where one confessed to the Rajah, who sent them straight back to Singapore for punishment.[27]

Duncan acted as Croupier at a highly successful farewell dinner on 8th February 1847 for Whampoa, the younger, who was about to set off for China. About this time one of his Chinese employees broke his forearm and had it set by Dr Oxley in a trial splint of Gutta Percha, it healing completely in three weeks and leading to a standard medical procedure.[28]

[24] *Singapore Free Press* 1841.10.28.
[25] *Singapore Free Press* 1843.6.1.
[26] *Singapore Free Press* 1846.0.3.
[27] *Singapore Free Press* 1845.1.2.
[28] *Singapore Free Press* 1847.7.8.

His old friend Clunis, in partnership with one Gow in a shipyard, was in some financial difficulty, and his creditor advertised on 4th January 1848 that Clunis' stock–in–trade was to be auctioned. Joining Mrs. Clunis, Duncan advertised an objection to this and was able to get the auction postponed indefinitely.

Duncan was the owner of a 60–ton schooner, named *Dolphin* after his cutter, which was trading along the north coast of Borneo. In Maludu Bay in November 1851 she was attacked by Illanun pirates who killed Burns, the Supercargo, Robertson the Master and four others. Sheriff Yassin was able to get possession of the schooner and the rest of the crew, whose lives had been spared to sail the vessel to the coast, and took her up river to Benggaya. The East India Company steamer *Pluto* was in the area and Yassin handed *Dolphin* over to them, having appropriated nothing.[29]

Business was not so good in the early 1850s, although in 1851 he is recorded as exporting 256 cases of gin to Manila, 150,000 cigars, 15 anchors and 7 cables to Calcutta while importing 46,000 baskets of rice from Arracan. The following year in September he opened in Flint Street a *'Singapore Auction & Commission Mart'* and advertised storage for coals or timber on the beach at Teluk Ayer.[30]

It was in 1853 that Duncan, coming out of his house to the chicken coops 50 yards away, found the body of a Chinese bound hand and foot, the throat cut to the bone and wrapped in a Chinese quilt. He had lived nearby for about five years, a quiet inoffensive man with no known enemies. Although Duncan had servants and dogs, nobody had heard any noise in the night. There was no clue as to the assailant. All 45 ducks and chickens were missing.[31]

It was in March 1855 that a number of leading residents recommended him in writing to Government as being most suitable for appointment as Superintendent of Police, but this was not to be.

Duncan died, aged 60, on 15th May 1867, leaving behind him his long–term Chinese mistress, Nonya Ah Thak, who was, under his will, to be paid eight dollars a month as long as she remained of good behaviour

---

[29] *Singapore Free Press* 1851.12.5.

[30] *The Straits Times* 1852.9.11.

[31] *The Straits Times* 1853.6.21.

and did not marry or form a connection with any other person. He provided for the maintenance and education of his two daughters by her,
Agnes, and Flora. By the same mother he had two sons, named Andrew
Hay and Robert Jack and he stipulated that when the daughters reached
16 years of age the estate should be sold and the proceeds split between
the four children and his sister Isabella in Shetland.[32]

The estate which he had probably purchased in 1842 was of 250 acres
located in Siglap near the sea and planted with coconut palms.

21.6 William Renshaw George

Aged about 28, he arrived in Singapore on 19th February 1825 without a
licence to settle but obtained employment with Charles Thomas & Co. as
bookkeeper at least until April 1827.[33] In May 1828 he was balloted as a
member of the Grand Jury and the following month was described in the
Singapore Chronicle as '*a gentleman of skill and experience in mercantile
affairs.*' He left the company and for a short time worked in partnership
with Claude Queiros but this did not last and was dissolved at the end of
June 1830.[34] Whether or not he re–joined Charles Thomas & Co. at this
stage is not known but he was made a partner of the firm on 1st November
1833. His illegitimate daughter Louisa was born on 4th January 1829 and
three months later he bought the *Singapore Chronicle* and *Commercial
Register* from its owner James Loch, who had offended the authorities. He
promised more attention to local commercial affairs and over time
increased the average size of the paper to six pages. In 1830 he was
Secretary of the short-lived Billiards Club and in September he started his
own printing press. He is recorded as leaving on a visit to Penang in
Hoopoe on 4th March 1831 and the following year got married on 9th
January to a daughter of William Farquhar.[35] His bride, Elizabeth Caroline
Burton, now about 32 years old, had been living in Calcutta and was the
widow of John Campbell Burton. It was agreed that she should manage

---

[32] *The Straits Times* 1951.6.9, Cecil Street.
[33] SSR N1, 315.
[34] *Singapore Chronicle* 1828.7.3
[35] *Singapore Chronicle* 1832.1.12.

her own financial affairs, an unusual arrangement at the time, but they were happily married until her death in 1858, living in a rented property in Beach Road, facing the sea on the site of the present Raffles Hotel.

Elizabeth produced a son on 28th September 1832 but he died in infancy and on 16th October 1834 their daughter, christened Helen Maria Gilman, was born. George sold the *Singapore Chronicle* in September 1835 to W. S. Lorrain as agent for J. F. Carnegy of Penang. Following this he made a trip overseas, returning to Singapore in the *Cowasjee Family* from Calcutta or Penang on 28th January 1836. The following year, his son John Chadwick Farquhar was born on 17th March. It was about this time that Charles Thomas & Co ceased to do business. In 1840 he was officially appointed Deputy Sheriff and on 2nd May wrote to the Registrar:"

> 'I beg leave to bring to your notice the present state of the Sheriff's Department arising from increasing business of the Court and the consequent inability of one person serving the numerous [illegible] required. I have therefore to request that you make an application to Government for an additional Bailiff to be allowed to the Establishment.'[36]

It was in 1842 that he bought the *Singapore Free Press* and *Mercantile Advertiser* which he owned for six years before selling out to Abraham Logan in 1848.

In November 1843 he went with numerous other Europeans to see a tiger caught in a deep pit near the present site of the Botanic Gardens. It made valiant attempts to escape and, after it was shot, he offered to show them a short cut to the Bukit Timah Road back to their carriages. After following him for several miles uphill and down dale, they found themselves at Tanglin Road with two miles to walk home under an extremely hot sun.

In 1847 he was in financial difficulties. This led to extensive property being seized and auctioned on the orders of the Sheriff, initiated by the shipwright Joseph Melany who had obtained a judgement against him. The property included 200 acres of orchard land in the Tanglin District, a small coconut plantation at Katong, two building lots in Upper Cross

---

[36] SSR AA11 dated 1840.5.2.

Street, two in Nankin Street and four in Rochor Canal Road. Difficulties continued and in December 1850 he petitioned to be discharged from insolvency, the case to be heard on the following 12th March.[37]

Following this, he joined Jose d'Almeida and Sons in 1852 as Senior Assistant. Following the death of his wife, he moved to a boarding house in River Valley Road kept by Mrs Nugent. It was reported that *'He goes out for a walk every morning at five o'clock, [before dawn] coming back to his tea at half-past six which he has done for forty years and has reaped his reward in still robust health, strong nerve, clear head and yet a lively enjoyment of the good things of life.'*

In 1864 he retired from the d'Almeidas, perhaps foreseeing their bankruptcy in 1865, and joined Wm. Spottiswoode & Co as bookkeeper until his death in 1873. He was diligent, public spirited, perhaps not over intelligent or imaginative but an ordinary, normal sort of man, father of a bastard, second husband of a widow with four children, labouring for many years at an office desk.[38]

21.7 Thomas Harrington

Thomas Talbot Harrington had joined the East India Company Marine service in about 1790. He was well-connected, his wife being the niece of the Earl of Seaforth and William Moffat, the owner of many of the ships in which he sailed, being his brother–in–law. His three brothers all reached high positions in the East India Company. Harrington had made several voyages to China and by April 1805 had been promoted, now in his mid–20s, to the command of *Ganges* bound for China and in convoy with seven other East Indiamen, protected by HMS *Blenheim* from possible attacks by the French. They did cross paths with two French ships and shots were fired but both sides sailed away without further ado. Among Harrington's passengers on that voyage were Thomas Raffles, Raffles' wife Olivia and sister Mary Anne as well as 16–year–old Robert

---

[37] *Singapore Free Press* 1850.12.27.

[38] JMBRAS, (1973). *150th Anniversary of the Founding of Singapore: Previously published as JMBRAS Volume XLII, Part I in 1969 Republished with additional illustrations and articles in 1973*, Times Printers Sdn. Bhd, Malaysia, p.189.

Ibbetson, all destined for Penang. They disembarked at Madras in mid–
August to join another vessel while *Ganges* continued on to Calcutta
reaching Penang only in November and Malacca in December. On her
homeward voyage from China she became increasingly prone to leaks,
had to be escorted to Bombay where she remained for nearly seven
months under repair before sailing for home once more, accompanied by
Earl St Vincent. A constant battle was waged to keep the sea out but when
south of Cape Agulhas, the most southerly point of Africa, it became evident that all was lost, with 10 feet of water in the well. Boats from *Earl St
Vincent* rescued all the passengers and crew and *Ganges* foundered on 29th
May 1807, losing her cargo valued at over £126,000, part of which was
Harrington's.

Harrington was given command of two more East Indiamen, the second being *Scaleby Castle* in which he made two voyages to Batavia and
China and was as usual allowed to trade to a certain extent for his own
account. The passing of an Act in 1813 opening most of the East India trade
to private competition was followed by an increase in salaries for ship's
officers but the withdrawal of their trade privileges. This he did not find
acceptable and, for some unexplained reason, now planned to settle at St
Helena. This bleak mountainous island in the South Atlantic, with at that
time a population of possibly 2,500 of whom some 400 to 600 were
Chinese labourers brought in by the Company from Canton initially in
1810, was an important stop for almost all ships sailing from the eastern
shore of America or Europe to the East on both the outward and return
voyages.[39] He had verbal permission from Beatson, the Governor at the
time, to lease certain land in the small town and, on the strength of this, had
had prepared in England a prefabricated house and warehouse which he
shipped in *Scaleby Castle*. On her arrival the newly appointed Governor,
Wilks, refused to make the land available. He had spent some £16,000 so
far and saw no alternative but to go on to Simons Bay on the eastern side
of the Cape of Good Hope taking with him 23 Chinese craftsmen to erect
his prefabricated house and establish its gardens at Simonstown. On his
return voyage he tarried too long at the Cape overseeing the construction

[39] Giese, K. and Marfaing, L. (2018). *Chinese and African Entrepreneurs: Social Impacts of Interpersonal Encounters*, BRILL, p. 88.

and arrived at St Helena on 11th September. He sailed for England before
the arrival on 15th October, to the surprise and dismay of the local inhabitants, of HMS *Northumberland* with the defeated French Emperor Napoleon
Bonaparte aboard. On the *Scaleby Castle*'s return to England he was cen-
sured and finally dismissed from the Company's service on 22nd March
1816, by which time he was back at the Cape having already negotiated a
deal with Admiral Malcolm which allowed him 30 tons of spare tonnage on
board the naval store–ships and transports for the purpose of shipping articles for the supply of Napoleon's establishment and the regimental messes.
At the same time the Admiral decreed that no tonnage on private account
should be granted to any other individual, giving Harrington a short but
effective and profitable monopoly, no private ships being allowed to
approach St Helena in case attempts were made to rescue Bonaparte. He
initially enjoyed the support of Lord Charles Somerset, the Governor of the
Cape Colony[40] and later the enmity of Lieutenant General Sir Hudson
Lowe, who had taken over as Governor of St Helena on 14th April 1814 and
who wrote on 20th November 1819 to Earl Bathurst in London:

'Mr. Harrington has made various attempts to have a vessel employed
between the Cape and this Island, sent once a Super Cargo on board
a passing Ship and at another time a relation of his own, without any
authority, and has in fact never ceased using his endeavours to establish
some communications by shipping with the Island. It is now his object, I
understand, to secure the consent of the Naval Authorities at Home to his
obtaining a Contract for the supply of Grain and Flour to the Squadron. It
would of course be presumptuous on my part to offer any objection, nor

---

[40] 1818.1.25 Lord Somerset to General Sir Hudson Lowe at St Helena:

'He is the only person here in the mercantile line for whom I feel any peculiar
interest. He came out here with the strongest recommendations to me from
persons of great respectability and to whom I am attached by ties of personal
regard. Exclusive however of every private feeling for Mr. Harrington's success,
he merits all the support the Governor of this settlement can afford him, being
the only person who has embarked a very large capital in the colony. Indeed
his buildings & other preparation for a widely extended trade are upon a scale
so expensive that I fear they can never repay him altho' they cannot fail to be a
lasting benefit to the colony.'

in fact am I aware of any, to his becoming the contractor for the supply of this, or any other Articles, whether for the Squadron or of the Island itself.'

Alexander Guthrie's arrival to join him in 1816 was welcome and his quickly acquired business capability enabled Harrington to leave for London with his wife and daughter in October 1819. His wife died whilst there in March 1820 and on his return, Alexander was sent off to Singapore where he arrived in February 1821. Harrington, having presumably found some other employee to carry on in Cape Town, set out with his daughter for China and passed through Singapore. Returning there early in 1823 he commenced business with Alexander. There is a record in a letter from Raffles' secretary to Farquhar dated 10th February 1823 of his having made a tender of 1,500 bags of Mooghey rice at 3 Spanish Dollars per bag payable by bills on Calcutta at the exchange of 204 Sicca Rupees per 100 Spanish Dollar.

> 'The same has been accepted by the Lt Governor on condition that the rice is landed and stored free of charge to the Government and that store rooms be granted for the same until the Company store is ready to receive it, which may be calculated not to exceed a month. The rice in question is understood to be stored in Mr. Guthrie's godowns and on the certificate of the storekeeper that it is so stored you will be pleased to grant bills on Bengal for the amount.'[41]

The Storekeeper Captain Flint had some concerns about the quality of the rice and requested that an official committee of inspection be set up. Before this could be done, Captain Murray confirmed that the Sepoys would accept it under certain conditions. These Guthrie had accepted on behalf of Harrington, who remained in Singapore until March 1824, when he departed for Malacca and Calcutta.

Harrington arrived in Calcutta in September 1824 and had made up his mind to find a new partner at the Cape before basing himself in London with their London agents and consignors W. J. Burnie & Co. This was not a success and in due course he left them and carried on trade in partnership with a William Gadney of the Cape but was declared bankrupt

---

[41] SSR L17 346 Hull to William Farquhar.

in London on 7th May 1829. (*London Gazette* of 22nd November 1831). He set out for Madras by *Andromachie* arriving on 23rd August 1830 and became Deputy Master Attendant Calcutta, marrying for a second time on 26th November 1831. It may be that Captain Harrington was assisted in obtaining his position at Calcutta by his elder brother Henry Hawes Harington (1770–1832) who was a proprietor of the Carnatic Bank in Madras (but was now living in London) as well as by his connections to the East India Company through the Moffat family. By 1840, he had become Master Attendant, Bengal, and he died on 29th November 1841 at his residence, Somerset Place, Colvin's Ghaut, Calcutta aged 61.

21.8 Graham Mackenzie

He arrived early in 1821 and in April assisted some merchants from Trengganu who had been cheated by Captain Methven. By July he was in possession of a plot of ground No. 8 on the East Beach on Campong Glam Plain and, bought from P. Christie, Lot No. 5 on River Street for building godowns, but which he had not yet occupied. He also had a lot on the Singapore River upstream of the reservoir which had been *'pagared in'* but not yet built on. Construction went ahead until Raffles arrived in October 1822 and cancelled all previous land transactions.

Writing to Lieutenant Nilson Hull, Raffles' secretary, on 30th October he stated:

'I this morning received your circular letter of yesterday's date and in compliance with the Lt. Governor's request have to state in reply that I have no written document authorising me to build the house which I now occupy. After arriving here I was of course anxious to erect a building somewhere or other for the protection of my property and in a situation calculated for carrying on trade. I therefore applied to the Resident Lt Col Farquhar and was allowed by him to build the house in question. I commenced my operations I think about the beginning of May 1821 and occupied the godown the latter end of December following. The whole amount of expenses I calculate at dollars four thousand three hundred and fifty, but I am sorry to say that I cannot give such a statement as the Lt. Governor requires, distinguishing the cost of erection from the charge of workmanship, not having paid for the same separately.'

To this he may or may not have received an reply and on 4th December he wrote again:

'Having to this day observed a Proclamation and Advertisement of the Hon'ble the Lt. Governor dated 2nd inst. and also a Proclamation dated yesterday, regarding the rescinding of all Certificates of Grants of Land by the Resident Lt. Col. Farquhar, and the resumption of the same by Government, as also intimating that certain lots of ground will be disposed of by Public outcry, I beg leave to request that you will enquire of the Hon'ble the Lieutt. Governor whether or not he intends previously to give me the choice of one of the new lots of ground agreeable to his promise on the day on which he called the merchants together to explain to them his plans. From what was then hinted and from the advertisements which have lately been issued, I suppose it is the intention of Government to resume possession of the piece of ground on which my present godown stands, and therefore I should wish to know whether the Government will reimburse me for the buildings which I have erected on the same. Without being made [privy] with those circumstances I should not, of course, think of purchasing another piece of ground, removing the present [illegible] and erecting buildings at a heavy expense, more particularly as there is as yet no regular confirmation of the Settlement and consequently a chance of losing every Rupee of expense which may be incurred. In most new settlements the merchant inhabitants chiefly consist of young men setting out in the world, who seldom have more capital than is absolutely necessary, and therefore no surplus to sink in extensive and frequent building. I remain, Sir, Your most obedient servant, Graham Mackenzie, Singapore 4th. Decr. 1822.'

He received a reply, the text of which is missing, to which he replied at length on 6th December:

'Sir, In reply to your letter to me of yesterday in which you were directed by the Hon'ble the Lieutt. Governor to state that my claim for compensation for the expense of the buildings which I have raised on the piece of ground now occupied by me must lay over pending reference to the Governor General in Council, and also that in case the same should be found valid whether I would be inclined to accept if certain terms therein stated should they be offered [words missing] four months — I beg leave to state as for [myself] 1ˢᵗ that should the Government resume possession of my present piece of ground I have no doubt whatever, from the general just and liberal system which it is well-known to pursue, that I shall receive full compensation for the godown which I presently occupy as well as to obtain another lot of ground equally well adapted for commercial purpose, more particularly as I erected my present building under the eye and with the knowledge of the Resident — as the ground was [word missing] out by him, and in fact that I was prohibited from erecting any other than a substantial godown of brick and mortar. If under those circumstances I should not be found entitled to indemnification, I shall in future be at a loss to know whether to obey commands of any authority other than the Supreme Government itself. I allow that I have heard Col. Farquhar state that it was possible the Government might resume possession of all the lots of ground granted by him, but I could never have supposed but full compensation would be given for whatever might be so taken. No man in his senses would build a single house if he had a chance of losing it six or twelve months afterwards. 2ⁿᵈ. That I am ready to acquiesce in the [illegible] proposed by the Hon'ble the Lieutt. Governor with the exception that should I not be able to finish the intended new godown for want of materials or otherwise within six months, I shall be allowed to possess my present one until the same is completed, pledging myself that no unnecessary delay shall take place on my part. I beg leave, however, to request that you will call the attention of the Hon'ble the Lieutt. Governor to my letter of 30ᵗʰ October last in which I have stated the exact amount of expenditure in building my present godown to be Dollars four thousand three hundred and fifty. As the difference between this sum and that stated in your letter can be of little moment to the Government it will be so to me as a private individual, I feel confident that the full amount [will] be readily awarded. I am Sir, your most obedient and humble servant, Graham Mackenzie. Singapore 6ᵗʰ December 1822.'

No details of the final arrangement exist but a part payment of 2,173 Company Rupees on account of compensation granted to him for removing to the opposite side of the river was authorised before Raffles left Singapore.[42]

---

⁴⁷ SSR L17 314 dated 1823.3.1.

A couple of months later, Mackenzie shipped on board the brig *Malacca* various piece goods for sale at Muntok or Palembang under charge of one of his own people. For reasons unknown, Captain Gardner sailed without that person, and Lt. Col. Farquhar had to be asked to write on 18th January 1823 to the Dutch Residents at both ports advising them that Mackenzie had now sent an Indian, Narayanasamy, in pursuit to reclaim the goods from Captain Gardner and also to get from him the proceeds of a sale of glassware he had sold for him previously in Malacca.[43]

In May the same year, Mackenzie joined Queiros, A. L. Johnston, Harrington and one other appealing to the Resident on behalf of another merchant, Francisco de Pastania, who was in financial difficulty. At a meeting of his creditors, he showed that the house he occupied which had been mortgaged to him for 800 Spanish Dollars, had now become his, the deed having expired. The property was to be resumed by Government and the Town Committee had only awarded him 300 Dollars whereas his neighbours in adjoining properties had been allowed the costs of their various houses. The signatories (who were probably his creditors) asked for the compensation to be raised to the full amount of the mortgage. There is no record of their success or otherwise.

In 1827, according to an official list, W. D. Shaw was with the company, probably a partner, and J. Brown was an employee.[44]

Misfortune befell on 24th October 1827 when *Asia*, a Hamburg ship sailing from Manila to China carrying a cargo of lead, spelter, quicksilver and specie was wrecked in a typhoon on an island about 45 miles from Manila. Two lives were lost. It is not clear whether Mackenzie was aboard or in Manila but on 6th November he was reported as being on the island, which implies he had an interest in the ship or her cargo.[45]

The following year Captain Pearl who had left Singapore wished to sell his property Mount Stamford and appointed Mackenzie & Co as his agent to handle the sale to Government. After stiff negotiations, the price of Sicca Rupees 10,000 was agreed until the Resident Councillor's assistant, Bonham refused to settle it in bills on Bengal. Mackenzie then withdrew the offer which caused some embarrassment to Government. Their Executive Officer was instructed in a hurry to discontinue any operations he might have commenced with reference to the Sepoy Lines and to withdraw all the artificers, convicts and implements of every description therefrom, reporting exactly as possible the extent of what had been done, with reference to the damage the property might have sustained. In the end, following suggestions from the Governor in Penang, the sale went through and operations to construct the new Sepoy Lines continued.

The company advertised two ships, *America* for freight or passage to London in April 1828 and *Eliza* for the same destination in October. Another in July, *Reaper*, arrived from London with a full cargo but no return freight could be found, and they dispatched her to China instead.

Although Mackenzie, in the words of the *Singapore Chronicle* on his arrival, possessed a frame and constitution which promised well for health and length of days, these hid signs of an incurable disease and he departed aboard *Lord Lowther* for China, with Miss Mackenzie *'to recruit his health'*. He died at Macao on 29th October, the news reaching Singapore nearly a month later. His remaining partners agreed to continue the firm.[46]

21.9 David Skene Napier

Born in Edinburgh on 12th July 1798, as a young man he went to Calcutta where John Adam, the Political Secretary introduced him to Raffles (Figure 39).[47] Thinking he could be of use, possibly provisionally in Pahang if a Resident were needed there or else in Bencoolen. Raffles wrote to Farquhar on 26th June to expect him in Singapore where he arrived in September 1819 with an indenture permitting him to reside in India. Writing to Raffles on 2nd November 1819 Farquhar begged to propose:

'Mr Napier is a person well adapted to fill the situation of Assistant or Agent in the Police Department as this gentleman has made a

---

[46] *Singapore Chronicle* 1828.11.20.

[47] Bastin, J. S. (2014). *Raffles and Hastings: private exchanges behind the founding of Singapore*, National Library Board Singapore [and] Marshall Cavendish Editions, Singapore, p.75.

considerable proficiency in the native language and has in other respects qualified himself for discharging the duties of such an office with efficiency. I therefore propose tending the present reference to you to avail myself of the services [of] Mr Napier to assist me generally [in] the Police Department and take the liberty to recommend the monthly sum of Spanish Dollars one hundred and fifty.'[48]

He was taken on immediately pending a reply but in his letter of 20th March, received on 14th April 1820, Raffles did not approve and Farquhar refused to pay the allowances, telling Napier the position had been retrenched. He therefore left for Penang and Calcutta on 20th April in *Coromandel* after writing a letter of complaint to Raffles which did not reach Bencoolen until 25th July.[49] Following investigation, in a letter dated 2nd January 1821 from Jennings in Bencoolen, Raffles did not hesitate to admonish Farquhar:

'The Lieutt. Governor has no hesitation in considering Mr. Napier fully entitled to the allowance of 150 dollars per month during the period he officiated in that capacity. It is perfectly clear to the Lieutt. Governor that whatever may have been your intention, Mr. Napier was impressed with the conviction that at any rate he would be entitled to the allowances until a reply from the Lieutt. Governor was received and it cannot be expected that a gentleman who is not in the service should officiate without an adequate compensation.'[50]

Long before the latter was received, Napier came back and with Charles Scott, the son of Robert Scott of Penang, formed after March 1821 the firm of Napier & Scott. On one occasion they supplied the Government with six weeks' supply of rum for the European troops at a rate of one dollar a gallon as the official supplies were exhausted and the troops presumably thirsty. Napier was in Calcutta to marry Ann Margaret Dixon on 15th November 1821.

In 1822 Napier & Scott are recorded as having *'a lot of ground on the bank of the Singapore River within Cantonment Plain and one in River*

---

[48] SSR L10 189 dated 1819.11.2.

[49] SSR L4 133-5.

[50] SSR L4 526-7.

Street. Held under the provisional sanction of the Resident. 2ⁿᵈ under certificate by the Resident 20ᵗʰ June 1820.' One of these sites was land which had originally been granted to Lieutenant Crossley but given after his departure by him to Napier when he realised he would not be going back to Singapore.[51]

In April 1822, Farquhar asked various merchants for their opinion as to the most eligible site for godowns for the purpose of carrying on an extensive trade. He gave a very definite response:

'I have no hesitation in saying that the ground pointed out between the village at Campong Glam and the Cantonment would be extremely incommodious for carrying on trade to any extent. The inconvenience arising from the shallowness of the water and the some times heavy surf would totally prevent boats of any size from approaching your godown and particularly at low water when your boats must be at a very great distance from your godowns, and the heavy expense of boat hire would come very heavy on merchants trading to any extent. The Singapore River is certainly the place best adapted for carrying on trade & you have every convenience that can possibly be required for trading to any extent, and the facility with which boats can approach your godown to enable you to ship goods with great expedition. I hope that the Supreme Government will alter their determination in not allowing individuals to build on the bank of the river. As I wish to apply for permission to build a godown in the space of ground allotted to Napier & Scott, you will oblige me by directing me thro' what channel I am to apply. I remain, Sir, your most obedient servant. D. S. Napier Singapore 13ᵗʰ April 1822.'

It is interesting that when granted a lot on River Street only the frontage on High Street was measured and the ground between that and the riverbank was still occupied by Malay houses the occupants of which had to be paid to move.

The Napiers were the most intimate of Raffles and Lady Raffles' friends during their stay in Singapore from October 1822 to June 1823, to whom they were known as *'the Naps'*.[52] Raffles was glad to write to Rev. Morrison, on his way back to Bencoolen in *Hero of Malown* on 9ᵗʰ June,

---

[51] SSR L7 204.
[52] Bastin, op. cit. p. 120.

that Mrs Napier had agreed to take the lead in favour of Mrs Thomsen's girls' school.

For some time there had been a dispute over a small bit of land between Napier's godown and that of Andrew Farquhar. Crawfurd, still fairly new to the job, persuaded him to give up his claim, writing on 11th June 1823:

'I beg to offer you my acknowledgement for the handsome manner in which you are pleased to surrender to Government your claims to the ground in dispute between yourself and Mr. A. Farquhar & for thus relieving me from the embarrassment of further agitating an unpleasant question. In reference to the manner and language stated by you to have been used by Mr. Farquhar in the progress of the discussion respecting the ground, I can feel no hesitation in expressing my regret that such a line of conduct should have been pursued and to express on this, as on all similar occasions, an unqualified disapproval of all personal altercation tending like that now alleged to injure the harmony & happiness of our little community.'[53]

Together with Captain Davis he was appointed by Crawfurd in 1824 to superintend the construction of the Malay (or Missionary) Chapel. Under Farquhar's regime church services had been held in a building in his own compound but now a new venue was needed. The building was completed the following year at the corner of Bras Basah Road and North Bridge Road, at a cost of $2,679.50 of which Government had subscribed $250.

Business was good and he contracted George Coleman, the architect, whom he had persuaded to come over from Java, to design and build for him a grand house on his large grounds fronting the East Beach. This was completed towards the end of 1826, but on 3rd November his wife Ann died, and on Christmas Eve he took his young children home to Scotland, sailing in *Exmouth*. While in London en route to his father in Edinburgh, Napier called on Lady Raffles, as she mentioned in a letter dated 23rd May 1827.[54]

---

[53] SSR L19 127.

[54] Baston, J and Kit, T. W. (2009). *Letters and Books of Sir Stamford Raffles and Lady Raffles: The Tang Holdings Collection of Autograph Letters and Books of Sir Stamford Raffles and Lady Raffles*, Editions Didier Millet, US, p. 310.

While he was away the Government rented his house for the use of the Governor when visiting Singapore or of other important visitors while he was not there. One example of this was it being allotted to Admiral Gaye during his stay in Singapore.[55]

While away he remarried in 1827, this time to Anna Margarita who, by the time they arrived back in Singapore in *Castle Huntly* on 24th August 1828 with his brother Robert, had produced a daughter.

The partnership with Charles Scott was dissolved on 30th June 1829.[56] He carried on under the name of D. S. Napier & Co. making his younger brother William a partner the following day. Taking his wife and family with him he left for China, only returning on 29th December, and three days later took *Hoopoe* to Batavia from whence they departed for Scotland, never to return. His large house *'having a larger compound than any other house in the same situation'* was advertised on 17th December as being *'to let'*.

His interest in the firm ended on 11th March 1830 and on 30th April the River Street godowns and the house in Beach Road which William had been living in, were advertised for sale on 8th April. Robert, the third brother was made a partner on 2nd August 1830.

Napier died on 17th December 1836 at Cringletie House, Peebles, Scotland.

21.10 Claude Queiros

Queiros was the supposed natural son and protégé of John Palmer, well–known merchant of Calcutta, who wrote to him on 1st February before he sailed for Singapore:

'I have offered you an unequivocal proof of friendship by approving an entire confidence in your prudence and diligence, directions and activity. I look for corresponding results. I have hazarded a considerable property with you though aware of your inexperience and of your alleged extravagance. You cannot fail to feel the weight of the responsibility you

---

[55] SSR N1 338.

[56] *Singapore Chronicle* 1829.7.16.

have henceforward to sustain. At Penang seek for and follow implicitly the counsel of Mr David Brown or Robert Scott his partner. At Singapore put yourself, if he permit you, into Colonel Farquhar's hands. Scrupulously avoid all species of ostentatious appearance in manners, conduct, apparel or domestic arrangements. Limit your whole monthly expenses, private and official to $100 per month exclusive of the store which you must make your dwelling house. Sell nothing upon credit unless previously told by Colonel Farquhar that you may safely do so. Until you feel your security sell only for coin or bullion. In time, if advised by Colonel Farquhar sell on barter for articles of certain sale here. If sugars from Siam may be had, of good quality from 4 to 5$ per picul, hand it on here. Pepper exceeding 10$ should never be meddled with except for China. Tin from 14 to 15$ may answer and nuts at 1½ $. The whole returns from your investment must come back to us. .... Work hard at Malay during your voyages and constantly at Singapore where you had better engage an instructor in the language, it being of vast consequence to read and write it fluently, and keep your accounts in Malay. Be mild but strict with that people and persuade Mrs Q to acquire the language as soon as possible. She will soon become your most valuable coadjutor. Send me up a half yearly balance sheet that I may observe your progress as a merchant.'

Good advice, but much of it was not taken. Arriving in February 1820 with his family, they stayed some time with then Major (later Lt. Colonel) Farquhar as there was no other available accommodation suitable for them. Queiros swiftly did a deal with the troops' doctor Prendergast to buy for 700 Spanish Dollars his house in the Military Cantonment and moved in. He was at first refused a site for a godown and Raffles demanded in a letter from Bencoolen dated 6th February 1821 to know why.[57] In due course he was allocated what was probably the best site of all, No. 1 River Street near to Ferry Point and it was here he built his godown and wharf.[58]

The saga of his chartered vessel *Adventure* in the second half of 1820 is too lengthy to discuss here but it did not redound to his credit and cost Farquhar quite a sum.[59]

---

[57] SSR L4 309.
[58] SSR L9 119-123.
[59] SSR L4 404.

An early idea of a tie up with Johnston came to naught and one with Andrew Farquhar in early 1822 ruptured, to Palmer's fury:

'I was not prepared for and shall not soon be reconciled to the rupture of your engagements with young Farquhar and still less am I satisfied with the reasons assigned for it. Happily however you can go on without the connection if you will only be direct and economical, remembering that by industry and parsimony only can you possibly acquire independence.'

Queiros was out–station in Calcutta from February 1822, arriving back in Singapore on 19 May.

His relationship with Raffles in early 1823 over the requirement to move his godown across to Lot 119 on the south bank of the river went from bad to worse. As Palmer wrote on 10th May 1823:

'I have received your letters of the 14th March and 3rd April and thank you for the local and personal information they bring me. Your grievances affect me the more because I cannot repair or redress them and if you have not followed my previous counsel respecting the Lieut. Govr. I can suggest nothing at all likely to be useful to you. If his measures infringe upon acknowledged or tacit privilege which you enjoyed under his own or Farquhar's concessions this government will listen to a calm and respectful representation of the case: but not to a private one, through any channel.'

This was followed by two letters both dated 18th June:

'Letter of April received by the *Wellington*. I have thought fairly of your pretension and proceedings in regard to your river premises until this day when I discover such evasion and twisting of the obvious sense of your claims that I predict you will be utterly disappointed of all redress, and be enjoined to atone for your unbecoming language to the Lieutenant Governor. If you shall continue pertinacious of your title to the lands you must have recourse to a petition but under the disadvantage you had not created for yourself when I first suggested that measure.'

and (second letter):

'I have just received your letter of 28th May and its voluminous enclosures and am perfectly astonished at your presumption and folly in regard to your storehouse and throughout the correspondence with Sir SR. It does not seem to me that you have a leg to stand on. By your own showing, compensations having been offered to you and timely notice given for the removal of your property. I see nothing for reference to counsel nor for redress except in reference to the original grant of land and the question of compensation which was fit matter for a memorial to the Supreme Government and would doubtlessly have been attended to if submitted through the proper channel and in respectful terms. In such a form I would have assisted your just or reasonable pretensions but I will not move in an affair, to say the best of it, so equivocal and inducted with so little discretion, temper or relative consideration.'

Compensation for the move was finally agreed at 10,000 Spanish Dollars and Queiros built his new godown between the plots of Flint (later Johnston) and Mackenzie on Boat Quay, his wharf having been demolished.

Relations between Palmer and Queiros continued to be fraught with accusations as his conduct was unsatisfactory. A letter dated 25th May 1826 accuses him of having *'caused a defection of friends to me [and I] am obliged to avail myself of the services of Mr. C. Thomas.' 'I fear you will be annihilated'*.

He departed for China in *Merope* on 29th July 1827. It was on 9th October that tenders were called by Government for the purchase of three lots of ground on the reserved Plain situated immediately in front of the premises belonging to Messrs Thomas, Montgomerie and himself. As this was contrary to previous undertakings there was an outcry and in due course the call for tenders was cancelled.

His partnership with W. R. George under the firm of Claude Queiros & Co. was dissolved on 30th June 1828. There is no indication when it had been started.[60]

Palmer & Co. in Calcutta failed, and it is not known exactly when Queiros left Singapore, but the sale of his plot to J. S. Clark was registered in August 1831.

---

[60] *Singapore Chronicle* 1828.7.3.

Queiros drowned in 1837 when disembarking from the vessel *Clairmont* in the roads off Madras.[61]

21.11 Tan Che Sang

An underworld figure whose wealth later gave him respect from the Chinese community in Singapore, Che Sang, as he was known, was born about 1763 in Guanzhou, China. This has over the years been misread as Guangzhou (Canton) and the mistake been perpetuated in countless articles. If he had been Cantonese his name would have been Chan but as a Hokkien it was their pronunciation of the same character, Tan, by which he was known. He left his native city at the age of 15 to seek his fortune among the gambier cultivators in Rhio and then moved to Penang where he spent 10 years and got married. His next move was to Malacca, now under British administration. After that city's return to the Dutch, Singapore and its burgeoning commerce was an irresistible draw. Arriving in 1819 with ample supplies of cash and a reputation for tough action he very quickly established a dominating position in the town and was recognised by Farquhar, who had known him in Malacca, as someone with whom the authorities could conveniently deal while metaphorically holding their noses, and recognised him unofficially as Capitan China.

He was known as a miser, for his addiction to gambling and the fact that he had on one occasion, after losing a considerable sum of money, cut off the first joint of his little finger, swearing to cure himself of the habit. He failed in this and was notorious for sleeping on a tiger skin surrounded by iron chests where he kept his money. He was reputed to have boasted that his influence was such that he only had to say the word to empty the Settlement of all Europeans.

The Nakhodah of the first junk to arrive direct from Amoy in February 1821 was arrested by the Sultan and put in the stocks for not having paid him a courtesy visit or for not offering a valuable enough present. His interpreter immediately rushed to find Che Sang to arrange his release which was done through the Resident and Police Assistant. It is possible

---

[61] *The Asiatic Journal and Monthly Register for British and Foreign India, China, and Australasia*, Oct 1837, p. 75.

that Che Sang was an agent for the junk as he was for many others in later years.

He had fingers in every pie. As an example in the last quarter of 1821, he held the licence to sell arrack through two shops in Campong China, one in Singapore town and one in Campong Glam. He had at least six shops built of wood, three large and three small along River Street between the Temenggong's compound and the sea. When Raffles on 9th November 1822 ordered the removal of the Fish Market to a site in Teluk Ayer it was thought to be sensible to have the pork, poultry and vegetable market in the same place. Che Sang offered to build the new market at his own expense provided he could enjoy free of tax the revenues to be raised by renting out the stands on either side of the passages leading to the fish and poultry sections. Farquhar recommended this to Raffles, but it is unlikely that it was approved as the 40 stalls were, after construction, divided into eight lots for sale.

In 1823 he had rented the pork 'farm' and tried to prevent the import of salt pork. In this he failed. Other 'farms' he also rented, as can be found in an appeal re the opium farm in 1829 and a case referred to him, in the absence of a court, ignored the fact that he had a clear conflict of interest. W. S. Duncan's diary for February 1824 refers to him buying a number of chests of opium from Captain Pearl at $1435 per chest which in Duncan's opinion could hardly have covered Pearl's costs but was evidently potentially profitable to Che Sang.

He was in 1830 called as a witness in a trial concerning one Kong Tuan over a partnership. It was reported that *'for the defence Che Sang, having been sworn by cutting off a cock's head, stated that he was present in December last when Ong Tuan, Tong Lee, Tong Guan and Tong Koon dissolved partnership.'* This method of promising to tell the truth, the whole truth and nothing but the truth by a witness who would not swear on the Bible or the Koran was reportedly common practice. Another witness persisted in his refusal to swear by cutting off a cock's head. In this case the evidence was not taken, and the witness was given over in custody of the Sheriff, until he paid a fine of 20 dollars, for contempt of court.

By the 1830s Che Sang felt he could do much as he liked. 24th February 1831 saw a brief article in the *Chronicle* about an extraordinary occurrence *'within the last week in which Che Sang, a well–known Chinese merchant acted a very conspicuous part.'* The following week's issue on 3rd March gave a full report. The magistrates had held an emergency meeting over the affair which concerned a poor deranged woman who broke a large quantity of earthenware and crockery exposed for sale at the front of a shop in Teluk Ayer Street. The elderly Chinese owner was naturally furious and with the assistance of two of his employees struck the woman and pushed her into the drain. Her family was wealthy and felt they had been insulted. They insisted that the matter be referred to Che Sang for arbitration but he, before agreeing, went to Bonham, the Assistant Resident to get his approval, having first gone and slapped the face of the elderly Chinese. Bonham, without considering the matter deeply, gave his approval. Che Sang then condemned the three Chinese to undergo a dozen lashes each with a rattan cane which he inflicted personally and in public shortly afterwards. It was rumoured that both Che Sang and the mad woman's son–in–law had an old grudge against the shop owner and so used this occasion to gratify their feud. This was followed with *'We could here have expatiated on the danger and impropriety of any Magistrate delegating his power to another, especially to such a person as Che Sang (a man who has risen from the very dregs of the people, few know how, and whose character and mental acquirements are quite in unison with his origin) but we are given to understand that......'* The rest of the sentence of four lines was censored.

A week later on 10th March the *Singapore Chronicle* reported a case of highway robbery and false imprisonment which had occurred during the latter part of the previous month in which Che Sang's name appeared possibly in a better light. Tan Bu Loh, the son of the Capitan China of Minto was accosted shortly after his arrival by junk from China by a man who demanded 200 dollars which he said was due to him from Bu Loh's father. He knew nothing of his father's debts and refused. A few days later two Chinese told him Che Sang wished to see him and he went with a friend to Che Sang's house. Che Sang was not at home and they left. They had not gone far when the two Chinese came and seized him, forcing him into the interior. His friend who had followed the attackers had had to desist when they threatened to kill him but went to report to the Magistrate what had happened. On the way they robbed him of a gold betel box, a diamond ring, a gold seal and 21 dollars in cash before taking him by bye–paths in the jungle to the house of a man named Hu Quan where he observed about a hundred men smoking opium, drinking, and gambling. Here he was detained for 48 hours. During this period the man who had originally accosted him was told that if he paid the 200 dollars he would be released, and his property returned. On the third night the man came again and told him he had been sent by Che Sang to liberate him.

Later the same year a report on the hesitation of merchants in Canton to buy Straits tin and the investigation into this problem quoted *'A specimen marked H is a sample of a quantity sold here by Che Sang some four or five years ago, and which was afterwards resold at Canton at a loss of 4 dollars per picul, owing to alleged adulteration.'*

Up the Kallang River Che Sang had at one time some brick kilns as shown in a murder report published by the *Singapore Chronicle* on 5th June 1834.

In addition to his various shops Che Sang had early on bought from Farquhar and his son a site of about 20,000 square feet (Lease No.298) with a godown lying *'on the riverside above the old bridge'*. In accordance with Raffles' requirements, he transferred his godown to Commercial Square after 1823 but retained the site. In June 1826 Crawfurd who was about to leave the Settlement, bought, through his agent Johnston, 13 properties in the Commercial Square, Market and Malacca Streets area. Of these four were reluctantly sold by Che Sang. One was a large lot of over 36,000 square feet, No. 25, lying south along Market Street as far as the new market. The second was Lease No. 23 in Malacca Street with sea frontage, the third, Lease No. 32 on the opposite side of the street on the corner of Commercial Square and the last, No. 33 adjacent to it on the south side of Commercial Square, each of the three being of just over 7,700 square feet. At a later stage he built a house in Campong Glam but never occupied it and it was sold to a Mr. Ker.

Che Sang died on 2nd April 1835 (not 1836 as is given in most references) and all Europeans received a written invitation to attend the funeral.

It was not until nearly a year later that his executors, Yian Ling and Boon Yian, put a notice dated 9th March 1836 in the *Singapore Chronicle* calling for those indebted to the estate to pay their debts and those having claims to make them known to the executors.

Index

Cree, Edward, 245
Crossley (Lieutenant), 46, 262
Cruikshank, Isaac Robert, 100
Cubitt, Thomas, 182
Cumberland, 162
Cuthbertson, Thomas, 195
cutting paper, 118

Da Silva, Francisco Pinto y Maia,
  243, 244
David Scott, 8
Davidson, G. F., 238
Davis, Captain Charles Edward, 18,
  50, 55, 66, 68, 72, 80, 97, 111, 148
Deans, John, 9
Deans Scott & Co, 9, 42
Delta of Pegu, 109
Diggles, Robert of Syme & Co, 29,
  225, 226
Discovery, 3
dollars, currency, 85
dollars, hard, 85
Dolphin, cutter, 248
Dolphin, schooner, 249
Doveton College, Calcutta, 184,
  196
Drysdale, J. C., 34, 37, 39, 155
D. S. Napier & Co., 264
Dugdale, Helen, 181
Duncan, John, 176
Duncan, Walter Scott, 15, 101, 119,
  221, 246–250, 269
Dunman, Thomas, 185–191
Dunn, John, 56, 57, 215–216
Dutch, 11
  Anglo-Dutch talks, 103
  financial problems, 48
  home government, 11

naval vessel, 36
Ramunia Point, 139
regulations, 135
Dutch East Indies, 221
Dutch Guilder, 85
Dutrongquoy, Gaston, 176

Earl Fitzwilliam, 6, 7, 130
Earnshaw, Daniel, 209
Earl St Vincent, 253
East Beach, 70
East Coast of Malaya, 173
East End Juvenile Mission, 206
East India Company, 4–6, 11–12, 14,
  25, 30, 32, 45–47, 53, 57, 111, 161,
  163, 165, 193, 213, 230–231, 252,
  256
  Bonham's introduction, 111
  Court House sale, 230–231
  Court of Directors in London,
    29, 161
  trade monopoly, 163
East Indiaman, 49, 215, 252
East India Railway stock, 201
Edinburgh, Duke of, 194
Edward Boustead, 174
Elgin Bridge, 167
Elliot, Captain Charles, Royal Navy,
  35, 150
Eliza, 96, 260
Elizabeth, 98, 129
Elliot, Clara, 36, 153
Elliot, Rear Admiral George, 153
Ellis, John, 119
England, 109
Enterprise, 111
Erskine, J. J., 71
Esplanade House No 1, 176

prisoners, 78, 79, 116, 123, 124, 140
  death in Police custody, 30
  escaped, 70, 115
  flooded out, 124
  hanged, 124
  sent to Calcutta, 140
profitable employment, 9
property tax assessment, 30
Providence, 15, 57
Public Auction, 40
pukka bridge, 223
Pulau Tekong, 104
Purvis, John, 57, 84

Quay, Collyer, 41
Queiros, Claude, 12, 18, 50, 52, 68, 72, 74, 105, 119, 170–171, 259, 264–268

Radical, yacht, 247, 248
Raffles Club, 108, 117, 164
Raffles, Sir Stamford (Lieutenant Governor), 3–6, 10, 14–21, 24, 31, 37, 43, 45–47, 49–52, 56, 62, 64–84, 86, 90, 95–97, 99, 101, 103, 105, 108, 110–113, 122, 134, 163, 213–215, 217–219, 223, 252, 260–262, 265, 266
  A. L. J's house, 21, 22
  Banker to, 31
  castigation, 97
  connection with Flint, 4, 47, 62, 65
  correspondence with A. L. J., 27, 101
  death, 113
  dismissal of Farquhar, 23, 80
  dispute with Captain Pearl, 75–77
  inclination to micro-manage, 45

  instructions to Crawfurd, 83
  letter of introduction for
    A. L. J., 19
  loss of *Fame*, 99
  relations with Farquhar, 72
  Town Committee, 18
Raffles, Thomas, 213
Rajah of Singapore, 58
Ralfe (Lieutenant), 12, 21, 48, 55, 57, 128
Ramunia Point, 91, 139, 142
Rangoon, Burma, 109
Read, C. R., 15, 16, 20, 22–24, 38, 57, 92, 106, 119, 135, 142, 240
Read, W. H., 38–39, 155, 172
Reaper, 260
Red-headed, 91
Reed, R. P., 49–50, 111
religious, 50, 110, 197, 200
Rembang, 239
Remmington, Samuel, 9
Repulse ship, 94–95, 107
Residency House, 84
Resident, 11, 14, 49, 87, 88, 95, 109, 121, 224
  Bonham, 136, 137
  Church, 137
  Crawfurd, 22, 26, 28, 80, 81, 83, 89, 103, 106, 220, 223
  Dutch, 32, 143, 259
  Farquhar, 4-6, 23, 45, 46, 61, 70, 97, 111, 216-218, 231, 239, 256–258, 262, 268
  Malacca, 46, 48
  Nattal, 50,
  Pahang, 260
Resident Councillor, 29, 109, 115, 122, 126, 133, 224, 226, 259
  Bonham, 30
  Garling, 136

pepper from, 94
piracy, 139
Sutton, H. T., 40
Sydney, 9
Syed Omar bin Ali Al Juneid, 78
Syed Yassin, 78
Sykes, Adam, 164–166, 174, 175, 177
Sykes Bleaching Company in
  Edgeley, 165
Sylph, clipper, 31, 32
Syme, John, 28
Syme & Co., 107, 225

Tabor, Captain Clement, 22
Tambora Volcano, Sumbawa, 162
Tan Beng Swee, 184, 188–192, 204
Tan Che Sang, 54, 57–59, 68, 97,
  110, 122, 146, 155, 268–271
Tan Kim Seng, 177, 184, 187, 188
Tan Tock Seng, 148, 232, 233
Tanglin Road, 251
Tanjong Katong, 244
Tanjong Malang, 79
Tanjong Pagar, 219, 233
Tanjong Pagar Dock Company Ltd.,
  124, 190–192, 203, 207
Tanjong Tangkap, 21, 36, 40, 131
Tappanooly, 50, 94, 112
Tartar, 128
Tek Sing, 77
Teluk Ayer, 69, 71, 86, 90, 131, 134,
  152, 249, 269, 270
Teluk Blangah, 104
Temenggong, 3, 23, 44, 47, 53, 62,
  70, 71, 73, 75, 79, 81, 96, 103, 104,
  105, 217
Temperton, widow of John, 128
Thames, 53

The Friends, 174
Thetis, 239
Thomas, Charles, 116, 170, 250, 251,
  267
Thomas Ripley & Co., 177
Tiger Hill, 151
Tigers, 150, 151, 251
Tillson, Herrmann & Co., 196–197
topes, 93
Town Committee, 18, 66, 259
Tracy, Rev. Ira, 31, 144
Travancore, 194
Travers, Major O. T., 5–6, 11, 15, 45,
  47–50, 111
Treaty of Nanking, 175
Trengganu, 55, 56
troops, 84, 96
  food supplies, 84
troublemaker, 56
True Briton, 111
Tunku Besar, 138
twacow, 144

Union Bank of Calcutta, 175
United Kingdom, 177, 179, 194
United States Consul, 102
Upper Cross Street, 251

Valetta, 102
Vasco da Gama, 243
Viall (Captain), 196
Victoria Road, or Street, 174, 175,
  186, 189
violence, 140
Viscount Melbourne, 173

Wallace, Captain, 31, 32
Wallace, Miss, 145

CPSIA information can be obtained
at www.ICGtesting.com
Printed in the USA
JSHW042157110622
26918JS00001B/3